SOFTWARE TESTING AND USER EXPERIENCE

Nastaran Nazar Zadeh

Toronto Academic Press

Software Testing and User Experience

Nastaran Nazar Zadeh

Toronto Academic Press
224 Shoreacres Road
Burlington, ON L7L 2H2
Canada
www.tap-books.com
Email: orders@arclereducation.com

ISBN: 978-1-77469-786-3

ABOUT THE AUTHOR

Nastaran Nazar Zadeh is a highly experienced computer engineer, researcher, and advisor in the fields of robotics, artificial intelligence and computer science. She holds a Master of Science in Computer Engineering from Mapua University of the Philippines and pursed her Ph.D. in Electronic Engineering at the same institution. With over seven years of teaching experience, Nastaran has taught electronic and computer engineering programs at several reputable academic institutions, where she has also led numerous thesis studies. Her research focuses on developing robotics systems with A.I. and machine learning, which enables her to stay up-to-date with the latest advancements in the field and implement cutting-edge technologies.

Contents

List of Figures

List of Tables

List of Abbreviations

BDD	Behavior-Driven Development
CBSFG	Component-Based Software Flow Graph
COTS	Commercial Off Shelf
MCDC	Modified Condition Adequacy
ODC	Orthogonal Defect Classification
SCC	Successful Completion Criteria
TDD	Test-Driven Development
UCD	User-Centered Design
UML	Unified Modeling Language
XP	Extreme Programming

PREFACE

Software testing is an essential aspect of the software development process that ensures software applications' quality, reliability, and functionality. However, more than testing is needed to guarantee a great user experience. Integrating user experience design and testing throughout the entire software development process is crucial to create intuitive, efficient, and enjoyable software applications.

This book aims to provide an in-depth understanding of software testing and user experience design and testing. We will explore the different types of software testing, the goals, scope, and history of software testing, and how testing goes beyond just unit testing. We will also delve into the fundamentals of user experience design and usability testing, as well as the process of conducting a test.

The first chapter begins with an introduction to software testing. It also explores what software testing is, why it is important, and its role in the software development process. It also covers the different types of testing and their significance in ensuring the quality and reliability of software applications.

The second chapter delves into the various types of software testing. It discusses unit testing, integration testing, system testing, acceptance testing, and other types of testing. It also explores the strengths and weaknesses of each type of testing and the best practices for implementing them.

The third chapter will explore the goals, scope, and history of software testing. It examines the evolution of software testing from its early days to its current state. It also discusses the different goals of software testing, such as detecting defects, verifying software requirements, and improving software quality.

The fourth chapter will look beyond unit testing and explore other types of testing, such as exploratory testing, regression testing, and performance testing. It also discusses the challenges and opportunities presented by these testing methods.

The fifth chapter will focus on user experience design. It also examines what user experience is, its importance, and how it affects the success of software applications. It also explores the different elements of user experience design, such as usability, accessibility, and aesthetics.

The sixth chapter will explore usability testing. It also examines the importance of usability testing, the different methods used in usability testing, and the best practices for conducting a usability test.

The seventh chapter will delve into the process of conducting a test. It also examines the different stages of testing, including planning, preparation, execution, and reporting. We will also discuss the different tools and techniques used in software testing.

The final chapter discusses how to expand from usability testing to designing the user experience.

—Author

CHAPTER 1

INTRODUCTION TO SOFTWARE TESTING

UNIT INTRODUCTION

Large software system development is a difficult and error-prone process. Errors can emerge at any level of development; however, these errors need to be found and fixed as quickly as possible in order to limit their propagation and reduce the expenses associated with verification. Engineers specializing in quality assurance need to be a part of the product development process from the very beginning so that they can determine which qualities are necessary and evaluate how those qualities will affect the process (DeMillo et al., 1988). Their responsibilities encompass the entirety of the development cycle, extending beyond product release into areas such as maintenance and post-mortem examination. It is not a simple task to develop and implement an effective quality process. However, in order to do so, the integration of a large number of quality-linked operations with product attributes, process establishment, available skills and resources, and the limitations of the financial resources are required (Baresi & Pezze, 2006).

Building huge software products require a lot of different operations, all of which need to be coordinated effectively in order to achieve the objectives that have been set. Among these responsibilities, the actions that primarily contribute to the building of the product and operations that must inspect the standards of the evolution, as well as the artifacts that are generated, can be distinguished. This categorization is not as clear as it could be given that most actions contribute, even if only slightly, to promoting progress and monitoring the quality. This characterization of tasks is not always accurate. Still, it helps to recognize a significant thread of the development process, including all quality-related tasks and is frequently known as the quality process (Causevic et al., 2010).

The quality process is not a stage but extends across the entire development cycle. It begins with the practicality study and continues well after product categorization, including servicing as well as post-mortem assessment. In the feasibility study, the characteristics that are pertinent to the product must be stated; the pre-requisites and design parameters must be thoroughly checked and evaluated in order to discover and eliminate design deficiencies that would otherwise be difficult to disclose and costly to eliminate; tests must be developed and scheduled in the initial design stages in order to minimize the likelihood of delivering poorly evaluated and substandard goods, and they must be carried out several times using different types of equipment (Juristo et al., 2006).

The quality process is comprised of a large number of supplementary activities, all of which need to be skillfully combined in order to accommodate the particular development process and fulfill all of the quality and cost requirements. The quality engineer must occasionally deal with conflicting requirements, such as minimizing expenses while maintaining a high level of quality, preventing interference with the product's development while adhering to rigorous deadlines, and so on. The selection of an appropriate collection of quality activities is challenging and calls for extensive experience in software verification, a solid understanding of design and expansion, a solid know-how of leadership and organization, and the potential to help settle among various aspects and requirements (Garousi & Mäntylä, 2016).

Identifying flaws and evaluating whether or not the product is ready are two distinct categories of issues that quality operations handle. It is impossible to add quality at the very end of the process; rather, it should be maintained consistently throughout the entire process. Identifying the key characteristics of flaws is hard and even more challenging to eradicate them from the ultimate output. A great deal of testing and analysis aims to unearth flaws in something so that they can be repaired or removed. Finding and fixing bugs during development undoubtedly helps to improve the quality of the finished product. Still, it does not guarantee that there will be no bugs left over after the product has been shipped out to customers (Candea et al., 2010). Continuing the search for problems until they are all located, identified, and corrected would lead to the execution of quality operations indefinitely and without any logic (Lemos et al., 2018). Users are more concerned with finding solutions to issues and evaluating the condition of software products based on their reliability, serviceability, prices, and, finally their capacity to meet users' expectations (Ciortea et al., 2010). Users are less concerned with preventing or eliminating errors in the software. Users are willing to overlook a small number of annoyance failures in exchange for cost-effective solutions to their problems; nevertheless, they will not tolerate serious failures, regardless of how infrequent they are, nor will they tolerate too many annoyance failures. So, it is essential to combine quality activities that seek to expose flaws with activities that evaluate a product's readiness in terms of its reliability and usability (Barr et al., 2014).

The majority of quality assurance operations are performed in isolation from the development process, yet, the efficiency of these activities is largely reliant on the quality of the advancement. Integration testing is more successful when software is executed in accordance with better design guidelines than when it is evolved without a coordinated scheme. By offering feedback on the factors that contribute to failures and the most common mistakes, quality activities can boost the development practice's overall quality (Nidagundi & Novickis, 2017).

TIPS

The benefits of testing include preventing bugs, reducing development costs and improving performance.

Learning Objectives

At the end of this chapter, readers will be able to:

1. Understanding the basics of software testing
2. Learning the different types of software testing
3. Understanding the software testing life cycle
4. Understanding the testing challenges
5. Understanding the importance of documentation

Key Terms

- Integration Testing
- Model Based Testing
- Module Testing
- Quality Process
- Software Testing
- Testing Levels
- Verification and Validation

1.1. QUALITY PROCESS

Several actions are involved in the quality process, which can be divided into five categories: planning and monitoring, specification validation, test case production, test case implementation and software verification, and process advancement (Harvey, 2005). The goal of monitoring and planning operations is to drive quality operations toward a product that meets the quality parameters. The process of planning operations commences during the initial phases of development by recognizing the essential features and outlining an early analysis and testing period. This continues throughout the development cycle by overseeing the quality process and improving and adapting it to address emerging challenges and prevent deviations from the preliminary plan that can cause project breakdown (Arditi & Gunaydin, 1997).

Remember

Software testing is the process of evaluating and verifying that a software product or application does what it is supposed to do.

Specifications allow for checking both consistency and internal consistency with relevant standards or requirements. Inspection of inter-specification consistency tries to reveal variations in the development phase that manifest them; inspection of intra-specification consistency helps to reveal as well as eliminate inconsistencies of specifications. – Either as differences from the appropriate specifications or as missing components in the comprehensive specifications. Many technologies, ranging from straightforward syntactic tests and low-tech inspections to model testing and formal verification, can be used to validate specifications (Meyers et al., 2012).

Typically, test cases are built from specifications and combined with data from the code coverage and development technologies. Information about common problems and dangers can be obtained from the application environment, and development technology a lot of companies collect extensive sets of tests taken from older systems that define specific application settings. These can be used either as regression tests for particular applications or as general tests for commonly used functionalities (Steenkamp, 1990). Different programming languages and development tools have their own weaknesses, which could result in particular types of errors. For example, C++ memory management flexibility comes with hazards that cause memory leaks, which can be mitigated — but not prevented — with structured design and programming training, appropriately combined with evaluation as well as testing. Code coverage identifies areas of code that have not been thoroughly verified and recommends further test cases to fulfill functional test suites or identify poorly written code (Porteus, 1986).

The moment necessary specifications become accessible, test cases can and should be developed. The obvious advantage of an early generation of test cases is that it alleviates scheduling issues: tests can be developed in conjunction with development operations, avoiding critical pathways. Therefore, test execution can begin once the appropriate code is complete, minimizing testing time after writing (Phillipsen et al., 1997). The before-time production of test cases has the drawback of assisting in the validation of specifications. Many specification problems, according to experience, are more convenient to uncover initially than during design or verification. Delaying the use of specifications until the coding phase can lead to significant expenses for recovery and cause expensive project delays. Several latest techniques advocate for before-time test case establishment, all the way up to extreme programming (XP), which replaces module specification with test case establishment (Mentzer et al., 2001).

In the absence of the entire system, test cases might have to be conducted. This can be owing to the decision to test modules progressively rather than waiting for the entire system to be developed or to the requirement to isolate the modules under test in order to concentrate on certain qualities and allow fault identification. Running test cases without the entire system necessitates the creation of suitable scaffolding, i.e., a framework that replaces the absent system's components. Drivers, stubs, and oracles are examples of adequate scaffolding (Donabedian, 1968). Drivers and stubs simulate the behavior of lacking elements that may be needed for the module-under-implementation tests by gearing up the activation environment for the module-under-test (drivers) and simulating the behavior of missing components that may be required for the module-under-execution tests (stubs). Oracles analyze the outcomes of performed test cases and flag abnormal behavior. To construct suitable scaffolding, engineers strike a reasonable balance between benefits and expenses. Correct scaffolding is undoubtedly incredibly valuable for quick test execution, but it can also be overpriced and alarmingly wrong. Inexpensive scaffolding saves money, but it can be ineffective for testing (Reichert et al., 2001).

Testing can detect several types of failures, but it can be insufficient for others. Thus it should be supplemented with alternate verification operations. The Cleanroom technique, for example, advises that testing be supplemented with code examination to discover defects at the basic level (Wu et al., 2009).

Process improvement concentrates on groups of projects with standard procedures, engineering teams, and development environments. Quality experts gather and evaluate data on in-process projects to detect and prevent common errors. Issues can be eradicated by modifying development operations, or they can be mitigated by implementing particular quality actions to eliminate errors at the earliest. Although certain corrective actions may be implemented in the present project, corrective actions are frequently claimed for future projects (Slot et al., 2015).

1.2. QUALITY PLAN

The quality engineer should create the quality plan early in the design cycle. The initial plan is based on the company's test scheme and the engineer's expertise. The test scheme explains the company's quality infrastructure, which includes process issues, such as the acquisition of a certain technique, and business-related concerns, such as the decision to outsource specific testing operations, equipment, and development elements (Berke & Godschalk, 2009).

The original plan is then processed to account for new information relating to the actual project, such as specifying module testing operations once design features are accessible. If the original plan cannot adapt to the project's requirements, an alternative plan should be devised to deal with any unanticipated scenario (Berke & French, 1994).

A comprehensive quality plan should contain all the necessary details to regulate the quality process, ranging from basic details like the products to be tested to extensive information such as a timetable of individual quality tasks and the assigned workforce to execute them. The following are the essential components of a high-quality plan (Moore et al., 2012):

i. Test items describe the elements that must be tested, such as the versions of the system that will be verified.
ii. Features to be tested denotes the specific characteristics that must be tested out of all the features provided by the objects to be evaluated.
iii. Features not to be tested denote features that are included in the plan.
iv. The approach is the strategy that will be used. For instance, according to company standards, it can be made compulsory that all modules should be analyzed and undergo specific testing procedures for system and subsystem testing.
v. Pass/Fail criteria specify the acceptance criteria, which are used to determine the competence of the software under test. For instance, some ordinary errors can be permitted while requesting that no severe or severe errors exist before providing a module (Van et al., 2019).
vi. The criteria for suspending or resuming testing activities are established to ensure that they can be conducted effectively. If the failure rate of the system being tested is impeding its performance, it may be decided to stop testing temporarily. However, before resuming testing, a "sanity test" should be administered to verify the basic functionality of the unit under test.
vii. Contingencies and risks point out risks and develop appropriate contingency measures. The testing process is not immune to the various hazards that commonly arise during development. These may

include staff attrition, inadequate familiarity with technology, and delays in task completion due to planning issues. In addition, specific risks are associated with testing, such as the provision of substandard components by the development team, unforeseen delays in test case implementation, and critical requirements that must be met (Brody, 2003).

viii. Deliverables include a list of all expected outcomes.

ix. Task and Schedule express the whole quality process in tasks planned to fulfill deadlines based on development, timing, and resource restrictions. The early plan is elaborated as the development progresses in order to react to the project structure. The preliminary plan, for instance, highlights general module assessment and verification chores that will be defined once the design defines the system's specific modules (Lyles & Stevens, 2014).

x. Personnel and responsibilities identify and assign responsibilities to qualified personnel.

xi. Environmental needs denote any requirements derived from the environment, such as specific equipment necessary to conduct the test cases (Shah et al., 2006).

1.3. QUALITY PROCESS MONITORING

The quality process should be analyzed in order to detect fluctuations and contingencies and to adjust quality operations to recent conditions at the earliest. Surveillance has two forms: traditional supervision of activity progress and quantitative parameter assessment of testing findings.

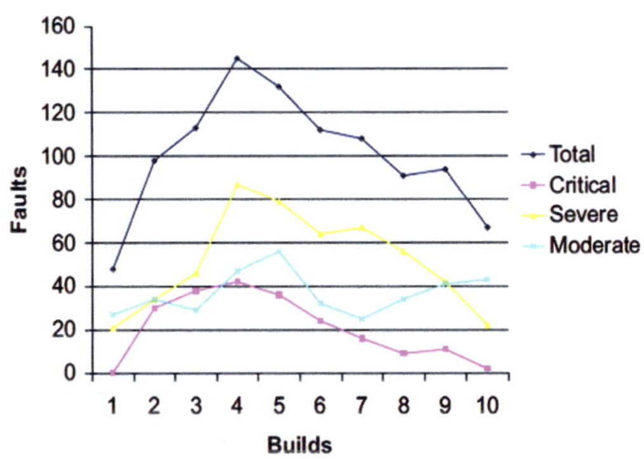

Figure 1.1. A typical fault distribution for a system grows over time.

Source: Atle Rotevatn et al., creative commons license.

The quality engineer notes the start and end dates, used resources, and advances of each activity and responds to variances from the current plan by either adapting it when deviations are acceptable or adopting a when devi-actions are severe to the current plan. The evaluation of quantitative development is extremely challenging and has only lately been used. It entails acquiring details on fault dispersion and competing it with previous data (Kano & Nakagawa, 2008).

Figure 1.1 is a figure from that depicts the allocation of faults over releases while accounting for three degrees of intensity. The graphic shows that the quantity of faults increases for the first buildings before dropping. The number of defects reduces at varying rates: intense faults drop quicker than ordinary faults, and average faults may even increase slightly. Different fault distributions suggest potential quality issues: If the frequency of faults does not decrease in the initial versions, it could be a sign of inadequate testing. On the other hand, if the frequency of faults does not decrease in the subsequent releases, it may indicate poor detection and resolution of the faults (Gowen et al., 2008).

The orthogonal defect classification (ODC), established by IBM in the 1990s, gives a thorough division of defects and advocates overseeing different distributions to identify potential quality issues (Gowen et al., 2012).

Figure 1.2. The distinction between validation and verification.

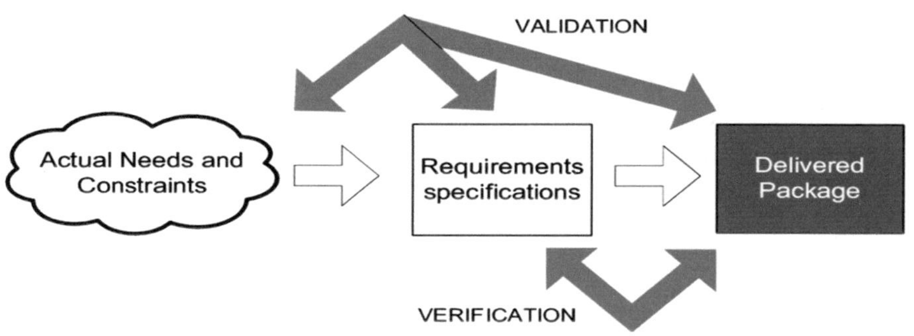

Source: Testing diaries, creative commons license.

Regardless of the known methods and techniques, the quality process is highly reliant on humans. The assignment of tasks is an important component of quality plans and strategies, and it can affect the project's likelihood of succeeding. Like with many other issues, there is no one-size-fits-all solution; instead, techniques vary depending on organizations, processes, and projects. Big businesses often segregate development and quality teams, whereas small organizations and frisky methods (for example, extreme programming) combines quality and development duties. Segregating quality and development teams promotes objective quality judgment and protects it from being undermined by scheduling pressure. Still, it limits scheduling freedom and necessitates good interaction methods between the two groups (Smidt & Schwanninger, 2005).

1.4. VERIFICATION AND VALIDATION

Verification operations are those that try to check the correlation of execution with its specification. In contrast, validation activities are those that aim to check the correspondence between a system and user expectations. The difference between verification and validation is depicted in Figure 1.2. It has been well-explained (Carson, 2002). Who brilliantly defined validation as "building the correct system" and verification as "building the system right?"

Verification and validation actions are complementary. Validation encompasses all phases of development, including evaluations from users on requirements and design specifications. However, the scale of user reviews may be constrained by their comprehension of development intricacies. Thus, the main emphasis of validation activities is directed toward the final product, which can be subjected to thorough testing during user acceptance testing (Sargent, 2015). Late execution of validation activities and considering user needs may pose considerable costs and risks. Therefore, validation activities should be closely integrated with verification activities that can be conducted early on without costly or unavailable user involvement (Sargent, 2010).

Several properties define software, including dependability, usability, security, interoperability, and so on. Certain qualities can be verified spontaneously. For example, by imitating the detection of N users and monitoring response time, a Web application's ability to serve up to a specific number N of users with response time below a predefined limit can be tested. Additional properties, which can be challenging to test, are an obvious target for validation. The user's potential to quickly access the necessary data via a web application, for example, is difficult to check but can be validated, for example, by tracking a sample population of users (Oberkampf & Trucano, 2002).

In the end, how qualities are expressed determines how reliable they are. For instance, as it refers to subjective sensations ("easily" and "bothersome"), a Web application's property stating that users must be able to simply add an item to the shopping basket without encountering irritating delays cannot be possibly verified. The expression of subjective emotions in quantifiable terms such as "number of mouse clicks" and "delays in seconds" allows for the verification of a property (Oberkampf & Trucano, 2008). For example, one can verify that users can add a specific item to their shopping cart with no more than four mouse clicks from the home page and that the application responds within one second after the click when the application is serving up to ten thousand users working concurrently can be verified. As a result, system testing begins as soon as requirements specifications are written. Mature development methods plan inspection tasks to evaluate their testability and maximize the software product's verifiability (Babuska & Oden, 2004).

Certain methods are needed for the validation and verification of various properties. Usability attributes, for instance, need special-purpose procedures for their validation, unlike dependability properties, which can be verified through model-based testing methodologies outlined below. In this instance, a typical process consists of the following key steps:

i. Checking specifications using custom checklists and traditional inspection methods.
ii. Evaluating preliminary prototypes created by simulating user interfaces.
iii. Testing periodic releases with end users and usability professionals (Wallace & Fujii, 1989).
iv. Final system and acceptability testing should take into account user-based testing, comparative testing, expert-based assessment and evaluation, and automatic analysis (Sargent, 1987).

In contrast to functional and model-based testing, which do not need user involvement, usability testing largely depends on users. The usability team point outs the categories of users, choose appropriate samples of the population based on the identified classes, defines groups of communications that accurately reflect important usages of the system, observes the communication of the specific users with the system, and then analyzes the results (Ryan & Wheatcraft, 2017).

1.5. FUNCTIONAL AND MODEL-BASED TESTING

The fundamental method for creating test cases is functional testing. Functional test cases can be used for any explanation of program behavior; they can be applied to all degrees of the requirements specification and design process, from system to module testing; they are productive in finding some categories of faults that generally elude code- and fault-based testing and they are usually cheaper to design and implement than tests designed using other methods (Hartman & Nagin, 2004).

A functional specification outlines the program's anticipated behavior. There are numerous ways to provide specifications. In terms of testing, we distinguish between specifications given in the usual language and those represented in a few formal languages. Functional testing methodologies include a series of procedures that aid in the analysis of specifications to produce an acceptable group of test cases. Functional testing is the process of selecting a group of test cases using appropriate criteria when specifications are provided as semi-formal models. This process is also known as model-based testing (Pretschner, 2005).

1.5.1. Functional Testing

Three contemporary techniques to general-purpose functional testing are category-partition, combinatorial, and catalog-based. The three major steps of category partition testing are applicable to requirements stated in natural language (Howden, 1980). The designer recognizes specification products that may be evaluated separately and pinpoints environmental factors that affect the performance of the examined feature as we begin to break the specification down into individually testable features (categories). When testing a Web application, for instance, we might recognize the catalog handler capability as a feature that can be independently tested. According to the sales and stock in the most recent sale period, the following specification extract affects the manufacturing and sale of items (Miller et al., 2005).

"If, during the most recent sales period, the quantity of orders drops below a specified level (t1), or if it does so while the inventory level is above a specified threshold (t2), the manufacture of that item is discontinued. If an item is not in manufacturing, the number of orders during the preceding era remained below t1, and the amount of stock drops below a level s1 s2, then the product is removed from the index. If the quantity of orders during the prior era is greater than t2 and the quantity on hand is less than t3, the manufacture of an item from the catalog is resumed. Products that are sold in conjunction with other products are dealt with in the same manner as compiled products, i.e., manufacturing is not postponed if one of the compiled products is still in production despite sales and stock of the considered product, and the considered item is retained in the catalog even if it is releasable if the compiled products are retained in the catalog. There cannot be more inventory than what each object can hold."

The following criteria that affect how the feature behaves can be inferred from the informal specification: number of orders in the most recent time frame, stock level, status of the item, and constructed products (Crapo, 1994).

Now the pertinent values are determined. For each parameter characteristic, the designer chooses a group of representative classes of values (options). Values are chosen separately from the other properties. For instance, Figure 1.3 displays a potential range of options for the categories taken from the catalog handler's specification. Options don't necessarily represent single values; instead, they typically represent groups of related values (Ranu et al., 2011).

Test designers must consider both normal and error values, and values on the edge of two categories while making choices (Muñoz, 2010). Finally, the test case specifications are produced. Combinations of the options found in the previous phases can easily be used to construct test case specifications.

Unfortunately, extremely huge test suites result from the simple combination of all options. For instance, the straightforward set of options in Figure 1.3 yields more than 1,000 combinations. In addition, a lot of combinations could be meaningless or absurd. For instance, it makes no sense to combine individual items with assembled objects that have a different status, or test designers can want only to test the boundary instances once (Le et al., 2007).

By setting straightforward limitations, the designers can avoid incorrect amalgams and restrict singletons: Pairs ["label," "if-"label"] restrict one value to exist in conjunction with a value denoted by the label. [error] denotes incorrect values and needs, at most one test case for that value. [Single] marks singleton values and needs at most one test case for them as well. By applying the limitations shown in Figure 1.3, the created test cases are reduced from over 1,000 to 82, constituting an appropriate group of test cases (Douglas et al., 2015).

The category division strategy is useful when there are fewer possible combinations, as in the case of the straightforward catalog handler. At times, however, options are not generally limited, and the number of test cases produced by taking into account every potential combination of options may be greater than the testing budget. Take the informal definition of a discount policy, for instance (Michelson, 2004). The eligible discount is determined based on the customer's status and the total quantity of purchases, as shown in the following excerpt (Brahme & Abraham, 1984).

orders in the period	**amount in stock**	**status of the item**
0 *[single]*	0 *[single]*	in production
$< t_1$	$< s_1$	in catalog
t_1 *[single]*	s_1 *[single]*	not available *[error]*
$< t_2$	$< s_2$	**status of assembled item**
t_2 *[single]*	s_2 *[single]*	in production *[if assmbl]*
$> t_2$	$< s_{max}$	in catalog *[if assmbl]*
$>> t_2$	s_{max} *[single]*	not available *[if assmbl][error]*
type of item	$> s_{max}$ *[error]*	
individual		
assembled *[assmbl]*		

Source: Testing diaries, creative commons license.

Figure 1.3. Testing a partition based on categories, a basic set of categories, options, and restrictions; this is the example catalog handler. Options for each grouping appear in their respective columns. Limits are denoted by square brackets.

Both people and educational institutions are eligible for the discount. If the quantity of orders during the evaluated sale time surpasses a level o_1 or a level $o_2 > o_1$, additional discounts are claimed (Piwowarski et al., 1993). Discounts are also applied if the current invoice amount or the sum of all bills for the current sales period surpasses the predefined criterion (i_1 and $i_2 > i_1$ for the present invoice, and t1 and $t_2 > t_1$ for the full sum of invoices for the period). Discounts can be added to indefinitely. No discounts are available to customers with questionable credit histories (Cooper, 2011).

Thus, we have a limitless number of test cases, as the options shown in Figure 1.4 that stem from the aforementioned specification have no inherent limitations (Kehrel & Brodde, 2013). It expands exponentially as the number of groups or options increases, as it does in most real-world situations (up to 182 test cases in this example). While the number of created test cases decreases due to the elimination of combinations of values that could show critical flaws, imposing artificial limits does not assist. One alternative is to put constraints on the possible permutations (Chowdhury & Forsmark, 2003).

customer type	# of orders in the period	amount in the invoice	total invoices in the period	credit situation
individual	$\leq o_1$	$\leq i_1$	$\leq t_1$	ok
business	$\leq o_2$	$\leq i_2$	$\leq t_2$	risky
educational	$> o_2$	$> i_2$	$> t_2$	

Figure 1.4. An unrestrained set of classifications and options.

Source: MDPI, creative commons license.

There are an infinite number of test cases because none of the options in Figure 1.4, which are derived from the previous specification, are bounded. In the current example, it increases exponentially as the number of categories or options rises, as it does in the majority of real-world situations, reaching up to 182 test instances (Lieb & Draganov, 2008). Artificial constraint forcing is ineffective because it decreases the amount of test cases generated by excluding configurations of values that could expose significant flaws. A different strategy involves limiting the combinations by only considering pairwise combinations of options. For instance, less than 18 test cases can cover all of the paired combinations in Figure 1.4 (Thapa & Walia, 2007). Combinatorial testing, which creates test cases that only cover pairwise possibilities, is dependent on the experimental finding that most failures are caused by single choices and infrequently by specific combinations of various choices. For test suites of restricted size, covering all pairwise combinations of options can thus expose the majority of likely failures. Combinatorial testing and category partition can be successfully integrated by first restricting the combination of options and then only considering pairwise possibilities (Caldwell et al., 1985).

We identify both abnormal values as well as boundary and error criteria while choosing options for the categories that have been defined. Many flaws typically lurk in unique situations that rely on the kind of factors being taken into account (Wuyts et al., 2007). For instance, test experts advise taking into account at least one value inside the limits, the low and high bounds themselves, the values before and after each bound, and at least one other value outside the limit when dealing with a range of values [low, high]. Expert test designers' knowledge can be preserved in catalogs that identify all scenarios that must be taken into account for each specification (Favaloro et al., 2010). We have the option of creating both general-purpose and niche catalogs. The first can be applied in the majority of situations, whereas the second only applies to special fields that are distinguished by specific cases. Specifications with a clear structure can benefit from catalogs. In order to provide a full set of test cases, catalog-based testing generally translates specifications into pre- and post-conditions, variables, definitions, and functions first (Kuvin & Karas, 2003).

1.5.2. Model-Based Testing

When specifications are given in a semi-formal language, test cases can be derived by using these models in conjunction with test-generating criteria. The development of the finite state model is one of the creative processes in testing that test designer's focus on. For repeated work, they use automatic procedures. Although this study concentrates on finite state automata, the same methodology can be used with a variety of models (Dalal et al., 1999). For the purpose of creating test case specifications, it is frequently reasonable to build a finite state model from specifications that describe transitions between a finite numbers of states. For instance, take into account the following basic specifications for a Web application's shopping cart functionality (Schieferdecker & Hoffmann, 2012):

The following commands can be used to control a shopping cart:

i. **createCart()** method produces a new, empty cart.
ii. **addItem(item, quantity)** function adds the specified number of items to the cart.
iii. **removeItem(item, quantity)** eliminates the specified number of things from the shopping cart.
iv. **clearCart()** empty the cart, no matter what is in it (Pretschner et al., 2005).

v. **purchase()** calculates the price and freezes the contents of the cart (Binder et al., 2015).

Alternatively, the finite state machine shown in Figure 1.5 might be used to model the shopping cart. Although it contains state-related characteristics, it does not replace the informal specification. Deriving invocation sequences that encompass various finite state machine components can be used to create test cases. All transitions must be covered according to a straightforward criterion (transition coverage). Many types of pathways must be traversed in order to satisfy sophisticated criteria (Utting et al., 2012).

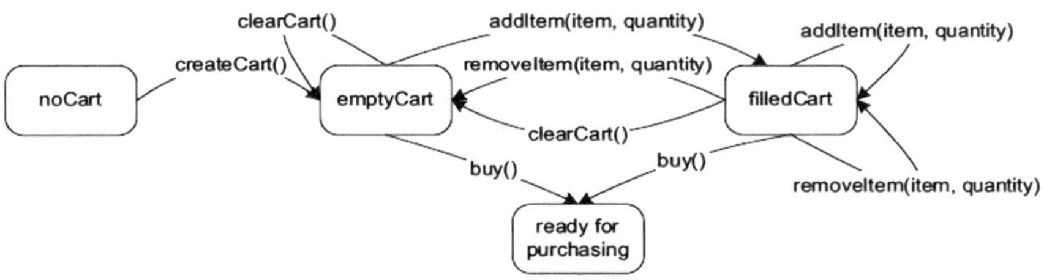

Figure 1.5. A model of the shopping cart's finite state machines derived from its vague specification.

Source: Mauro Pezzè et al., creative commons license.

Frequently, models that offer characteristics for model simplification are used to portray finite-state behaviors. Among the most common examples is a StateChart, which can substantially simplify a finite state machine by including default states, histories, and/or-decomposed states (Aichernig et al., 2018). For instance, the two buy edges of the finite state machine of Figure 1.5's empyCart, and filledCart states can be combined into a single state in the StateCharts of Figure 1.6. Most of the time, it is simple to expand the finite state machine-specific criteria and add new ones that make use of the new model's unique structure. By focusing only on the transformation of the StateCharts and not all the transformations of the identical finite state machine, for instance, the size of the created test cases for big StateCharts can be reduced (Dias & Travassos, 2010).

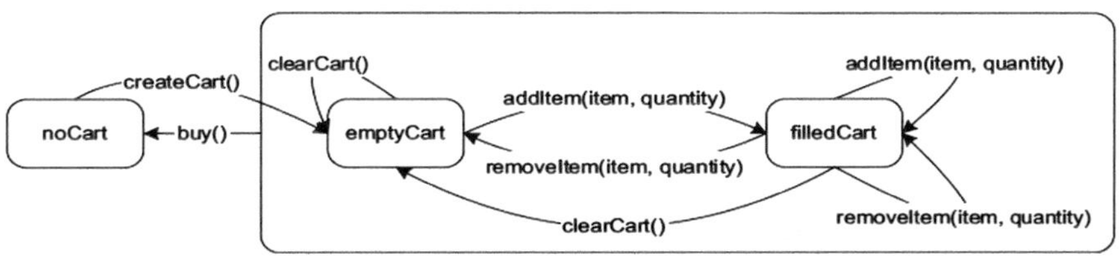

Figure 1.6. A stateCharts description of the shopping cart from the previous section.

Source: Mauro Pezzè et al., creative commons license.

1.6. TESTING LEVELS

Various abstraction levels are used in the development of software: modules may be created specifically for a system or may be repurposed from other systems; subsystems are created by incorporating sets of repurposed elements; (Pyc & Rawson, 2009) and the final system is created by compiling elements and subsystems into an application that fulfills the pre-requisites. As shown by the conventional V model in Figure 1.7, testing is done at each level. Module, integration, system, and acceptability testing are frequently distinguished (Labiche et al., 2000).

1.6.1. Module Testing

Typically, the developers themselves do an initial isolation test on each module or component to ensure that it behaves as planned (module testing) (Hayes, 1986). Comprehensive module testing is essential for finding and fixing errors that would otherwise be challenging to find and expensive to fix in later development stages. Structural and functional testing are both a part of module testing. Functional test cases can be produced from module specifications by employing an effective functional or module-based test method, such as those described in the previous section (Alexander et al., 2006).

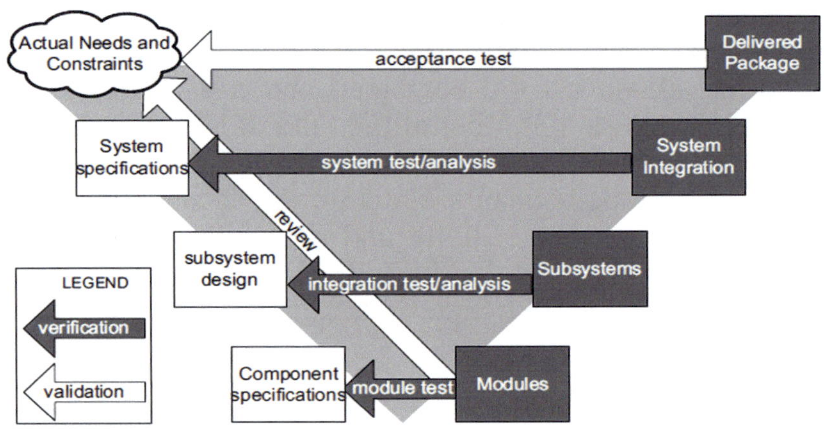

Figure 1.7. The V-shaped progression of development and evaluation.

Source: Tutorialspoint, creative commons license.

Functional testing may fail to identify some types of issues because engineers may create the same function in various ways, and the test cases created from a particular element may not encompass all available versions. An understandable example is an effective sorting technique that handles extremely small sets, sets that are somewhat large, and sets that are larger than the available memory (Marinissen et al., 2002). A straightforward quadratic algorithm, such as bubblesort, is sufficient for sorting small sets, that quicksort may be recommended for sorting large sets that exist in storage, and that treesort is better for sorting sets that are larger than the available memory (Li et al., 2005).

Functional testing covers the functionality of the code; structural testing examines the code's structure and addresses scenarios that are not covered by functional testing. The application of structural testing typically occurs in two steps: first, programmers determine the code coverage using straightforward coverage tools that show the percentage of covered code and emphasize the missing portions of the code, and then they create test cases that range covered portions of the code. Several code components might be considered when calculating coverage (Jha et al., 2009). The simplest coverage criteria measure the proportion of statements that are actually executed by the test cases and is statement-centric. The number of branches that are exercised by the tests is measured by branch coverage criteria. The number of paths that the tests cover is measured by path coverage criteria. Depending on how paths are chosen, several path coverage requirements can be found. Data flow is referred to in additional criteria. Readers can find more details on code coverage in (Abuelnaga et al., 2021).

Coverage requirements include non-executable items because they consist of all the components. Unfortunately, there is no solution to the problem of recognizing executable elements. Therefore, we are unable to choose only the appropriate subset of implementable elements automatically (Cappa et al., 2018).

Code coverage is typically used as an approximatively metric to track module testing operations rather than as an absolute indicator. For instance, if we talk about statement coverage, the presence of up to 10–15% of non-implementable statements may be tolerable. Still, a higher percentage may indicate either a poor design that results in an excessive number of non-executable statements. This poor specification makes it impossible to derive an appropriate set of functional test cases. When the coverage drops below a desirable level, test developers and designers look more closely at the module to find and fix the issue (Wohlgemuth & Kurtz, 2011).

In some serious situations, all components that are not tested are evaluated to see if they can be tested or what factors lead to the appearance of non-executable statements. For instance, the quality standards generally used in the avionics industry, RTCA/DO-178B "Software Considerations in Airborne Systems and Equipment Certification," and its European equivalent, EUROCAE ED-12B, mandate MCDC coverage for on-board software and manual testing of components (Yan et al., 2013).

The modified condition adequacy (MCDC)Z& criterion applies to basic conditions. It demands that each basic condition be proved to have an independent impact on each choice. In other words, there are two test instances for each basic condition C in which the truth values of all conditions other than C are the same, and the compound condition as a whole assesses to true for one of those test cases and false for the other (Wohlgemuth & Kurtz, 2014).

1.6.2. Integration and Component-Based Testing

The quality of individual modules is essential but insufficient to ensure the quality of the final system. The breakdown of low-quality modules results in devastating system breakdowns that are frequently hard to detect and costly to eradicate. Sadly, unexpected interactions between well modules generate numerous subtle failures. Unexpected connections among well-developed software components are reported in the investigative statements of the Ariane 5 accident that resulted in the rocket's destruction on July 4th, 1996 and the Mars Climate Orbiter's failure to attain Mars orbit on September 23rd, 1999 (Kim et al., 2008).

A module that had been successfully tested and utilized on earlier Ariane 4 missions collapsed on the first Ariane 5 mission, which set off a series of unfortunate events that resulted in the loss of the rocket in the Ariane accident. The horizontal bias computation module malfunctioned due to an overflow brought on by the Ariane 5 rocket's higher horizontal velocity than the Ariane 4 rocket. Software created by the JPL laboratory and software created by the main contractor Lockheed Martin unexpectedly interacted, leading to the loss of the Mars Climate Orbiter. While the spacecraft operational data required for map reading were anticipated to be in metric units, the software created by Lockheed Martin delivered data in English units. When used in systems relating to homogenous measurement systems, both modules performed admirably; however, when used improperly, they failed (Wu et al., 2003).

Incomplete specifications or poor executions of interfaces, resource utilization, or necessary attributes are ultimately responsible for integration errors. Unfortunately, it could be challenging or expensive to fully identify all module communications. For instance, it might be challenging to forecast communications between distant and seemingly irrelevant modules that transmit an interim hidden file that just so happens to have the same name as two different modules, especially if the name clash only occasionally occurs and only in specific patterns. Many factors can lead to integration errors (Schlatow et al., 2017):

- A parameter or value being interpreted inconsistently, such as when the Mars Climate elucidated both English and metric units;

- Unintentional non-observance of capacity or size, such as the overflowing of a buffer in some versions of the Apache 2 Web server;
- Effects on resources, such as those that can occur when modules use resources that aren't quoted in their interfaces (Yau & Dong, 2000);
- Functionality that is either missing or incorrect, which can occur when incomplete specifications are poorly read;
- Dynamic mismatches, which result from unpredicted dynamic bindings (Wu et al., 2001); and
- Non-functional difficulties, which arise from under specified non-functional attributes.

Many connecting modules are examined during integration testing. Big bang testing, which awaits until all modules have been assembled, is fruitless because integration flaws may spread across other modules and go undetected, or they may show up as defects much later than when they actually occur and become challenging to identify and eliminate. The majority of integration testing approaches advise testing integrated parts gradually (Crnkovic, 2001). The two types of integration strategies are structural and feature-driven. Structural strategies, which include bottom-up and top-down techniques as well as their combination—sometimes known as a backbone strategy—define the order of integration in accordance with the design structure. They involve integrating modules based on the use and include relationships, starting from the top, bottom, or both sides, as appropriate (Beydeda et al., 2001).

Thread and critical module strategies are examples of feature-driven methods that specify the sequence of integration in accordance with the dynamic interaction trends among modules. Thread testing recommends integrating modules in accordance with execution threads that match system features (Vitharana, 2003). Modules are integrated as part of critical module testing in accordance with the related risk factor that characterizes the singularity of modules. However, feature-driven test approaches typically involve more complicated preparation and administration than structural strategies since they better align with development strategies that result in early implementable systems. Thus, they are only preferred for large systems where the benefits outweigh the additional expenditures (Weyuker, 1998).

Integration testing is further complicated by the use of COTS components. Components are distinct from conventional modules in that they can be used in a variety of contexts without regard to how they were originally developed. Designers who reiterate components frequently do not have access to the source code and must instead depend on the interface standards (Gill & Grover, 2003). Moreover, components are frequently reused in situations that were not necessarily anticipated during creation, and as a result, their behavior could not quite fit the requirements. When determining test suites specific to the contemplated environment, designers should compare their requirements with the offered profiles and re-run the compilation tests connected with the profiles (Mahmood et al., 2007).

1.6.3. System, Acceptance, and Regression Testing

Module and integration testing can give assurance regarding the quality of the individual modules and their communications, but not regarding how the system will behave as a whole. For instance, the implementation of the discount rules as specified in the system requirements may not be guaranteed even if a module precisely manages the product database and it interacts with the module that calculates costs in a proper manner (Davis, 1993). Furthermore, just because a system complies with the requirements and specifications does not guarantee its performance. So, we must test the entire system against its requirements and those of its users in order to finalize the validation and verification process. System testing confirms the entire system's compliance with its specifications, whereas acceptance testing confirms the system's compliance with users' expectations (Alegroth et al., 2013).

System and acceptability testing take into account both the functional and non-functional aspects of the entire system's behavior. The internals of the software constitutes a major foundation for module and integration testing (Fawzy & Esawai, 2017). As a result, they concentrate on verification processes that yield valuable information without necessitating the installation of the entire system or the presence of users. As was covered before in this section, the majority of module and integration testing operations concentrate on functional features (Ali et al., 2005).

Simple static analysis tools and human investigation can be used to check some non-functional qualities, such as modularity, maintainability, and testability, although comprehensive testing is not necessary. Other crucial non-functional characteristics, such as performance, can also be enforced by better design practices, but users and the entire system must be present during testing to be effective (Hasan, 2006). Early prototypes can be subjected to usability and performance tests and analyzes to evaluate important design choices and catch some development faults. Still, tests on the deployed system are necessary to produce accurate results. Additional non-functional features, such as security and privacy, are taken into account by specialized teams of specialists who operate along with the testing team rather than by the testing team (Sek et al., 2010).

Because of the scale of the software, structural testing is not very helpful in system testing. It is of limited use to measure code coverage to detect a way that hasn't yet been used. However, determining the set of available features and taking into account all scenarios is crucial for spotting system faults. As a result, functional and model-based testing are the main foundations of system testing. The most significant challenge in system testing is comprehending the often enormously complex requirements specifications (Leung & Wong, 1997). Thankfully, specifications are created for software architects who must comprehend the entire system and recognize a unified software architecture. As a result, specifications are frequently well-organized, and good designers may spot aspects that can be verified separately. The basic processes of system testing are shown in Figure 1.8. Individually testable features, or characteristics that can be managed cogently by a single test designer are first identified by quality engineers. Test designers choose the optimal testing strategy for each of the identified features; this strategy may be model-based testing or functional testing (Nurhayati et al., 2019).

Instead of being created in a sequential fashion, the software is built and released frequently. Every new project or version has the potential to add or expose errors, leading to problems not seen in earlier iterations. It is crucial to ensure that any newer version does not go backward in comparison to earlier ones. Such testing is frequently referred to as regression testing, or non-regression testing, in short (Faisal et al., 2021).

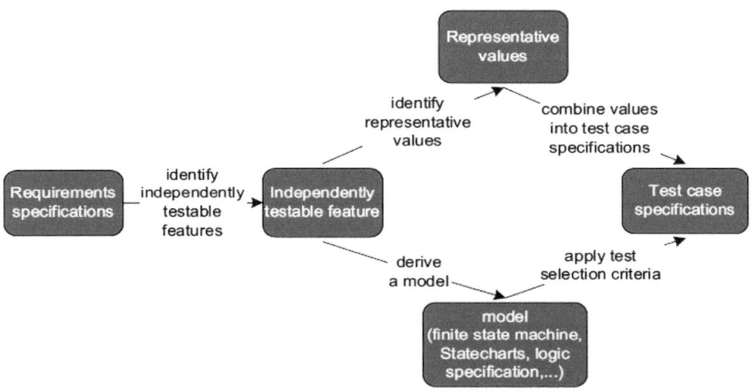

Figure 1.8. A systematic approach to system testing.

Source: Mauro Pezzè et al., creative commons license.

Restarting all the test cases created for the prior versions is a straightforward regression testing strategy known as the "retest all approach," and it is used to see if the new version exhibits any odd behaviors that weren't present in the previous versions. This straightforward method could result in significant expenses and nontrivial issues because it requires changing test cases that aren't quickly relied on the recent version. Also, the price of performing all test cases again could be prohibitive and perhaps useless (Seymour et al., 2007).

With ad-hoc procedures created for the particular application, the quantity of test cases that need to be re-run can be decreased. Techniques for selection are based on codes. The people who work on the code keep track of the program elements that were put to the test in earlier versions and choose test cases that put the current release's altered elements to the test (Davis, 1989). Several code-based selection methods concentrate on various programming features, such as control-flow, data-flow, etc. Code-based selection techniques have good tool support and function even when specifications are not kept up to date, but they are difficult to scale up: they work well for small, local modifications, but offer challenges when changes affect significant areas of the product (Khorasani & Zeyun, 2014).

Techniques for selection that are based on changes to the specifications are emphasized. Compared to code-based solutions, they scale up significantly better because they are not constrained by the quantity of altered code but rather call for adequately maintained specifications (Roubtsov & Heck, 2006). They perform especially well with model-based testing methodologies, which can be enhanced using trackers to pinpoint tests that need to be run again. For instance, if the system is described using finite state machines, it is simple to modify traditional test generation parameters to concentrate on the finite state machine components that have been altered or added in the most recent build (Ding et al., 2019).

Techniques for prioritizing test cases define preferences among tests and provide various execution plans rather than choosing a subset of test cases. Priorities are set up to delay the implementation of cases that are less likely to uncover flaws in order to maximize the effectiveness of tests. The effectiveness of defect detection, execution histories, and code structure are the foundations of common priority schemas (ALraja, 2015). Recent test cases are given low priority by history-based priority schemas. By doing this, we can ensure that every test case will eventually be run again. For some releases, like overnight regression testing, this technique excels. Priority schemas that concentrate on fault-identification increase the priority of tests that expose flaws in the latest versions, making them more likely to work out unstable sections of the code and expose flaws that have been present for a while. Schemas with structural priorities provide precedence to either test cases that exercise recently run elements or test cases that produce good coverage (Liker & Sindi, 1997).

In the first scenario, they work to reduce the likelihood that certain sections of code would go untested for a long period of time; in the second scenario, they work to reduce the number of tests that must be run repeatedly in order to attain sufficient coverage (Hanssen & Haugset, 2009). By locating, eliminating, and appropriately marking redundant test cases, high-quality test suites can be maintained throughout versions. Planning, test specifications, and reporting papers all belong in good test documentation. Test plans, which are discussed in Section 2, and test strategies, which list the company's or group's quality strategies, are examples of planning papers. Test suites and lone test cases are the main subjects of test specification documents. The coordination of specification and reporting documents is necessary for regression testing (Reinke, 2003).

ACTIVITY 1.1.

What is software testing? Give a detail presentation.

SUMMARY

Since software testing has been a topic of ongoing research for many years, quality engineers today can gain from a variety of findings, tools, and approaches. Even if many conventional study fields are still available, there are still plenty of challenges to be overcome due to advancements in design and application. The majority of the outcomes from research on testing theory to date have been negative, indicating the discipline's limitations yet urging further research. We still need a solid foundation for contrasting various standards and methods. While useful, the testing methods now in use are still not entirely satisfactory. In order to address new programming paradigms, we need new approaches, but more importantly, we need greater test automation assistance.

Complex computer systems, heterogeneous mobile applications, and component-based development provide additional difficulties. For modern software systems, it is often difficult to forecast all potential applications and execution frameworks, so we must shift from traditional testing schemes that primarily function before deployment, to those that function after deployment, such as dynamic analysis, and self-organizing software.

REVIEW QUESTIONS

1. What is software testing, and why is it essential in the software development process?
2. What are the different types of software testing, and what are the advantages and disadvantages of each approach?
3. What is the difference between functional and non-functional testing, and why is it important to test both?
4. What are some common challenges associated with software testing, and how can they be addressed?
5. How do you design an effective testing strategy, and what factors should be considered when creating a test plan?
6. What are some best practices for managing and reporting software defects, and how can defect tracking systems help streamline the process?

MULTIPLE CHOICE QUESTIONS

1. What is software testing?

a. The process of finding errors in software code
b. The process of fixing errors in software code
c. The process of writing software code
d. The process of designing software code

2. **What is the main goal of software testing?**
   a. To ensure that software code is free of errors
   b. To ensure that software code is delivered on time
   c. To ensure that software code is designed properly
   d. To ensure that software code is profitable
3. **Which of the following is NOT a type of software testing?**
   a. Unit testing
   b. Integration testing
   c. Documentation testing
   d. Performance testing
4. **Which type of testing focuses on testing the functionality of the software?**
   a. Unit testing
   b. Integration testing
   c. System testing
   d. Acceptance testing
5. **Which of the following is a benefit of software testing?**
   a. Decreased development time
   b. Increased development costs
   c. Increased customer satisfaction
   d. Decreased quality of the software

Answers to Multiple Choice Questions

1. (a); 2. (a); 3. (c); 4. (c); 5. (c)

REFERENCES

1. Abuelnaga, A., Narimani, M., & Bahman, A. S., (2021). A review on IGBT module failure modes and lifetime testing. *IEEE Access, 9*, 9643–9663.
2. Aichernig, B. K., Mostowski, W., Mousavi, M. R., Tappler, M., & Taromirad, M., (2018). Model learning and model-based testing. In: *Machine Learning for Dynamic Software Analysis: Potentials and Limits: International Dagstuhl Seminar 16172, Dagstuhl Castle, Germany, April 24–27, 2016, Revised Papers* (pp. 74–100).
3. Alegroth, E., Nass, M., & Olsson, H. H., (2013). JAutomate: A tool for system-and acceptance-test automation. In: *2013 IEEE Sixth International Conference on Software Testing, Verification and Validation* (pp. 439–446).

4. Alexander, A., Bergman, P., Hagströmer, M., & Sjöström, M., (2006). IPAQ environmental module; reliability testing. *Journal of Public Health, 14*, 76–80.
5. Ali, A. S. B., & Money, W. H., (2005). A study of project management system acceptance. In: *Proceedings of the 38th Annual Hawaii International Conference on System Sciences* (pp. 234c).
6. ALraja, M. N., (2015). User acceptance of information technology: A field study of an e-mail system adoption from the individual students' perspective. *Mediterranean Journal of Social Sciences, 6*(6 S1), 19.
7. Arditi, D., & Gunaydin, H. M., (1997). Total quality management in the construction process. *International Journal of Project Management, 15*(4), 235–243.
8. Babuska, I., & Oden, J. T., (2004). Verification and validation in computational engineering and science: Basic concepts. *Computer Methods in Applied Mechanics and Engineering, 193*(36–38), 4057–4066.
9. Baresi, L., & Pezze, M., (2006). An introduction to software testing. *Electronic Notes in Theoretical Computer Science, 148*(1), 89–111.
10. Barr, E. T., Harman, M., McMinn, P., Shahbaz, M., & Yoo, S., (2014). The oracle problem in software testing: A survey. *IEEE Transactions on Software Engineering, 41*(5), 507–525.
11. Berke, P. R., & French, S. P., (1994). The influence of state planning mandates on local plan quality. *Journal of Planning Education and Research, 13*(4), 237–250.
12. Berke, P., & Godschalk, D., (2009). Searching for the good plan: A meta-analysis of plan quality studies. *Journal of Planning Literature, 23*(3), 227–240.
13. Beydeda, S., & Gruhn, V., (2001). An integrated testing technique for component-based software. In: *Proceedings ACS/IEEE International Conference on Computer Systems and Applications* (pp. 328–334).
14. Binder, R. V., Legeard, B., & Kramer, A., (2015). Model-based testing: Where does it stand? *Communications of the ACM, 58*(2), 52–56.
15. Brahme, D., & Abraham, J. A., (1984). Functional testing of microprocessors. *IEEE Transactions on Computers, 33*(06), 475–485.
16. Brody, S. D., (2003). Are we learning to make better plans? A longitudinal analysis of plan quality associated with natural hazards. *Journal of Planning Education and Research, 23*(2), 191–201.
17. Caldwell, G., Gow, S. M., Sweeting, V. M., Kellett, H. A., Beckett, G. J., Seth, J., & Toft, A. D., (1985). A new strategy for thyroid function testing. *The Lancet, 325*(8438), 1117–1119.
18. Candea, G., Bucur, S., & Zamfir, C., (2010). Automated software testing as a service. In: *Proceedings of the 1st ACM Symposium on Cloud Computing* (pp. 155–160).
19. Cappa, C., Mont, D., Loeb, M., Misunas, C., Madans, J., Comic, T., & De Castro, F., (2018). The development and testing of a module on child functioning for identifying

children with disabilities on surveys. III: Field testing. *Disability and Health Journal, 11*(4), 510–518.

20. Carson, J. S., (2002). Model verification and validation. In: *Proceedings of the Winter Simulation Conference* (Vol. 1, pp. 52–58).
21. Causevic, A., Sundmark, D., & Punnekkat, S., (2010). An industrial survey on contemporary aspects of software testing. In: *2010 Third International Conference on Software Testing, Verification and Validation* (Vol. 1, pp. 393–401).
22. Chowdhury, R. S., & Forsmark, C. E., (2003). Pancreatic function testing. *Alimentary Pharmacology & Therapeutics, 17*(6), 733–750.
23. Ciortea, L., Zamfir, C., Bucur, S., Chipounov, V., & Candea, G., (2010). Cloud9: A software testing service. *ACM SIGOPS Operating Systems Review, 43*(4), 5–10.
24. Cooper, B. G., (2011). An update on contraindications for lung function testing. *Thorax, 66*(8), 714–723.
25. Crapo, R. O., (1994). Pulmonary-function testing. *New England Journal of Medicine, 331*(1), 25–30.
26. Crnkovic, I., (2001). Component-based software engineering—New challenges in software development. *Software Focus, 2*(4), 127–133.
27. Dalal, S. R., Jain, A., Karunanithi, N., Leaton, J. M., Lott, C. M., Patton, G. C., & Horowitz, B. M., (1999). Model-based testing in practice. In: *Proceedings of the 21st International Conference on Software Engineering* (pp. 285–294).
28. Davis, F. D., (1989). Technology acceptance model: TAM. In: Al-Suqri, M. N., & Al-Aufi, A. S., (eds.), *Information Seeking Behavior and Technology Adoption* (pp. 205–219).
29. Davis, F. D., (1993). User acceptance of information technology: System characteristics, user perceptions and behavioral impacts. *International Journal of Man-Machine Studies, 38*(3), 475–487.
30. DeMillo, R. A., Guindi, D. S., McCracken, W. M., Offutt, A. J., & King, K. N., (1988). An extended overview of the Mothra software testing environment. In: *Workshop on Software Testing, Verification, and Analysis* (pp. 142, 143).
31. Dias-Neto, A. C., & Travassos, G. H., (2010). A picture from the model-based testing area: Concepts, techniques, and challenges. In: *Advances in Computers* (Vol. 80, pp. 45–120).
32. Ding, Z., Saide, S., Astuti, E. S., Muwardi, D., Najamuddin, N., Jannati, M., & Herzavina, H., (2019). An adoption of acceptance model for the multi-purpose system in university library. *Economic Research-Ekonomska Istraživanja, 32*(1), 2393–2403.
33. Donabedian, A., (1968). Promoting quality through evaluating the process of patient care. *Medical Care, 6*(3), 181–202.
34. Douglas, P. S., Hoffmann, U., Patel, M. R., Mark, D. B., Al-Khalidi, H. R., Cavanaugh, B., & Lee, K. L., (2015). Outcomes of anatomical versus functional testing for coronary artery disease. *New England Journal of Medicine, 372*(14), 1291–1300.

35. Faisal, A., Handayanna, F., & Purnamasari, I., (2021). Implementation technology acceptance model (tam) on acceptance of the zoom application in online learning. *Jurnal Riset Informatika, 3*(2), 85–92.

36. Favaloro, E. J., Lippi, G., & Franchini, M., (2010). Contemporary platelet function testing. *Clinical Chemistry and Laboratory Medicine, 48*(5), 579–598.

37. Fawzy, S. F., & Esawai, N., (2017). Internet banking adoption in Egypt: Extending technology acceptance model. *Journal of Business and Retail Management Research, 12*(1), 109–118.

38. Garousi, V., & Mäntylä, M. V., (2016). When and what to automate in software testing? A multi-vocal literature review. *Information and Software Technology, 76*, 92–117.

39. Gill, N. S., & Grover, P. S., (2003). Component-based measurement: Few useful guidelines. *ACM SIGSOFT Software Engineering Notes, 28*(6), 4.

40. Gowen, A. A., O'donnell, C. P., Cullen, P. J., & Bell, S. E. J., (2008). Recent applications of chemical imaging to pharmaceutical process monitoring and quality control. *European Journal of Pharmaceutics and Biopharmaceutics, 69*(1), 10–22.

41. Gowen, A. A., O'Sullivan, C., & O'Donnell, C. P., (2012). Terahertz time domain spectroscopy and imaging: Emerging techniques for food process monitoring and quality control. *Trends in Food Science & Technology, 25*(1), 40–46.

42. Hanssen, G. K., & Haugset, B., (2009). Automated acceptance testing using fit. In: *2009 42nd Hawaii International Conference on System Sciences* (pp. 1–8).

43. Hartman, A., & Nagin, K., (2004). The AGEDIS tools for model-based testing. *ACM SIGSOFT Software Engineering Notes, 29*(4), 129–132.

44. Harvey, L., (2005). A history and critique of quality evaluation in the UK. *Quality Assurance in Education, 13*(4), 263–276.

45. Hasan, B., (2006). Delineating the effects of general and system-specific computer self-efficacy beliefs on IS acceptance. *Information & Management, 43*(5), 565–571.

46. Hayes, I. J., (1986). Specification directed module testing. *IEEE Transactions on Software Engineering*, (1), 124–133.

47. Howden, W. E., (1980). Functional program testing. *IEEE Transactions on Software Engineering*, (2), 162–169.

48. Jha, P. C., Gupta, D., Yang, B., & Kapur, P. K., (2009). Optimal testing resource allocation during module testing considering cost, testing effort and reliability. *Computers & Industrial Engineering, 57*(3), 1122–1130.

49. Juristo, N., Moreno, A. M., & Strigel, W., (2006). Guest editors' introduction: Software testing practices in industry. *IEEE Software, 23*(4), 19–21.

50. Kano, M., & Nakagawa, Y., (2008). Data-based process monitoring, process control, and quality improvement: Recent developments and applications in steel industry. *Computers & Chemical Engineering, 32*(1, 2), 12–24.

51. Kehrel, B. E., & Brodde, M. F., (2013). State of the art in platelet function testing. *Transfusion Medicine and Hemotherapy, 40*(2), 73–86.

52. Khorasani, G., & Zeyun, L., (2014). Implementation of technology acceptance model (TAM) in business research on web-based learning system. *International Journal of Innovative Technology and Exploring Engineering, 3*(11), 112–116.

53. Kim, S., Park, S., Yun, J., & Lee, Y., (2008). Automated continuous integration of component-based software: An industrial experience. In: *2008 23rd IEEE/ACM International Conference on Automated Software Engineering* (pp. 423–426).

54. Kuvin, J. T., & Karas, R. H., (2003). Clinical utility of endothelial function testing: Ready for prime time? *Circulation, 107*(25), 3243–3247.

55. Labiche, Y., Thévenod-Fosse, P., Waeselynck, H., & Durand, M. H., (2000). Testing levels for object-oriented software. In: *Proceedings of the 22nd International Conference on Software Engineering* (pp. 136–145).

56. Le Traon, Y., Mouelhi, T., & Baudry, B., (2007). Testing security policies: Going beyond functional testing. In: *The 18th IEEE International Symposium on Software Reliability (ISSRE'07)* (pp. 93–102).

57. Lemos, O. A. L., Silveira, F. F., Ferrari, F. C., & Garcia, A., (2018). The impact of software testing education on code reliability: An empirical assessment. *Journal of Systems and Software, 137*, 497–511.

58. Leung, H. K., & Wong, P. W., (1997). A study of user acceptance tests. *Software Quality Journal, 6*, 137–149.

59. Li, H. Y., Li, W. H., Wong, L. Y., & Hwang, N., (2005). Built-in via module test structure for backend interconnection in-line process monitor. In: *Proceedings of the 12th International Symposium on the Physical and Failure Analysis of Integrated Circuits, 2005; IPFA 2005* (pp. 167–170).

60. Lieb, II. J. G., & Draganov, P. V., (2008). Pancreatic function testing: Here to stay for the 21st century. *World Journal of Gastroenterology: WJG, 14*(20), 3149.

61. Liker, J. K., & Sindi, A. A., (1997). User acceptance of expert systems: A test of the theory of reasoned action. *Journal of Engineering and Technology Management, 14*(2), 147–173.

62. Lyles, W., & Stevens, M., (2014). Plan quality evaluation 1994–2012: Growth and contributions, limitations, and new directions. *Journal of Planning Education and Research, 34*(4), 433–450.

63. Mahmood, S., Lai, R., & Kim, Y. S., (2007). Survey of component-based software development. *IET Software, 1*(2), 57–66.

64. Marinissen, E. J., Iyengar, V., & Chakrabarty, K., (2002). A set of benchmarks for modular testing of SOCs. In: *Proceedings. International Test Conference* (pp. 519–528).

65. Mentzer, J. T., Flint, D. J., & Hult, G. T. M., (2001). Logistics service quality as a segment-customized process. *Journal of Marketing, 65*(4), 82–104.

66. Meyers, D. C., Durlak, J. A., & Wandersman, A., (2012). The quality implementation framework: A synthesis of critical steps in the implementation process. *American Journal of Community Psychology, 50*, 462–480.

67. Michelson, A. D., (2004). Platelet function testing in cardiovascular diseases. *Circulation, 110*(19), e489–e493.

68. Miller, M. R., Crapo, R., Hankinson, J., Brusasco, V., Burgos, F., Casaburi, R., & Wanger, J. A. T. S., (2005). General considerations for lung function testing. *European Respiratory Journal, 26*(1), 153–161.

69. Moore, K. L., Brame, R. S., Low, D. A., & Mutic, S., (2012). Quantitative metrics for assessing plan quality. In: *Seminars in Radiation Oncology* (Vol. 22, No. 1, pp. 62–69). WB Saunders.

70. Muñoz, J. E. D., (2010). Diagnosis of chronic pancreatitis: Functional testing. *Best Practice & Research Clinical Gastroenterology, 24*(3), 233–241.

71. Nidagundi, P., & Novickis, L., (2017). Introducing lean canvas model adaptation in the scrum software testing. *Procedia Computer Science, 104*, 97–103.

72. Nurhayati, S., Anandari, D., & Ekowati, W., (2019). Unified theory of acceptance and usage of technology (UTAUT) model to predict health information system adoption. *KEMAS: Jurnal Kesehatan Masyarakat, 15*(1), 89–97.

73. Oberkampf, W. L., & Trucano, T. G., (2002). Verification and validation in computational fluid dynamics. *Progress in Aerospace Sciences, 38*(3), 209–272.

74. Oberkampf, W. L., & Trucano, T. G., (2008). Verification and validation benchmarks. *Nuclear Engineering and Design, 238*(3), 716–743.

75. Phillipsen, L. C., Burchinal, M. R., Howes, C., & Cryer, D., (1997). The prediction of process quality from structural features of child care. *Early Childhood Research Quarterly, 12*(3), 281–303.

76. Piwowarski, P., Ohba, M., & Caruso, J., (1993). Coverage measurement experience during function test. In: *Proceedings of 1993 15th International Conference on Software Engineering* (pp. 287–301).

77. Porteus, E. L., (1986). Optimal lot sizing, process quality improvement and setup cost reduction. *Operations Research, 34*(1), 137–144.

78. Pretschner, A., (2005). Model-based testing. In: *Proceedings of the 27th International Conference on Software Engineering* (pp. 722, 723).

79. Pretschner, A., Prenninger, W., Wagner, S., Kühnel, C., Baumgartner, M., Sostawa, B., & Stauner, T., (2005). One evaluation of model-based testing and its automation. In: *Proceedings of the 27th International Conference on Software Engineering* (pp. 392–401).

80. Pyc, M. A., & Rawson, K. A., (2009). Testing the retrieval effort hypothesis: Does greater difficulty correctly recalling information lead to higher levels of memory? *Journal of Memory and Language, 60*(4), 437–447.

81. Ranu, H., Wilde, M., & Madden, B., (2011). Pulmonary function tests. *Ulster Med J., 80*(2), 84–90.

82. Reichert, P., Borchardt, D., Henze, M., Rauch, W., Shanahan, P., Somlyódy, L., & Vanrolleghem, P., (2001). River water quality model no. 1 (RWQM1): II. Biochemical

process equations. *Water Science and Technology, 43*(5), 11–30.

83. Reinke, S. J., (2003). Does the form really matter? Leadership, trust, and acceptance of the performance appraisal process. *Review of Public Personnel Administration, 23*(1), 23–37.
84. Roubtsov, S., & Heck, P., (2006). Use case-based acceptance testing of a large industrial system: Approach and experience report. In: *Testing: Academic & Industrial Conference-Practice And Research Techniques (TAIC PART'06)* (pp. 211–220).
85. Ryan, M. J., & Wheatcraft, L. S., (2017). On the use of the terms verification and validation. In: *INCOSE International Symposium* (Vol. 27, No. 1, pp. 1277–1290).
86. Sargent, R. G., (1987). An overview of verification and validation of simulation models. In: *Proceedings of the 19th Conference on Winter Simulation* (pp. 33–39).
87. Sargent, R. G., (2009). Verification and validation of simulation models. In: *Proceedings of the 2009 Winter Simulation Conference (WSC)* (pp. 162–176).
88. Sargent, R. G., (2010). Verification and validation of simulation models. In: *Proceedings of the 2010 Winter Simulation Conference* (pp. 166–183).
89. Sargent, R. G., (2015). Model verification and validation. *Modeling and Simulation in the Systems Engineering Life Cycle: Core Concepts and Accompanying Lectures*, 57–65.
90. Schieferdecker, I., & Hoffmann, A., (2012). Model-based testing. *IEEE Software, 29*(1), 14–18.
91. Schlatow, J., Möstl, M., Ernst, R., Nolte, M., Jatzkowski, I., & Maurer, M., (2017). Towards model-based integration of component-based automotive software systems. In: *IECON 2017–43rd Annual Conference of the IEEE Industrial Electronics Society* (pp. 8425–8432).
92. Sek, Y. W., Lau, S. H., Teoh, K. K., Law, C. Y., & Parumo, S. B., (2010). Prediction of user acceptance and adoption of smart phone for learning with technology acceptance model. *Journal of Applied Sciences (Faisalabad), 10*(20), 2395–2402.
93. Seymour, L., Makanya, W., & Berrangé, S., (2007). End-users' acceptance of enterprise resource planning systems: An investigation of antecedents. In: *Proceedings of the 6th Annual ISOnEworld Conference* (pp. 1–22).
94. Shah, N. N., Bowd, C., Medeiros, F. A., Weinreb, R. N., Sample, P. A., Hoffmann, E. M., & Zangwill, L. M., (2006). Combining structural and functional testing for detection of glaucoma. *Ophthalmology, 113*(9), 1593–1602.
95. Slot, P. L., Leseman, P. P., Verhagen, J., & Mulder, H., (2015). Associations between structural quality aspects and process quality in Dutch early childhood education and care settings. *Early Childhood Research Quarterly, 33*, 64–76.
96. Smidt, E., & Schwanninger, M., (2005). Characterization of waste materials using FTIR spectroscopy: Process monitoring and quality assessment. *Spectroscopy Letters, 38*(3), 247–270.

97. Steenkamp, J. B. E., (1990). Conceptual model of the quality perception process. *Journal of Business Research, 21*(4), 309–333.
98. Thapa, B. R., & Walia, A., (2007). Liver function tests and their interpretation. *The Indian Journal of Pediatrics, 74*, 663–671.
99. Utting, M., Pretschner, A., & Legeard, B., (2012). A taxonomy of model-based testing approaches. *Software Testing, Verification and Reliability, 22*(5), 297–312.
100. Van, D. B. A., Mummery, C. L., Passier, R., & Van, De. M. A. D., (2019). Personalized organs-on-chips: Functional testing for precision medicine. *Lab on a Chip, 19*(2), 198–205.
101. Vitharana, P., (2003). Risks and challenges of component-based software development. *Communications of the ACM, 46*(8), 67–72.
102. Wallace, D. R., & Fujii, R. U., (1989). Software verification and validation: An overview. *IEEE Software, 6*(3), 10–17.
103. Weyuker, E. J., (1998). Testing component-based software: A cautionary tale. *IEEE Software, 15*(5), 54–59.
104. Wohlgemuth, J. H., & Kurtz, S., (2011). Using accelerated testing to predict module reliability. In: *2011 37th IEEE Photovoltaic Specialists Conference* (pp. 003601–003605).
105. Wohlgemuth, J., & Kurtz, S., (2014). Photovoltaic module qualification plus testing. In: *2014 IEEE 40th Photovoltaic Specialist Conference (PVSC)* (pp. 3589–3594).
106. Wu, C. W., Pearn, W. L., & Kotz, S., (2009). An overview of theory and practice on process capability indices for quality assurance. *International Journal of Production Economics, 117*(2), 338–359.
107. Wu, Y., Chen, M. H., & Offutt, J., (2003). UML-based integration testing for component-based software. In: *COTS-Based Software Systems: Second International Conference, ICCBSS 2003 Ottawa, Canada, February 10–12, 2003 Proceedings 2* (pp. 251–260).
108. Wu, Y., Pan, D., & Chen, M. H., (2001). Techniques for testing component-based software. In: *Proceedings Seventh IEEE International Conference on Engineering of Complex Computer Systems* (pp. 222–232).
109. Wuyts, F. L., Furman, J., Vanspauwen, R., & Van De, H. P., (2007). Vestibular function testing. *Current Opinion in Neurology, 20*(1), 19–24.
110. Yan, F., Noble, J., Peltola, J., Wicks, S., & Balasubramanian, S., (2013). Semitransparent OPV modules pass environmental chamber test requirements. *Solar Energy Materials and Solar Cells, 114*, 214–218.
111. Yau, S. S., & Dong, N., (2000). Integration in component-based software development using design patterns. In: *Proceedings 24th Annual International Computer Software and Applications Conference; COMPSAC 2000* (pp. 369–374).

CHAPTER 2

TYPES OF SOFTWARE TESTING

UNIT INTRODUCTION

In beginner programming courses, the need for testing in high-quality software development is often underestimated. Learning is enhanced and emphasis on quality and correctness is fostered through unit tests and specific test-driven development (TDD) components. Tools like JUnit greatly simplify the creation of test cases. These systems can also be used to automate subject grading, which is an added benefit to teachers (Basili & Selby, 1987).

The purpose of a technique called validation is to increase the user's confidence that the program is working as intended. Inspection often requires inspection. The purpose of testing is to ensure that a program meets its requirements, but as Edsger Dijkstra pointed out, testing can only prove the existence of bugs, not the existence of bugs. Nonetheless, thorough testing significantly boosts confidence that performs as planned (Kuhn & Reilly, 2002).

Never presume that your code is correct, as a programmer. Yet, novice programmers frequently believe that success is defined as a program that executes without syntax problems. Early testing can help children develop a trusting mindset and sense of accountability for the accuracy of their work (Hooda & Chhillar, 2015).

Debugging print statements that cluttered a program's source code and caused "scroll blindness" had long been used in software testing. To interpret test findings, one must sift through a lot of output, which is a time-consuming and extremely subjective procedure. Another significant drawback of this method is that it lacks the automation and versatility necessary to run tests frequently and quickly in the development process (Fraser & Arcuri, 2012).

Learning Objectives

At the end of this lesson, students will able to:

- Identify and describe the different types of software testing
- Understand the advantages and disadvantages of each testing type
- Comprehend the testing process
- Develop testing strategies
- Learn about the tools and techniques used in software testing

Key Terms

- Software Testing
- Test-Driven Development
- Types of software Testing
- Unit Testing
- Unit Testing in Java

2.1. UNIT TESTING

The advent of object-oriented programming has changed the way programmers approach software testers. Bottom-up object-oriented programming favors a testing approach that emphasizes classes, and that makes sense. A unit test runs a "unit" of code individually and compares the results to the expected results. A Java entity is usually a class. Unit tests use one or more methods to create observables that can be tested automatically (Daka et al., 2014).

Proponents of Extreme Programming (XP) advocate test-driven development (TDD) as the preferred and efficient way to build software. With this approach, you must first design the behavior of the class to complete the test cases. Tests are performed on each modification class during implementation (Mackinnon et al., 2000).

TIPS

The three basic types of software testing categories are discussed below: Functional Testing, Non-Functional Testing and Maintenance.

2.2. UNIT TESTING IN INTRODUCTORY COURS-ES

The decision of when (or whether) to implement complex tools may change, but unit testing is perfectly appropriate to be introduced in CS1. For instance, the teacher could assign a straightforward class with clear specs and ask the students to try out the techniques by creating a test driver.

Reading instructions, how to use prewritten software systems, and testing to see if they perform as intended are all objectives of this exercise (Latorre, 2013). The restrictions of software and the significance of identifying and documenting these restrictions can both be demonstrated using such exercises. The inclination of starting students to program just for a particular application, as opposed to creating useful reusable components, may be lessened by experimentation outside of context (Patterson et al., 2003).

It is recommended to do both positive and negative tests. Positive tests put the test object's anticipated functionality to the test. Negative testing makes advantage of scenarios where failure is anticipated and where the code should robustly manage the error.

Students can test different argument values to see which ones are effective. Such a strategy promotes reviewing class and method declarations. The parameters that can be restricted by this analysis can then be created, along with preconditions, post conditions, and invariants (Olan, 2003). Without having to create a test driver, the BlueJ IDE offers a straightforward mechanism for interactively testing classes and functions. BlueJ's object bench allows for the interactive execution of an object's methods. Inspectors make it possible to see the object's current state, providing quick reviews on the results of using the method.

BlueJ's correlative analyzing features have some restrictions. As a result, tests that find defects must be manually run again after improvements have been made because they cannot be automated or reused. This is especially problematic when a huge amount of manually provided data is required, such as when filling a big array. Regression testing is necessary in these circumstances, which entails redoing tests to make sure that changes have fixed the issue and haven't caused any new faults. Such analysis must be automated to be useful (Barriocanal et al., 2002).

It is preferable to require as little human interaction as possible during testing. The tests should self-check, and results should be sent to the programmer indicating if each test was successful or unsuccessful. Regression test development can be time-consuming and sometimes error-prone. In actuality, more code may be required for tests than is being tested. However, the amount of work required to generate test cases can be significantly decreased by tools like J Unit (Janzen, 2005).

Testing can also be done with a debugger. An efficient technique to track the execution of a program to identify the root of a bug is to set markers, watches, etc. Regression testing, however, is not appropriate for an interactive debugger. Once an error has been found, it is then possible to isolate it by debugging. Unit testing can greatly lessen the need for debugging because it is best suited to the early identification and eradication of errors (Warren et al., 2014).

Tests run in the debugger or on the BlueJ object bench do not constitute correctly. They can only execute one procedure call or statement at a time, in essence. They also need judgment to interpret the outcomes (Morse & Anderson, 2004).

2.3. TEST-DRIVEN DEVELOPMENT (TDD)

One crucial aspect of software engineering is analyzing software at every stage of the development process. XP methodology goes one step further and suggests an evolutionary way of design that continuously alternates between coding and testing using a test-code cycle. In development of test-driven, the tests are created prior to implementation code is written (Fraser et al., 2003). The TDD cycle entails:

1. Provide a basic test;

2. Start each test (some or all will fail);
3. Make a minor adjustment;
4. Do the exams successfully; and
5. Refactoring to enhance the design (Spacco & Pugh, 2006).

Refactoring entails reworking already-existing classes as well as methods, for as by breaking a class or method up into several smaller ones. The source code may be reorganized to enhance its quality and design. Yet, since changes have the potential to introduce problems, tests must be run repeatedly.

Many facets of software design, such as unit testing, depending on specifications. Specifications and tests play complementary roles in TDD. Traditional black box and glass box testing are combined in unit testing.

The prerequisites and the intended outcomes of a method, or a "black box perspective," are provided in the specifications. The programmer also has a glass box view in TDD, where implementation code is produced concurrently with the analysis (Moe, 2019).

A class's features and intended functionality are better understood when tests are run first. The need for getter and setter methods, for instance, is made abundantly clear by the design of the JUnit testing framework. This method will more likely result in reusable code (Causevic et al., 2011).

Tools typically don't computerize the creation of test data. Creating suitable test inputs is a challenging and non-algorithmic procedure. Guidelines for using typical, boundary, and error circumstances continue to be valid.

Also, the tester must determine in advance which outcomes are suitable for different given collection of inputs. The execution of test procedures using predetermined inputs and evaluating the acceptability of the outcomes are both tasks that can be automated (George & Williams, 2003).

TIPS

The three basic types of software testing categories are discussed below: Functional Testing, Non-Functional Testing and Maintenance.

2.4. UNIT TESTING IN JAVA WITH JUNIT

The Java programming language will be used to demonstrate the unit test procedure in this section. The provided example will test a straightforward Java class that represents bank accounts and has procedures for account creation, deposit, and withdrawal requests, and account balance inquiries. The JUnit testing tool will be demonstrated using unit tests (Janzen & Saiedian, 2006).

Java unit testing is supported via the JUnit framework. A test case using JUnit is typically developed as a subclass of junit.framework. TestCase. Predicate functions, which also include assertTrue, assertNull, and their opposites, several assertEquals methods for various argument types, and other testing-related functionality, provide the basic testing functionality. These techniques contrast actual and predicted outcomes (Karac & Turhan, 2018).

The test fixture refers to the items that are being tested. The test fixture is set up using the setUp() function, and it is released using the tearDown() method. Any variety of test methods can be included in a test case. Typically, a test method examines one method from the class in question.

In JUnit, test method execution conforms to the following model:

testXXX()

tearDown()

setUp()

JUnit starts each test method with a setUp call and ends each test method with a tearDown call. The current test method is not continued if a test fails (Munir et al., 2014).

The aforementioned model is repeated in a JUnit test case, which searches all test methods using reflection. In order for reflection to know which methods to call, test methods need to be public, void, start with "test," and take no arguments.

The example that follows shows how a JUnit test case for a basic class representing bank accounts with a name and an integer balance should be written (Pancur et al., 2003).

```
import junit.framework.TestCase;

public class AccountTest extends TestCase {

public AccountTest(String arg0) {

super(arg0);

}

public void testDeposit() { a.deposit(200);

assertEquals("deposit error: ," 700, a.getBalance());

}
```

```
public void testWithdraw() { a.withdraw(200);
assertEquals("withdraw error: ," 300, a.getBalance());
}
}
public static void main(String[] args) {
junit.swingui.TestRunner.run(AccountTest.class);
}
Account a;        // test fixture
public void setUp() {
a = new Account("D. Morebucks," 500);
```

In this instance, the test fixture is the Account object a. Before each test method is executed, the setUp method initializes the fixture. A single process from the Account class is exercised in every test method, and the results are evaluated using assert Equals. This example does not require a tearDown function because Java automatically disposes of unused objects. To release resources, for as by terminating a file or database interactions, tearDown is typically utilized (Ivo et al., 2018).

There are text and GUI interfaces for JUnit. The outcomes of this example, which employs the Swing GUI interface for JUnit, are displayed in Figure 2.1. The JUnit window displays total number of test methods executed, the total errors and failures, and a "Green Bar" for a test that passed with flying colors. Which procedures succeeded and which failed are displayed on the Test Hierarchy tab. Any failed test methods would be described in detail under the Failures tab (Nagappan et al., 2008).

Let's say the Account class implements the withdrawl procedure in the following naive manner.

```
// Subtracts amt from the balance of this Account
public boolean withdraw(double amt) { balance = balance – amt;
}
```

The subsequent test would show a flaw if transactions that result in a negative balance are supposed to be denied.

```
public void testWithdraw2() { a.withdraw(800);
assertEquals("withdraw error: ," 500, a.getBalance());
```

```
}
```

It shows the result, which are represented as a "Red Bar," demonstrate that a failure took place. Once more, the number of test methods, mistakes, and failures are displayed. The assert Equals message string argument, the anticipated outcome, and the actual result are all displayed in the failures panel, which also indicates the method that failed.

You can run specific test methods in the hierarchy by using the Run button to the right of the Results window. Stack traces of the unsuccessful test methods are shown in the bottom panel.

JUnit distinguishes between failures and errors. The assert methods are capable of foreseeing failures. Errors are unexpected issues brought on by uncaught exceptions that have spread from a test procedure.

It is necessary to address the issue that has been identified with withdrawl. By raising an exception, we can enhance the method (Janzen & Saiedian, 2005).

```
// Subtracts amt from the balance of this Account
// Throws InsufficientFundsException if balance < amt
public void withdraw(double amt) {
if (balance < amt)
throw new InsufficientFundsException();
else
balance = balance – amt;
}
```

Now that the testWithdraw2 method has succeeded, another test is required to ensure that the exception is thrown when necessary.

```
public void testWithdraw3 () {
try {
a.withdraw(501);
fail("Expected InsufficientFundsException");
} catch (InsufficientFundsException e) {
// exception test succeeded
}
```

```
}
```

The test method fails right away as a result of the fail method if the anticipated exception is not raised. The test in this case passes from the Insufficient Funds Exception would be thrown and caught.

Test suites help organize test cases when a project expands and the quantity of test cases develops. The term "test suite" refers to a group of connected tests. A JUnit test suite can be created in a variety of methods. One is to add each test method by name separately, like in the example that follows (Bruzual et al., 2020).

```
public static Test suite() {
    TestSuite suite = new
    TestSuite("Test everything");
    suite.addTest(new
    AccountTest("testDeposit"));
    suite.addTest(new
    AccountTest("testWithdraw1"));
    suite.addTest(new
    AccountTest("testWithdraw2"));
    suite.addTest(new OtherAcct
    Tests("testWithdraw3")); suite.
    addTest(new OtherAcctTests("t
    estWithdraw4")); return suite;
}
```

Including all testing procedures from a test case, like in this instance, is a simpler solution.

```
public static Test suite() {
TestSuite suite =
new TestSuite("Test
everything"); suite.
addTestSuite(AccountTest.class); suite.
addTestSuite(OtherAcctTests.class);

return suite;

}
```

All procedures with titles that start with "test" from the specified classes will be covered by this. JUnit test cases are Java classes, making it simple to input remarks and create documentation pages. Consequently, the test plan's documentation is a straightforward and essential step in the process of developing tests as a whole. JUnit may be used manually or using an IDE with reasonable ease. Simple IDEs for educational purposes BlueJ and DrJava now come with built-in JUnit functionality. The open-source Eclipse IDE incorporates JUnit in a very adaptable manner at a more advanced level. A wizard in Eclipse can create test method stubs automatically. IDEs like eclipse, which also assist hot code updates, enable the execution of JUnit tests without the need to recompile the test suite. Eclipse can be set up to start a debugger if a failure happens (Artho et al., 2007).

2.5. EXTENSIONS AND ADVANCED FEATURES

Testing software with a user interface that is graphical can be very time-consuming and difficult. Users can randomly enter data and click buttons at random. By recording and replaying keystrokes, mouse clicks, and other user input, numerous JUnit modifications have been developed to test GUI programs (Abbot, Marathon). Additional add-ons have been created for J2EE web applications, server-side code testing (Cactus), and more. The purpose of unit tests is to analyze a single functional component, however, most non-trivial programs are challenging to test in isolation. Testing a code that interacts with other programs, accesses databases, etc., can be extremely difficult. By using fake implementations that simulate the actual functionality of complicated component interaction, a method known as Mock Objects substitutes domain code. For mock objects, many JUnit extensions are provided (EasyMock, Mock Maker) (Weikle et al., 2019).

The JUnit website contains details regarding extensions

Kent Beck, who also worked on the development of JUnit, created the first unit testing tools for Smalltalk. Ada, C, C++, Curl, Delphi, Eiffel, JavaScript, Perl, Python, and the Microsoft.NET languages are a few of the languages that have a growing family of tools that are comparable to other languages. For a few of these languages, the instructive article "JUnit Cookbook" has also been updated (Sherman et al., 2013).

2.6. UNIT TESTING FOR AUTOMATED PROJECT GRADING

Grading of projects can be at least somewhat automated with the help of technologies like JUnit. For instance, after the test harness is set up, it is possible to drag student contributions into an eclipse project and run the test from there. Java source files are automatically compiled when they are dropped into Eclipse. The JUnit test system can rerun a test utilizing the new code thanks to dynamic hot code updates (Combéfis & de Moffarts, 2019).

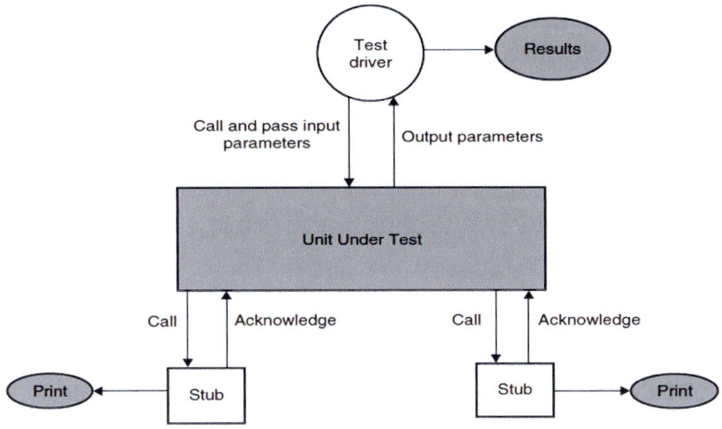

Figure 2.1. Dynamic unit test environment.

Source: Atle Rotevatn et al., creative commons license.

ACTIVITY 2.1:

What are the types of software testing? Give a detail presentation.

It would be simple to create a script on a Unix/Linux machine to further automate this procedure by cycling among submissions and sending output results to files (Olan, 2003).

The testing procedure can be further automated with Java's Ant build tools, and the outcomes are compiled in a structured report and sent via email to the intended recipient. Notwithstanding the need for more grader comments, there remains room for improvement in the grading process (Spacco et al., 2005).

Assembling the submission method in which students can run their code via a ready-made test driver to give feedback on failed tests is an additional option. Also, this system would emphasize how crucial accurate specifications and standards are. The test cannot be performed if a student's code does not adhere to a class's specifications for method names and declarations. As mistakes that students would probably miss might be found and fixed prior to final submission is due, it might also lower the number of submissions that are undesirable. It is consistent with Kent Beck's recommendations for TDD from, notwithstanding the possibility that this would encourage programming for the test drive (Desai et al., 2009).

SUMMARY

A testing framework is necessary for creating trustworthy software. The addition of unit testing to a programmer's toolbox can enhance the design and drastically cut down on time spent looking for enigmatic errors. Students can be effectively encouraged to extensively test the software they build by using tools like JUnit. Such tools are more than just extra bells and whistles for an IDE; they improve the learning process. If unit testing is introduced to students early on and is supported by these tools, students may also become "test infected."

REVIEW QUESTIONS

1. What are the different types of software testing, and how are they used in the software development life cycle?
2. How does functional testing differ from non-functional testing, and why is it important to test both aspects of a software system?
3. What are some of the most common techniques used in manual testing, and how do they compare to automated testing approaches?
4. What is regression testing, and why is it important in ensuring software quality over time?
5. How can performance testing help identify bottlenecks and other issues that might affect the overall speed and responsiveness of a software system?
6. What are some of the key considerations when designing and implementing a software testing strategy, and how can organizations ensure that their testing efforts are effective and efficient?

MULTIPLE CHOICE QUESTIONS

1. What is black-box testing?

a. Testing conducted in isolation
b. Testing conducted with full knowledge of the system
c. Testing conducted without knowledge of the system
d. None of the above

2. Which type of testing focuses on the performance of the software under normal and peak load conditions?

a. Functional testing
b. Usability testing
c. Load testing
d. Integration testing

3. **Which type of testing ensures that the software works as intended across different devices, platforms, and browsers?**
   a. Compatibility testing
   b. Regression testing
   c. Security testing
   d. Acceptance testing
4. **Which type of testing is conducted by developers to ensure that their code is working as expected?**
   a. Unit testing
   b. Integration testing
   c. System testing
   d. Acceptance testing
5. **Which type of testing verifies that the software meets the requirements and specifications agreed upon by the client and development team?**
   a. Regression testing
   b. Acceptance testing
   c. System testing
   d. Usability testing

Answers to Multiple Choice Questions

1. (c); 2. (c); 3. (a); 4. (a); 5. (b)

REFERENCES

1. Artho, C., Chen, Z., & Honiden, S., (2007). AOP-based automated unit test classification of large benchmarks. In: *31st Annual International Computer Software and Applications Conference (COMPSAC 2007)* (Vol. 2, pp. 17–22).
2. Barriocanal, E. G., Urbán, M. Á. S., Cuevas, I. A., & Pérez, P. D., (2002). An experience in integrating automated unit testing practices in an introductory programming course. *ACM SIGCSE Bulletin, 34*(4), 125–128.
3. Basili, V. R., & Selby, R. W., (1987). Comparing the effectiveness of software testing strategies. *IEEE Transactions on Software Engineering*, (12), 1278–1296.
4. Baumgärtel, P., Grundmann, P., Zeschke, T., Erko, A., Viefhaus, J., Schäfers, F., & Schirmacher, H., (2019). RAY-UI: New features and extensions. In: *AIP Conference Proceedings* (Vol. 2054, No. 1, p. 060034).
5. Bruzual, D., Montoya, F. M. L., & Di Francesco, M., (2020). Automated assessment of Android exercises with cloud-native technologies. In: *Proceedings of the 2020*

ACM Conference on Innovation and Technology in Computer Science Education (pp. 40–46).

6. Causevic, A., Sundmark, D., & Punnekkat, S., (2011). Factors limiting industrial adoption of test driven development: A systematic review. In: *2011 Fourth IEEE International Conference on Software Testing, Verification and Validation* (pp. 337–346).
7. Choi, J. S., Kim, E. K., Moon, H. J., & Kwak, J. Y., (2015). Higher body mass index may be a predictor of extrathyroidal extension in patients with papillary thyroid microcarcinoma. *Endocrine, 48*, 264–271.
8. Combéfis, S., & De Moffarts, G., (2019). *Automated Generation of Computer Graded Unit Testing-Based Programming Assessments for Education*. arXiv preprint arXiv:1911.12323.
9. Daka, E., & Fraser, G., (2014). A survey on unit testing practices and problems. In: *2014 IEEE 25th International Symposium on Software Reliability Engineering* (pp. 201–211).
10. Desai, C., Janzen, D. S., & Clements, J., (2009). Implications of integrating test-driven development into CS1/CS2 curricula. *ACM SIGCSE Bulletin, 41*(1), 148–152.
11. Fraser, G., & Arcuri, A., (2012). Sound empirical evidence in software testing. In: *2012 34th International Conference on Software Engineering (ICSE)* (pp. 178–188).
12. Fraser, S., Beck, K., Caputo, B., Mackinnon, T., Newkirk, J., & Poole, C., (2003). Test driven development (TDD). In: *Extreme Programming and Agile Processes in Software Engineering: 4th International Conference, XP 2003 Genova, Italy, May 25–29, 2003 Proceedings* (pp. 459–462).
13. George, B., & Williams, L., (2003). An initial investigation of test driven development in industry. In: *Proceedings of the 2003 ACM Symposium on Applied Computing* (pp. 1135–1139).
14. Hooda, I., & Chhillar, R. S., (2015). Software test process, testing types and techniques. *International Journal of Computer Applications, 111*(13).
15. Ivo, A. A., Guerra, E. M., Porto, S. M., Choma, J., & Quiles, M. G., (2018). An approach for applying test-driven development (TDD) in the development of randomized algorithms. *Journal of Software Engineering Research and Development, 6*, 1–31.
16. Janzen, D. S., & Saiedian, H., (2006). On the influence of test-driven development on software design. In: *19th Conference on Software Engineering Education & Training (CSEET'06)* (pp. 141–148).
17. Janzen, D. S., (2005). Software architecture improvement through test-driven development. In: *Companion to the 20th Annual ACM SIGPLAN Conference on Object-Oriented Programming, Systems, Languages, and Applications* (pp. 240, 241).
18. Janzen, D., & Saiedian, H., (2005). Test-driven development concepts, taxonomy, and future direction. *Computer, 38*(9), 43–50.
19. Kuhn, D. R., & Reilly, M. J., (2002). An investigation of the applicability of design of experiments to software testing. In: *27th Annual NASA Goddard/IEEE Software Engineering Workshop, 2002, Proceedings* (pp. 91–95).

20. Latorre, R., (2013). Effects of developer experience on learning and applying unit test-driven development. *IEEE Transactions on Software Engineering, 40*(4), 381–395.
21. Mackinnon, T., Freeman, S., & Craig, P., (2000). Endo-testing: Unit testing with mock objects. *Extreme Programming Examined*, 287–301.
22. Moe, M. M., (2019). Comparative study of test-driven development TDD, behavior-driven development BDD and acceptance test–driven development ATDD. *International Journal of Trend in Scientific Research and Development, 3*, 231–234.
23. Morse, S. F., & Anderson, C. L., (2004). Introducing application design and software engineering principles in introductory cs courses: Model-view-controller java application framework. *Journal of Computing Sciences in Colleges, 20*(2), 190–201.
24. Munir, H., Moayyed, M., & Petersen, K., (2014). Considering rigor and relevance when evaluating test driven development: A systematic review. *Information and Software Technology, 56*(4), 375–394.
25. Nagappan, N., Maximilien, E. M., Bhat, T., & Williams, L., (2008). Realizing quality improvement through test driven development: Results and experiences of four industrial teams. *Empirical Software Engineering, 13*, 289–302.
26. Olan, M., (2003). Unit testing: Test early, test often. *Journal of Computing Sciences in Colleges, 19*(2), 319–328.
27. Pancur, M., Ciglaric, M., Trampus, M., & Vidmar, T., (2003). Towards empirical evaluation of test-driven development in a university environment. In: *The IEEE Region 8 EUROCON 2003; Computer as a Tool* (Vol. 2, pp. 83–86).
28. Patterson, A., Kölling, M., & Rosenberg, J., (2003). Introducing unit testing with BlueJ. *ACM SIGCSE Bulletin, 35*(3), 11–15.
29. Schneider, S. A., Lang, A. E., Moro, E., Bader, B., Danek, A., & Bhatia, K. P., (2010). Characteristic head drops and axial extension in advanced chorea-acanthocytosis. *Movement Disorders, 25*(10), 1487–1491.
30. Sherman, M., Bassil, S., Lipman, D., Tuck, N., & Martin, F., (2013). Impact of auto-grading on an introductory computing course. *Journal of Computing Sciences in Colleges, 28*(6), 69–75.
31. Spacco, J., & Pugh, W., (2006). Helping students appreciate test-driven development (TDD). In: *Companion to the 21st ACM SIGPLAN Symposium on Object-Oriented Programming Systems, Languages, and Applications* (pp. 907–913).
32. Spacco, J., Strecker, J., Hovemeyer, D., & Pugh, W., (2005). Software repository mining with marmoset: An automated programming project snapshot and testing system. In: *Proceedings of the 2005 International Workshop on Mining Software Repositories* (pp. 1–5).
33. Sullivan, G. J., Topiwala, P. N., & Luthra, A., (2004). The H. 264/AVC advanced video coding standard: Overview and introduction to the fidelity range extensions. *Applications of Digital Image Processing XXVII, 5558*, 454–474.
34. Warren, J., Rixner, S., Greiner, J., & Wong, S., (2014). Facilitating human interaction in an online programming course. In: *Proceedings of the 45th ACM Technical Symposium on Computer Science Education* (pp. 665–670).

35. Weikle, D. A., Lam, M. O., & Kirkpatrick, M. S., (2019). Automating systems course unit and integration testing: Experience report. In: *Proceedings of the 50th ACM Technical Symposium on Computer Science Education* (pp. 565–570).

CHAPTER 3

GOALS, SCOPE, AND HISTORY OF SOFTWARE TESTING

UNIT INTRODUCTION

In the histories of the evolution of digital computers, software testing has been around since the dawn of time. Testing software is an essential part of evaluating and determining software quality. Hence testing should never be skipped. Testing often takes between 40 and 50% development efforts, & typically utilizes more work for systems requiring higher reliability levels. As a result, software engineering's important component is testing. 4th generation development of programming languages (4GL) that makes the software implementation process go more quickly increased the percentage of time spent on testing (Khan, 2010). Because of the increasing work needed to maintain and improve current systems, a large testing amount will be required to verify those systems after any modifications are implemented. Even though there have been advancements in verification approaches & formal methods, the system need still be evaluated before being put into use. Testing continues to be the only successful method to ensure the quality of software systems that are not trivial and the most complex yet poorly understood subfields of software engineering. Future trends suggest that testing, a significant area of research in computer science, will become even more significant (Baresi & Pezze, 2006).

This retrospective on 50 years of software testing technique research examines growth of software testing technique research by tracking significant research findings which may have led to field's development. In addition, this evaluates the evolution of research paradigms by tracing the types of research questions & methodologies employed at different periods. We utilize Redwine and Riddle's technology maturation approach as the basis for our study of how software testing approaches generate the idea, then utilize it provisionally, develop it, and expand it into a more comprehensive solution. Shaw provides an excellent framework of software engineering research paradigms in his book, classifies the research environments, methodologies, and research validations software researchers conduct. This chapter evaluates the research procedures for testing techniques using Shaw's model (Sawant et al., 2012).

Learning Objectives

At the end of this chapter, readers will be able to:

- Understand the concept of software testing and its importance in software development.
- Learn different types of software testing techniques such as black-box testing, white-box testing, gray-box testing, regression testing, and acceptance testing.
- Gain an understanding of the advantages and disadvantages of each testing technique and when to use them in software testing.
- Understand the process of creating test cases, test suites, and test plans, and how to execute them.
- Learn about test-driven development (TDD) and behavior-driven development (BDD) and how they are used in software testing.
- Understand the importance of test coverage, test automation, and continuous integration in software testing.
- Learn about the tools and technologies used in software testing such as test management tools, defect tracking tools, and performance testing tools.

Key Terms

- Redwine/Riddle Software Technology
- Software Testing Techniques
- Structural Techniques
- Testing Spectrum
- Testing Techniques Taxonomy

3.1. THE TESTING TECHNIQUES TAXONOMY

Software testing involves many non-technical & technical areas, including design & implementation, specification, process & management, maintenance, issues in software engineering. Our study focuses on state of the art in testing techniques and latest techniques representing this area's future direction (Rohlf, 1972).

3.1.1. The Goal of Testing

The testing definition varies in different publications according to the level of testing, process & purpose. Miller provides an excellent account of testing:

"An objective of testing is to confirm its software system quality by systematically putting the software through its paces under carefully controlled conditions."

According to Miller's testing description, most software quality assurance operations constitute testing. He argues that the primary objective of testing should be to identify error. A good test has a high possibility of uncovering error that has not yet been identified, and a successful test does so. This software testing activity broad classification can be subdivided. Testing, for this chapter, is a dynamic analysis of piece of software, which necessitates the execution of system to generate results compared to predicted outputs (Stroebe et al., 2008).

Remember

Testing has its own cycle; in each phase, all focus revolves around quality.

3.2. THE TESTING SPECTRUM

Each stage of the software life cycle includes testing, but testing performed at each level of software development has a distinct character and goals (Zhang et al., 2017).

- **Unit Testing** occurs at the most fundamental level. It tests the smallest testable bit of software, which is referred to alternately as "unit," "module," and "component" (Vegas et al., 2009).
- **Integration Testing** occurs bigger structure has formed by joining two or more previously tested units. The test is frequently performed on both the interfaces between the components and the larger structure being built in case if the building's quality cannot be determined from its components (Ipate & Holcombe, 1997).

- **System Testing** often verifies quality of overall system. Frequently, system testing is based on system's functional/requirement specification. Moreover, non-functional quality aspects such as dependability, security, and maintainability are examined (Borjesson & Feldt, 2012).
- **Acceptance Testing** is performed when the developers pass the finished system to the clients or end users. Acceptance testing is intended to ensure that the system is functional rather than identify errors (Hsia et al., 1997).

3.3. DYNAMIC ANALYSIS AND STATIC ANALYSIS

There are two basic sorts of quality assurance activities based on whether actual execution of the software being evaluated is required or not:

- **Static Analysis** focuses on the variety of techniques employed to assess or predict software quality without considering actual executions. The techniques in this field are symbolic analysis, code inspection, program analysis and model checking (Heckman & Williams, 2008).
- **Dynamic Analysis** focuses on specialized techniques for estimating and determining software quality by actual executions, using real data, & in realistic (or simulated) conditions. Input synthesis, the application of structurally determined testing processes, & the automation of testing environment development are techniques in this area (Mariani et al., 2010).

The static and dynamic approaches can nearly always be described independently, although occasionally intertwined. Testing in this paper refers to dynamic analysis because most testing activities (and all methodologies examined in this research) depend on the software being executed (Rountev et al., 2004).

3.4. STRUCTURAL TECHNIQUE AND FUNCTIONAL TECHNIQUE

Figure 3.1 depicts the flow testing information. As we can see, testing entails setting up appropriate inputs, running the software using the input, and analyzing the results. The "Software Configuration" consists of the source code, requirements specification, and design specification, among other things. The "Test Configuration" comprises testing tools, plans, and cases (Liu & Chen, 2008). A testing technique is used to choose input test cases and analyze test outcomes based on the testing information flow. There are 2 main branches of testing methodologies: functional and structural. Various techniques disclose different quality elements of a software system (Miller, 2012).

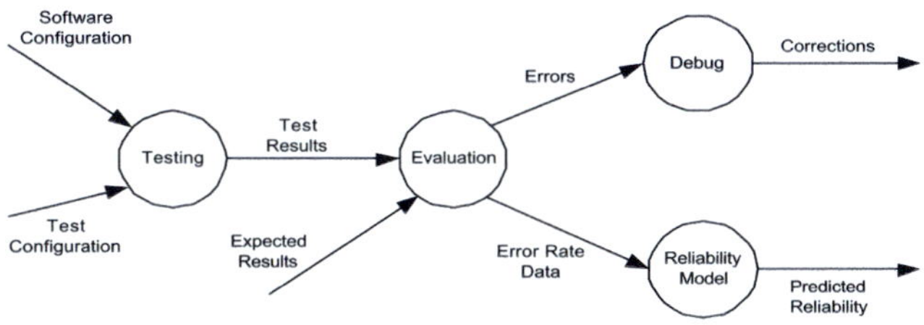

Figure 3.1. Testing information flow.

Source: Sheikh Umar Farooq et al., creative commons license.

- **Functional Testing**: A "black box" metaphor describes the software program or system being tested. To guide the selection of test cases for functional testing the requirement or design specification of the software item under test is used. Examples of expected results include manually calculated values, requirement/design requirements, & simulated results. These examples are mostly referred to as test oracles. Functional testing places a focus on the outward behavior of software's entity (Shi, 2010).
- **Structural Testing**: The computer program is considered a "white box." The software entity's implementation informs selection of test cases. Choosing such test cases is to make certain areas of the software entity, such as program branches, or paths, particular statements, execute. To assess the anticipated outcomes a set of coverage criteria are used.

Branch coverage, path coverage & data-flow coverage are a few examples of coverage criteria. The internal structure of the software entity is the focus of structural testing (Jones et al., 1996).

3.5. SCOPE OF THE STUDY

3.5.1. Technical Scope

In this chapter, we concentrate on the technological development of testing methodologies, including these structural and functional techniques that have had a significant academic and practical impact. We'll examine how the most widely used approach and strategy for choosing test cases and analyzing test results have developed. Theoretical and methodological research on software testing techniques can be loosely divided into two areas, and as both branches advance, so does testing technology. We are also interested in maturation inhibitors, which explains why in-depth research hasn't led to a revolutionary improvement in industrial testing techniques (Beutel, 1991). Software testing covers a wide range of additional fascinating topics. Even if some of the domains may be inextricably linked to our study, we restrict the scope of our research to the available testing methodologies. We will specifically avoid talking about:

i. How the software development cycle includes testing;
ii. How several testing levels are conducted;
iii. Testing process models;
iv. Management responsibilities, & testing policy; and
v. Software testability & stop testing criteria (Estublier et al., 2005).

3.5.2. Goal and Standard of Progress

Helping designers, developers, and managers build high-quality systems is the ultimate purpose of software testing. To efficiently carry out effective testing to uncover more requirements, design, and implementation problems, and to boost confidence that software has various attributes – research and development on testing are conducted. Testing technique research aims to find useful testing tools and procedures. Fundamental research and developing, improving, expanding, and popularizing better techniques are necessary for progress toward this goal (Sim et al., 2003).

The following criteria are used to measure testing technique research progress:

i. The technology's level of acceptance, both inside and outside the scientific community;
ii. Dependency on other software engineering domains to a certain extent;
iii. Research paradigms have changed in reaction to the advancement of software development tools;
iv. the feasibility of using certain methods in a large-scale, practical context; and
v. Technology adoption: seminars, training, and managerial focus (Vyatkin, 2013).

3.6. THE HISTORY OF TESTING TECHNIQUES

3.6.1. Concept Evolution

The software has already been tested since it was first written. With time, the idea of testing itself changed. The direction of testing technique research has changed along with the concept and goals of software testing. Before we start studying the history of testing approaches, let's quickly go through the concept progression of testing using the testing process model by Gelperin & Hetzel (1988) (Graham & Dayton, 2002).

1. **Phase I. The Debugging-Oriented Period. Before 1956: Testing Was Not Separated from Debugging**

   In 1950, Turing wrote the renowned piece on program testing regarded as the first. How can we tell if a program is intelligent? This question is addressed in the essay. In other words, this question is a particular case of "How would we know that the requirements are satisfied by the program?" if the requirement is to create such a program. Turing's operational test stipulated that a human interrogator could not tell the difference between a program's behavior and that of a reference system (a person) (tester). This might be regarded as functional testing in its embryonic stage. Debugging, testing, and program checkout were still not distinct ideas (Eickelmann & Richardson, 1996).

2. **Phase II. The Demonstration-Oriented Period. 1957~78: – Testing to Ensure that the Software Meets its Requirements**

   Testing, sometimes known as program checkout at the time, and debugging were not separated until 1957. Charles Baker observed in 1957 that "program checkout" was thought to have two objectives: "Make sure the program works" and "Make sure the program solves the problem." Although "making sure" was frequently interpreted as the testing aim of completing requirements, the latter objective was seen as the testing's primary objective. Debugging and testing are two distinct steps, as seen in Figure 3.1. The difference between testing and debugging depended on how success was defined. During this time, definitions emphasize that testing aims to show correctness: "Thus, an ideal test only passes when a program is error-free."

The notion that software might be thoroughly tested also became popular in the 1970s. This prompted other studies that focused on path coverage testing. "Exhaustive testing defined either in terms of program pathways or a program's input domain," as stated in the 1975 work by Goodenough and Gerhart (Luo, 2001).

3. **Phase III. The Destruction-Oriented Period. 1979~82: – Implementation Faults Detected by Testing**

   In 1979, The Art of Software Testing, written by Myers laid the groundwork for developing more efficient test technique design. The definition of software testing as "the process of executing a program to identify defects" was first used. It was stressed that finding errors greatly increases the utility of test cases. Similar to the demonstration-oriented stage, it is possible to unintentionally choose test data with a low likelihood of leading to software faults. Testing will be more successful if its goal is to demonstrate a program's flaws; in this instance, the test cases chosen will have a higher chance of doing so. Early associations between testing and other verification/validation activities resulted from this shift of emphasis (Burgin et al., 2009).

4. **Phase IV. The Evaluation-Oriented Period. 1983~87: Faults in Requirements and Design as Well as in the Implementation Detect by Testing**

   In 1983, the National Bureau of Standards Institute for Computer Sciences and Technology released the Guideline for Lifecycle Validation, Verification, and Testing of Computer Software, which outlined a methodology for integrating analysis, review, and test activities to provide product evaluation throughout the software lifecycle. The recommendation suggests that the creation and upkeep of high-quality software can be ensured with a well-selected group of VV&T strategies (Guo et al., 2021).

   5. Phase V. The Prevention-Oriented Period. Since 1988: Faults prevention in requirements, design, and implementation by Testing

   "The act of designing tests is one of the most effective bug preventers known" Beizer stated that in the influential book Software Testing Techniques which contains the most comprehensive catalog of testing techniques. This expanded the testing definition to include error prevention and detection activities. This produced a timeless realization of the value of early testing (Gelperin & Hetzel, 1988).

Hetzel defined testing as "planning, developing, building, maintaining, and carrying out tests and test environments" in 1991. Beizer provided four stages of testing-related thought a year earlier:

i. To make software functional
ii. To break the software
iii. To reduce risk
iv. A state of mind, i.e., a concern with testability across the entire life cycle.

Due to these concepts, software testing came to stress the value of early test design across the software life cycle.

Although both phases concentrate on software requirements and design to minimize implementation problems, the mechanism distinguishes the prevention-oriented phase from the evaluation-oriented phase. Whereas the evaluation approach mostly focuses on analysis & reviewing techniques other than testing, the prevention model emphasizes the importance of test preparation, analysis, and design activities (Neuderth et al., 2009).

3.7. MAJOR TECHNICAL CONTRIBUTIONS

Theoretical and methodological research on testing methodologies can be broadly categorized into two groups. Software testing uses various techniques, from programming languages, graph theory, reliable-testing theory, reliability analysis, etc. In this article, we concentrate on the important theoretical research findings that offer a solid foundation for developing and improving procedures thoughtfully and efficiently, such as testing criteria & test data sufficiency. The systematic approach, given a strong theoretical foundation, aims to use analytical techniques to enforce activity sequences* that, taken together, achieve some desirable testing-oriented consequence (Dyba, 2005).

First, the most important theoretical research contributions and key testing methodology foundations will be covered. In the next section, Redwine/Riddle maturity model show how approaches by testing have developed from an intuitive, ad hoc collection of methodologies into an integrated, systematic discipline. Figure 3.2, depicts notion of testing development, significant technical contributions to testing methods, & most important theoretical and methodological studies. An important principle should be noted when choosing a paper. As a result of the research's ability to define, shape, or fundamentally alter technology over its period, Figure 3.2 was chosen to represent the research's idea. It is not required that it be the first paper on the subject to be published (Orso & Rothermel, 2014).

Although software testing was frequently carried out as a crucial component of software development before 1975, it remained an intuitive, sometimes ad hoc collection of techniques. People mostly used functional and structural methodologies in their testing processes, but there was little systematic research on their methods or theories.

In their article Toward a Theory of Test Data Selection from 1975, fundamental theorem of testing provided by Goodenough and Gerhart. This is the first study that has been published that tries to establish a theoretical basis for testing, which states that a test data selection technique is entirely successful if it is certain to find any programming fault.

This allowed testing to identify problems rather than not find them, as indicated in section 2. The previous section also analyzes how this paper's concepts have limitations. Their study sparked a series of subsequent investigations into testing methodologies theory (Shull et al., 2002).

The same year, Huang argued that standard test data selection criterion, which requires each program statement to be run at least once throughout the test, misses several significant errors. The edge technique was provided as a clarification of the statement testing criterion. This strategy's major goal is to use the program digraph's each edge at least once. This study also provided information on probe insertion, a testing approach that will be very helpful in future testing procedures (Sharafi et al., 2015).

The path testing approach, another key test selection tool, was introduced in 1976. Howden recommended in his research that test data be chosen so every path through a program be taken at least one time. Only a portion of the potentially endless set of program pathways may be tested in practice since the set of program paths is always limitless. Research on the reliability of route testing is intriguing because they limit how reliable tactics require examining only a portion of a program's paths (Boehm & Sullivan, 2000).

Two important theoretical papers on testing methodologies, one on structural and the other on functional testing, were published in 1980. There was little theoretical research on functional testing, even though it was widely utilized and valued in academic and professional settings. In 1980, the first theoretical framework for constructing functional tests using systematic design methodologies was presented. Howden talked about the concept of design functions, which frequently equate to code lines with accompanying comments explaining the function's impact. The paper demonstrates how functional tests can be created using systematic design methodologies, such as structured design methodology (Broy & Denert, 2012).

The structural testing study from 1980 was the other study. A domain error occurs when a portion of a program's input domain leads program to proceed in the wrong direction. Variables in branch statement predicates or erroneous branching statement that predicates is affected by incorrect computations can result in domain errors. To discover domain mistakes, White & Cohen suggested a set of restrictions. The report also outlines future study directions and explains why tests succeed or fail (Sommerville, 2011).

In 1985, data flow analysis for structural testing saw the light of day. A set of criteria for choosing test data was provided by Rapps & Weyuker based on data flow analysis. They claim that one flaw in the path selection criterion is the possibility of undetected program flaws. The introduction of path selection criteria of a family is followed by an explanation of how these criteria interact. The issue of selecting acceptable test data is also covered in this essay. The theoretical foundation for data-flow-based program testing methodologies was laid forth in this study (Selby, 2007).

One of the early approaches focused on using specifications while choosing test cases was put up in 1989 by Richardson and colleagues. Traditional specification-based functional testing relies solely on heuristic criteria because test cases are manually chosen based on a requirement definition. On the other hand, structural testing can allow applications to be automated & determine customer satisfaction. The authors created a testing approach that blends specification-based and implementation-based techniques by extending implementation-based techniques to apply to formal specification languages. Structural testing, functional testing, and formal specifications all appeared to be combined for the first time in this study.

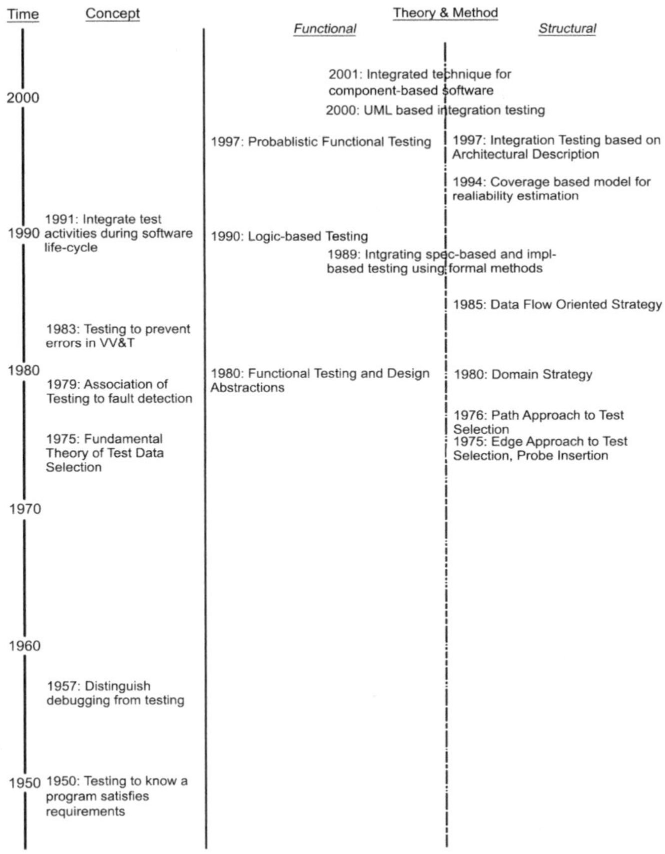

Figure 3.2. Major research results in the area of software testing techniques.

Source: Sheikh Umar Farooq et al., creative commons license.

In 1990, more research on specification-based testing was published. The most fundamental kind of logic is a Boolean algebra, and many tools for logical analysis use it to check, transform, and simplify specifications. Boolean algebra can be used to examine consistency and completeness and can also serve as the foundation for test design. Decision tables can specify all functional requirements of various programs, which serves as a valuable foundation for creating programs and tests. By utilizing Karnaugh-Veitch charts, Boolean algebra is made simple. In his book, Beizer defined functional requirements using decision tables and Karnaugh-Veitch charts. This was one of the early methods for choosing test data based on established, well-known Boolean algebra reasoning (Saleh et al., 2019).

Early in the 1990s, there was an uptick in demand for estimating and forecasting software system reliability. Several reliability models used before Jalote and colleagues' work in 1994 used functional testing strategies and made reliability predictions based on failure data gathered during testing. Data collection, calculation, expertise, and computation for result interpretation are necessary for these models. By modeling a software system as a graph and assuming that a node's dependability is a function of how many times it is performed during testing, the authors offer a novel method based on the coverage history of the program. The more times a node is executed during testing, the more reliable it is. The reliability and validity of the individual nodes are then used to simulate and calculate the dependability of the software system. With such a model, adding reliability computation functionality to coverage analysis tools is simple, totally automating reliability estimation.

Results from both functional and structural testing methods were successful in 1997. The framework for probabilistic functional testing was put forth this year. In their formulation of the testing activity, Bernot and colleagues estimate the reliability and confidence level in the accuracy of the system being tested. Additionally, they describe how to create suitable distributions for the most prevalent data domains, including unions, intervals of integers, inductively defined sets & Cartesian products (Boehm, 2006).

The other intriguing study from 1997 used a rigid, automatable method for complex system integration testing called formal architectural description. The authors suggest modeling the systems' desired behavior using the formal specification language CHAM in this study. A graph representing all potential system behaviors regarding interactions between its constituent parts is derived and simplified. Similar to how control & data flow graphs are used in structural testing, an appropriate set of reduction graphs can be used to highlight the system's key architectural characteristics and generate integration tests using a coverage method. The use of formal methods in testing procedures has been a trend since the later 1980s; this study is one example (Buffardi, 2020).

Many software developers have used Commercial Off Shelf (COTS) software and unified modeling language (UML) since the late 1990s. So, the proper testing methods for the UML components are required by this development trend. Hartmann and colleagues at Siemens integrated test generation and test execution technologies with industry-standard UML modeling tools like Rational Rose in their 2000 study to address the issue of testing components. The authors outline their method for modeling components and interactions, explain how test cases are created from these component models, and then walk through how to run them to check that they behave per expectations. The method is tested using examples in the Siemens TnT environment. Test cases are derived from StateCharts with annotations.

A method to test component-based software is also the subject of contemporary study. The component-based software flow graph (CBSFG) was proposed graphically by Beydeda and colleagues in 2001. Features unique to component-based software, such as the absence of component source code, hamper testing. The study suggests a method that combines black-box and white-box tactics. CBSFG, component software graphical representation that displays data from specification and implementation, is explained. The identification of test cases based on well-known structural methodologies can then be made using it. The conventional structural testing methods can locate test cases in this graphical form using data flow criteria. Functional testing is still being done on the key parts (Boehm, 1976).

3.8. TECHNOLOGY MATURATION

Figure 3.3 illustrates the maturation process of how software testing approaches have changed from an ad hoc, intuitive procedure to a structured, systematic technology discipline. The development of testing methodologies is analyzed and understood using three models. After that was a quick introduction to these models (Riddle, 1984).

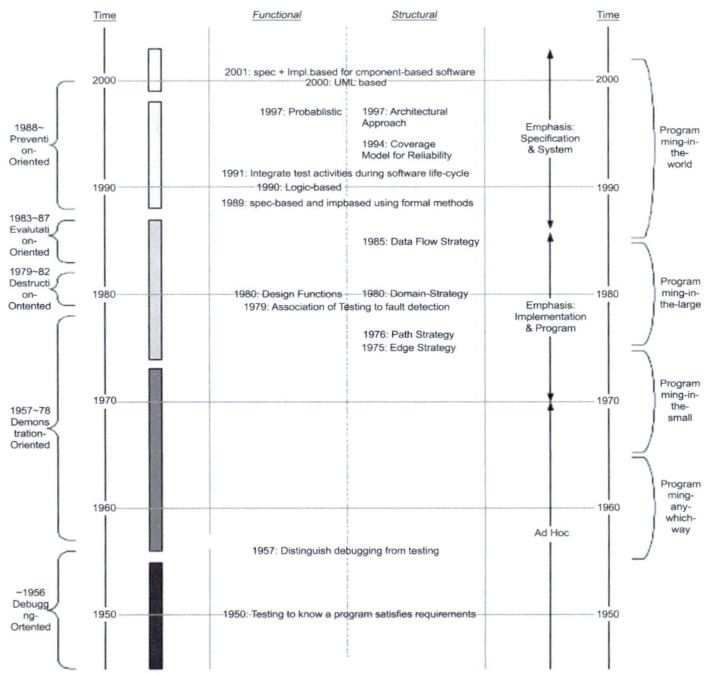

Figure 3.3. Technology maturation analysis of software testing techniques.

Source: Geeksforgeeks, creative commons license.

3.8.1. Redwine/Riddle Software Technology Maturation Model

The core of this maturation study is the Redwine/Riddle. To identify organic features of the process and guidelines and methods helpful in bringing contemporary software technology into wide use, Redwine & Riddle observed the development and diffusion of several software technologies in 1985. They studied how technological innovation is conceptualized, developed into something useable, and then "marketed" to the point where most professionals use it. In the Redwine/Riddles model, there are six phases defined (Clements & Shaw, 2009).

1. **Phase 1: Basic Research:** Analyze fundamental concepts and ideas, give the issue some framework, and develop important research questions. When the testing goals were established to ensure that the program complies with its specification in the mid- to late 1950s, the basic research period for testing methodologies ended. Early studies started to attempt to develop fundamental testing principles (Shaw, 2002).
2. **Phase 2: Formulation of Concept:** Informal ideas exchange, creation of research community, convergence on set of compatible ideas, and publication of answers to particular subproblems.

   The idea development process for testing was concentrated between the late 1950s and the middle of the 1970s when theoretical research started, and the discussions over the testing's actual aim ended. The Goodenough & Gerhart's paper publication on testing data selection marks the final milestone of this phase (Pfleeger, 1999).
3. **Phase 3: Extension & Development:** Use the technology in its early stages, define the fundamental concepts, and generalize the strategy. The testing procedure development and extension period spans from the middle of the 1970s to the late 1980s. Over this time, several testing approaches are suggested and assessed for functional & structural testing. Throughout this time, the fundamentals of testing methodologies were gradually developed (McKenzie, 1981).

4. **Phase 4: Internal Exploration & Enhancement:** Develop training materials, expand the strategy to another domain, apply technology to actual issues, stabilize technology, and demonstrate the worth of the outcomes.

   Software testing technique research reached the internal exploration stage in the late 1980s. The last period's ideals were broadly embraced and applied to more significant real-world issues, and technologies stabilized and advanced.

   Today, people can employ testing professionals or businesses to handle their testing needs. Universities and businesses are offering an increasing number of courses and training programs (Thomas, 2015).

5. **Phase 5: External Exploration & Enhancement:** Similar to internal, incorporating larger population of uninformed developers provides compelling evidence of their usefulness and application. The middle of the 1990s saw the rise of testing procedures. Testing was made easier and more difficult by the growth of programming languages, development methodologies, abstraction granularity, and specification power, as well as by the emergence of increasingly complicated scenarios and system needs. Testing makes use of efficient specification and development methodologies (Das et al., 2019).

6. **Phase 6: Popularization:** Create production-quality, supported versions of the technology, advertise, and sell it, and grow the user base. We don't believe that research on testing methodologies has entered its popularization phase, despite testing activities being conducted constantly and everywhere. With different systems & development methodologies come varied testing strategies. Although specialized firms can be employed to perform testing, the industry lacks a shared platform for exchanging and utilizing academic research findings and adopting successful business practices. This will be covered in later parts (Hill et al., 2013).

3.9. BRIEF HISTORY OF SOFTWARE ENGINEERING

It is impossible to isolate the development of software testing from initiatives in other branches of software engineering, such as formal specification, programming language, and software architecture.

Shaw's study, which can be seen as a brief history of this large field, describes the important shift in research concentration of software engineering. The shift in software engineering research paradigms, which began in the middle of the 1950s, is depicted in Table 3.1 (Wirth, 2008).

Table 3.1. Significant Shifts in Research Attention of Software Engineering

1960 ± 5 **Programming-any-which-way**	Mnemonics, precise use of prose Emphasis on small programs Representing structure, symbolic information Elementary understanding of control flow
1970 ± 5 **Programming-in-the-small**	Simple input-output specifications Emphasis on algorithms Data structures and types Programs execute once and terminate
1980 ± 5 **Programming-in-the-large**	Systems with complex specifications Emphasis on system integration, management Long-lived databases Program assemblies execute continually
1990 ± 5 **Programming-in-the-world**	Software integrated with hardware Emphasis on management process improvement, system structure Abstractions for system design (client-server, object...) Heavily interactive systems, multimedia

3.10. TESTING PROCESS MODELS

The key testing goals model presented by Gelperin & Hetzel is the third reference model. This was covered in great length in the section on testing concept evolution that came before it. Knowing how testing objectives have evolved greatly aids in our comprehension of the intellectual development of testing technique research, including how new concepts are built upon either established ones from the same field of study or on research from unrelated fields (Bodenhausen, 1988).

The Redwine/Riddle model offers metrics for determining where the research stands in the maturation phase and how a procedure can migrate to the following one. Shaw's model creates the global context for studies of technology maturation so they may be compared to other software engineering studies. The testing-specific goals of a testing technique research are evident in the Gelperin and Hetzel model. Each model helps us see the issue from a different angle, but none adequately explains the peculiar phenomena in the technological development of test methodologies. We provide our research inside the framework created using these models and offer our own opinions (Woods et al., 1975).

3.11. THE MAJOR STAGES OF RESEARCH & DEVELOPMENT TRENDS

The study & development of testing methodologies typically go through three key stages, each with a distinct pattern. By trend, we mean the methods most research and development activities use to identify and resolve problems.

Figure 3.3's "technology evolution" column illustrates how testing technique technologies and methods for choosing test data have evolved from an ad hoc, experienced implementation-based period to a current concentration on specification-based (Mujumdar, 2004).

3.11.1. 1950 – 1970: Ad Hoc

Figure 3.3 demonstrates that, aside from the conceptual notions of testing objectives, there were minimal research findings on testing methodologies between 1950 and 1970. Research findings from before 1970 could be too old to be included in the current bibliography collections (Fielding, 1989). We examined numerous testing survey papers from the 1980s, which ought to have had the "ancient" research in hand by the time they conducted their study to avoid being influenced by this aspect. We assume that their surveys, which were conducted before their times, at least covered the key technical advancements, and we can base our research for the years up to 1970 on their findings (Brown et al., 2005).

We describe the era between 1950 and the year 1970 as being ad hoc based on the presumption above. There have been many discussions about determining whether a test is good throughout this time, and the main focus of research is on the purpose of testing. As demonstrated in the GH88 model, testing has now evolved from proving that a program satisfies its requirements to be an independent process. At the same time, Shaw's point of view allows us to see that the entire field of software engineering was in the stage of programming in any manner. It makes perfect sense that testing has remained in the ad hoc phase, where test data is chosen randomly and arbitrarily, aimlessly (Schaffartzik et al., 2014).

3.11.2. 1971 – 1985: Emphasize Implementation and Single Program

The entire software engineering research community changed its paradigms from the program-in-the-small stage to the program-in-the-large stage starting in the middle of the 1960s and continuing through the middle of the 1980s. The primary changes brought about by this shift in software development were that the typical challenges transitioned from smaller programs to larger programs and algorithms and were on the verge of producing more complicated problems. Testing procedure research saw a boom in reaction to this huge change (Dezhina & Ponomarev, 2014).

On the structural side, four important papers were published in 1975, 1976, 1980, and 1985, each of which proposed a crucial structural testing technique.

These studies were adopted as the traditional standards for subsequent research followed them. Figure 3.3 shows that practically all significant theoretical structural testing research was published during this time. The transition from simple programs to huge systems challenged the whole software engineering community. Still, it took the testing community some time to adjust—about five years (Qvale, 2002).

The picture also shows that there was just one notable outcome for functional testing during this time. The cause is clear. Functional testing has only used heuristic criteria and is based on requirements. Without the ability to express the requirements effectively, strictly, and unambiguously, it isn't easy to establish when and if such criteria are satisfied. This served as one of the driving forces for the creation of implementation-based testing approaches, which had the advantage of being automated and able to measure customer satisfaction. Thankfully, the study that came out at this time set a great tone for further studies because it shifted the focus from the low-level, simplistic input/output requirements that testers frequently employed to a higher level—the system's architecture. The question of evaluating "software" rather than a "system" was still of interest to scholars and practitioners throughout this time. Nonetheless, the entire field of software engineering had started to prepare for the transition from the stage of large-scale programming to a higher level (Penuel et al., 2020).

3.11.3. 1986 – Current: Emphasize Specification and System

Starting in the middle of the 1980s, as software became more and more common, the engineering for this field changed from programming-in-the-large to programming-in-the-world. System structures and component interfaces replaced algorithms as the defining issues. System specifications have become more intricate. Research in formal techniques and software architecture has greatly facilitated and inspired how individuals specify their systems. Based on this research, software systems may now be characterized in more detailed, clear, and automated ways, creating excellent opportunities to advance functional testing methods. Meanwhile, software development is no longer just for stand-alone systems; distributed, object-oriented, and component-based systems are becoming increasingly necessary. The testing community's researchers have taken notice of this trend and are shifting their emphasis in line with it (Alagar et al., 2011).

Several studies have utilized the advancements of formal methods & logical analysis since the late 1980s. Researchers have been requesting new specification methods to improve their results because there are still limitations in the powers of specification. Developing software specification technologies has benefitted both functional and structural testing methods (Howitz et al., 2020).

Much testing research has been conducted on these systems due to the widespread development and use of object-oriented technologies, COTS software, and component-based systems. Early in the 1990s, the earliest OO testing experiments were published. Most components, such as classes and other elements, employ conventional functional and structural methodologies. Researchers have put up fresh challenges and solutions to examine components' relationships and inheritances. They employ structural and functional procedures, and combining the two techniques for testing complex systems has been a successful strategy (Ölveczky & Meseguer, 2004).

ACTIVITY 3.1:

What do you know about the history of software testing?

SUMMARY

To assist engineers in creating high-quality systems, testing has been widely adopted. The methods for testing have developed from ad hoc activities carried out by a small group of programmers to a disciplined area of study in software engineering. The development of testing methods has been successful yet insufficient. There is high pressure to generate software of higher quality at cheaper costs, yet current methodologies are insufficient for this. We should conduct fundamental research that tackles the tough problems, develop tools & methods, and conduct empirical investigations so that we may anticipate a big change in the way we test software.

To facilitate transfer of these techniques into practice, researchers should show efficacy of numerous existing techniques for large industrial software. The research's findings will be validated by their effective application in developing commercial software, inspiring further study. The widespread usage of software and the rising expense of validating it will spur industry-research partnerships to develop innovative methods and speed their implementation. One of the most important research fields will shortly be the invention of effective testing methods and tools to produce high-quality software.

REVIEW QUESTIONS

1. What is the difference between white-box testing and black-box testing? Give an example of a situation in which you would use each technique.
2. What is boundary value analysis? How can it help you design more effective tests?
3. Explain the difference between functional testing and structural testing. What are the advantages and disadvantages of each approach?
4. Describe the different types of test cases that you might use when testing software. When would you use each type?
5. What is regression testing? Why is it important, and how do you perform it effectively?
6. How do you measure the effectiveness of your testing? What metrics can you use to evaluate your test results, and what do they tell you about the quality of your software?

MULTIPLE CHOICE QUESTIONS

1. Which of the following testing techniques is used to identify defects in the early stages of development?

a. Unit testing

b. Integration testing

c. System testing

d. Acceptance testing

2. Which of the following is NOT a black-box testing technique?

a. Equivalence partitioning

b. Boundary value analysis

c. State transition testing

d. Statement coverage

3. Which of the following is a non-functional testing technique?

a. Regression testing

b. Load testing

c. User acceptance testing

d. Boundary value analysis

4. Which of the following is a white-box testing technique?

a. Equivalence partitioning

b. Boundary value analysis

c. Decision table testing

d. Statement coverage

5. Which of the following is a static testing technique?

a. Performance testing

b. Usability testing

c. Walkthrough

d. Exploratory testing

Answers to Multiple Choice Questions

1. (a); 2. (d); 3. (b); 4. (d); 5. (c)

REFERENCES

1. Alagar, V. S., Periyasamy, K., & Periyasamy, K., (2011). *Specification of Software Systems* (Vol. 1, pp. 105–128) London, UK: Springer.
2. Baresi, L., & Pezze, M., (2006). An introduction to software testing. *Electronic Notes in Theoretical Computer Science, 148*(1), 89–111.
3. Beutel, R. A., (1991). Software engineering practices and the idea/expression dichotomy: Can structured design methodologies define the scope of software copyright. *Jurimetrics J., 32*, 1.

4. Bodenhausen, G. V., (1988). Stereotypic biases in social decision making and memory: Testing process models of stereotype use. *Journal of Personality and Social Psychology, 55*(5), 726.
5. Boehm, B. W., & Sullivan, K. J., (2000). Software economics: A roadmap. In: *Proceedings of the Conference on the Future of Software Engineering* (Vol. 1, pp. 319–343).
6. Boehm, B. W., (1976). Software engineering. *IEEE Trans. Computers, 25*(12), 1226–1241.
7. Boehm, B., (2006). A view of 20th and 21st century software engineering. In: *Proceedings of the 28th International Conference on Software Engineering* (Vo. 1, pp. 12–29).
8. Borjesson, E., & Feldt, R., (2012). Automated system testing using visual GUI testing tools: A comparative study in industry. In: *2012 IEEE Fifth International Conference on Software Testing, Verification and Validation* (Vol. 1, pp. 350–359). IEEE.
9. Brown, D. G., Johnson, K. M., Loveland, T. R., & Theobald, D. M., (2005). Rural land - use trends in the conterminous United States, 1950–2000. *Ecological Applications, 15*(6), 1851–1863.
10. Broy, M., & Denert, E., (2012). *Software Pioneers: Contributions to Software Engineering* (Vol. 1, pp. 1–11). Springer Science & Business Media.
11. Buffardi, K., (2020). Assessing individual contributions to software engineering projects with git logs and user stories. In: *Proceedings of the 51st ACM Technical Symposium on Computer Science Education* (Vol. 1, pp. 650–656).
12. Burgin, M., Debnath, N., & Lee, H. K., (2009). Measuring testing as a distributed component of the software life cycle. *Journal of Computational Methods in Sciences and Engineering, 9*(s2), S211–S223.
13. Clements, P., & Shaw, M., (2009). "The golden age of software architecture." *IEEE Software, 26*(4), 70–72.
14. Das, S., Kim, S. W., Choi, Y. J., Lee, S., Lee, S. H., Kong, J. S., & Jang, J., (2019). Decellularized extracellular matrix bioinks and the external stimuli to enhance cardiac tissue development in vitro. *Acta Biomaterialia, 95*, 188–200.
15. Dezhina, I., & Ponomarev, A., (2014). Advanced manufacturing: New emphasis in industrial development. *Форсайт, 8*(2), 16–29.
16. Dyba, T., (2005). An empirical investigation of the key factors for success in software process improvement. *IEEE Transactions on Software Engineering, 31*(5), 410–424.
17. Eickelmann, N. S., & Richardson, D. J., (1996). An evaluation of software test environment architectures. In: *Proceedings of IEEE 18th International Conference on Software Engineering* (Vol. 1, pp. 353–364). IEEE.
18. Estublier, J., Vega, G., & Ionita, A. D., (2005). Composing domain-specific languages for wide-scope software engineering applications. In: *Model Driven Engineering Languages and Systems: 8th International Conference, MoDELS 2005, Montego Bay, Jamaica, October 2–7, 2005. Proceedings 8* (Vol. 2, pp. 69–83). Springer Berlin Heidelberg.

19. Fielding, A. J., (1989). Migration and urbanization in Western Europe since 1950. *The Geographical Journal, 155*(1), 60–69.
20. Gelperin, D., & Hetzel, B., (1988). The growth of software testing. *Communications of the ACM, 31*(6), 687–695.
21. Graham, M. H., & Dayton, P. K., (2002). On the evolution of ecological ideas: Paradigms and scientific progress. *Ecology, 83*(6), 1481–1489.
22. Guo, J., Wang, Q., & Li, Y., (2021). Evaluation-oriented façade defects detection using rule-based deep learning method. *Automation in Construction, 131*, 10–20.
23. Heckman, S., & Williams, L., (2008). On establishing a benchmark for evaluating static analysis alert prioritization and classification techniques. In: *Proceedings of the Second ACM-IEEE International Symposium on Empirical Software Engineering and Measurement* (Vol. 1, pp. 41–50).
24. Hill, R., Halamish, E., Gordon, I. J., & Clark, M., (2013). The maturation of biodiversity as a global social–ecological issue and implications for future biodiversity science and policy. *Futures, 46*, 41–49.
25. Howitz, W. J., McKnelly, K. J., & Link, R. D., (2020). Developing and implementing a specifications grading system in an organic chemistry laboratory course. *Journal of Chemical Education, 98*(2), 385–394.
26. Hsia, P., Kung, D., & Sell, C., (1997). Software requirements and acceptance testing. *Annals of Software Engineering, 3*(1), 291–317.
27. Ipate, F., & Holcombe, M., (1997). An integration testing method that is proved to find all faults. *International Journal of Computer Mathematics, 63*(3, 4), 159–178.
28. Jones, B. F., Sthamer, H. H., & Eyres, D. E., (1996). Automatic structural testing using genetic algorithms. *Software Engineering Journal, 11*(5), 299–306.
29. Khan, M. E., (2010). Different forms of software testing techniques for finding errors. *International Journal of Computer Science Issues (IJCSI), 7*(3), 24.
30. Liu, S., & Chen, Y., (2008). A relation-based method combining functional and structural testing for test case generation. *Journal of Systems and Software, 81*(2), 234–248.
31. Luo, L., (2001). *Software Testing Techniques* (Vol. 15232, No. 1–19, p. 19). Institute for software research international Carnegie Mellon university Pittsburgh, PA.
32. Mariani, L., Pastore, F., & Pezze, M., (2010). Dynamic analysis for diagnosing integration faults. *IEEE Transactions on Software Engineering, 37*(4), 486–508.
33. McKenzie, D., (1981). The variation of temperature with time and hydrocarbon maturation in sedimentary basins formed by extension. *Earth and Planetary Science Letters, 55*(1), 87–98.
34. Miller, T., (2012). Using dependency structures for prioritization of functional test suites. *IEEE Transactions on Software Engineering, 39*(2), 258–275.
35. Mujumdar, A. S., (2004). Research and development in drying: Recent trends and future prospects. *Drying Technology, 22*(1, 2), 1–26.

36. Neuderth, S., Jabs, B., & Schmidtke, A., (2009). Strategies for reducing test anxiety and optimizing exam preparation in German university students: A prevention-oriented pilot project of the University of Würzburg. *Journal of Neural Transmission, 116*, 785–790.

37. Ölveczky, P. C., & Meseguer, J., (2004). Specification and analysis of real-time systems using real-time Maude. In: *Fundamental Approaches to Software Engineering: 7th International Conference, FASE 2004. Held as Part of the Joint European Conferences on Theory and Practice of Software, ETAPS 2004, Barcelona, Spain, March 29-April 2, 2004; Proceedings 7* (Vol. 7, pp. 354–358). Springer Berlin Heidelberg.

38. Orso, A., & Rothermel, G., (2014). Software testing: A research travelogue (2000–2014). In: *Future of Software Engineering Proceedings* (Vol. 1, pp. 117–132).

39. Penuel, W. R., Riedy, R., Barber, M. S., Peurach, D. J., LeBouef, W. A., & Clark, T., (2020). Principles of collaborative education research with stakeholders: Toward requirements for a new research and development infrastructure. *Review of Educational Research, 90*(5), 627–674.

40. Pfleeger, S. L., (1999). Making change: Understanding software technology transfer. *The Journal of Systems & Software, 47*(2), 111–124.

41. Qvale, T. U., (2002). A case of slow learning?: Recent trends in social partnership in Norway with particular emphasis on workplace democracy. *Concepts and Transformation, 7*(1), 31–55.

42. Riddle, W. E., (1984). The magic number eighteen plus or minus three: A study of software technology maturation. *ACM SIGSOFT Software Engineering Notes, 9*(2), 21–37.

43. Rohlf, F. J., (1972). An empirical comparison of three ordination techniques in numerical taxonomy. *Systematic Zoology, 21*(3), 271–280.

44. Rountev, A., Kagan, S., & Gibas, M., (2004). Static and dynamic analysis of call chains in Java. In: *Proceedings of the 2004 ACM SIGSOFT International Symposium on Software Testing and Analysis* (Vol. 1, pp. 1–11).

45. Saleh, H., Avdoshin, S., & Dzhonov, A., (2019). Platform for tracking donations of charitable foundations based on blockchain technology. In: *2019 Actual Problems of Systems and Software Engineering (APSSE)* (Vol. 1, pp. 182–187). IEEE.

46. Sawant, A. A., Bari, P. H., & Chawan, P. M., (2012). Software testing techniques and strategies. *International Journal of Engineering Research and Applications (IJERA), 2*(3), 980–986.

47. Schaffartzik, A., Mayer, A., Gingrich, S., Eisenmenger, N., Loy, C., & Krausmann, F., (2014). The global metabolic transition: Regional patterns and trends of global material flows, 1950–2010. *Global Environmental Change, 26*, 87–97.

48. Selby, R. W., (2007). *Software Engineering: Barry W. Boehm's Lifetime Contributions to Software Development, Management, and Research* (Vol. 69, pp. 1–15). John Wiley & Sons.

49. Sharafi, Z., Soh, Z., & Guéhéneuc, Y. G., (2015). A systematic literature review on the usage of eye-tracking in software engineering. *Information and Software Technology, 67*, 79–107.
50. Shaw, M., (2002). What makes good research in software engineering? *International Journal on Software Tools for Technology Transfer, 4*, 1–7.
51. Shi, M., (2010). Software functional testing from the perspective of business practice. *Computer and Information Science, 3*(4), 49.
52. Shull, F., Basili, V., Carver, J., Maldonado, J. C., Travassos, G. H., Mendonça, M., & Fabbri, S., (2002). Replicating software engineering experiments: Addressing the tacit knowledge problem. In: *Proceedings International Symposium on Empirical Software Engineering* (Vol. 1, pp. 7–16). IEEE.
53. Sim, S. E., Easterbrook, S., & Holt, R. C., (2003). Using benchmarking to advance research: A challenge to software engineering. In: *25th International Conference on Software Engineering, 2003; Proceedings* (Vol. 1, pp. 74–83). IEEE.
54. Sommerville, I., (2011). *Software Engineering, 9/E* (Vol. 1, No. 2, pp. 1–23). Pearson Education India.
55. Stroebe, W., Mensink, W., Aarts, H., Schut, H., & Kruglanski, A. W., (2008). Why dieters fail: Testing the goal conflict model of eating. *Journal of Experimental Social Psychology, 44*(1), 26–36.
56. Thomas, T. K., (2015). Measuring community impact assessment for internal destination performance evaluation in an exploring tourist destination. *ATNA Journal of Tourism Studies, 10*(1), 53–71.
57. Vegas, S., Juristo, N., & Basili, V. R., (2009). Maturing software engineering knowledge through classifications: A case study on unit testing techniques. *IEEE Transactions on Software Engineering, 35*(4), 551–565.
58. Vyatkin, V., (2013). Software engineering in industrial automation: State-of-the-art review. *IEEE Transactions on Industrial Informatics, 9*(3), 1234–1249.
59. Wirth, N., (2008). A brief history of software engineering. *IEEE Annals of the History of Computing, 30*(3), 32–39.
60. Woods, S. S., Resnick, L. B., & Groen, G. J., (1975). An experimental test of five process models for subtraction. *Journal of Educational Psychology, 67*(1), 17.
61. Zhang, M., Li, X., Zhang, L., & Khurshid, S., (2017). Boosting spectrum-based fault localization using PageRank. In: *Proceedings of the 26th ACM SIGSOFT International Symposium on Software Testing and Analysis* (Vol. 1, pp. 261–272).

CHAPTER 4

BEYOND UNIT TESTING

UNIT INTRODUCTION

In the beginning of this chapter, we take a look at several different development life cycle models for the software and discuss the implications that each of these life cycles has for testing. We took a broad perspective and recognized 3 levels (unit, system and, integration) in terms of symmetrical relationships within the waterfall model (Luo, 2001). These levels are as follows: This perspective has been reasonably successful over the course of several decades, and all these levels continue to exist; however, the emergence of various life cycle models compels us to take a closer look at these testing perspectives. We start with the classic waterfall model in the beginning, mostly due to the fact that it is well known and serves as a reference model for more contemporary models. After that, we investigate variations on the waterfall paradigm, and then we finish up with some mainline agile variants (Jamil et al., 2016).

A significant change also occurs in the way that we think. Our capacity to recognize test cases may be hindered depending on how the item being tested is depicted, which is why we are more focused with how to depict the item being tested (Sawant et al., 2012). If you have a look at the papers that were presented at the most important conferences (either professional or academic), you will see that the number of sessions on the specification models and procedures is very close to the number of presentations on testing methodologies. Model-Based Testing, abbreviated as MBT, is the point at which all layers of software modeling and testing come together (Basili & Selby, 1987).

Learning Objectives

When they have finished reading this chapter, learners will be able to do the following:

Understand the importance of software testing

Differentiate between different testing techniques

Understand the process of test case design

Learn about different levels of testing

Understand how to measure test coverage

-Key Terms

- Agile Testing
- Beyond Unit Testing
- Scrum
- Traditional Waterfall Testing
- Waterfall Testing

4.1. TRADITIONAL WATERFALL TESTING

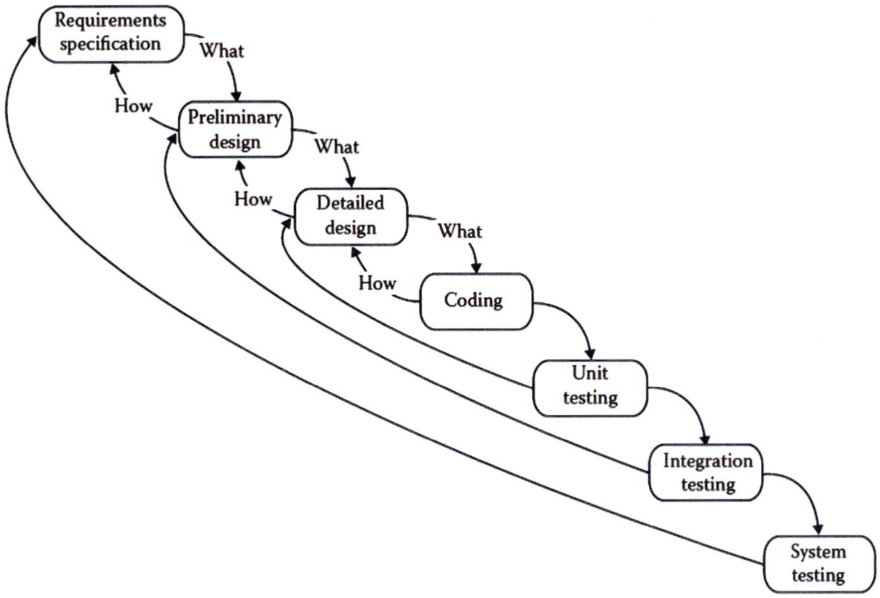

Figure 4.1. The waterfall life cycle.

Source: Wikipedia. Org, creative commons license.

The waterfall model, as can be seen in Figure 4.1, is widely considered to be the standard approach for the development of software. In order to illustrate the way that the fundamental levels of testing match the early waterfall phases, it is sometimes depicted as a V, as seen in Figure 4.2. According to this point of view, the knowledge that is produced during one of the stages of development serves as the basis for the identification of test cases at that level (Barr et al., 2014). Nothing here that might be considered controversial: we surely would expect that system test cases have a direct correlation with requirements specification, and also that unit test cases are developed from the thorough design of the unit. The what-and-how cycles that are very tight are very significant on upper left side of cascade (Thummadi et al., 2011). They emphasize those facts that comes before the one being worked on defines the tasks that are to be completed in the phase that comes after it. When it is finished, the successor phase will provide an explanation of how it achieves "what" was supposed to be done. They are also the best times to perform software reviews on the relevant products. The phases on the left are sometimes referred to as the fault formation phases, whereas the phases on the right are sometimes called the fault detection phases (Sinha & Das, 2021).

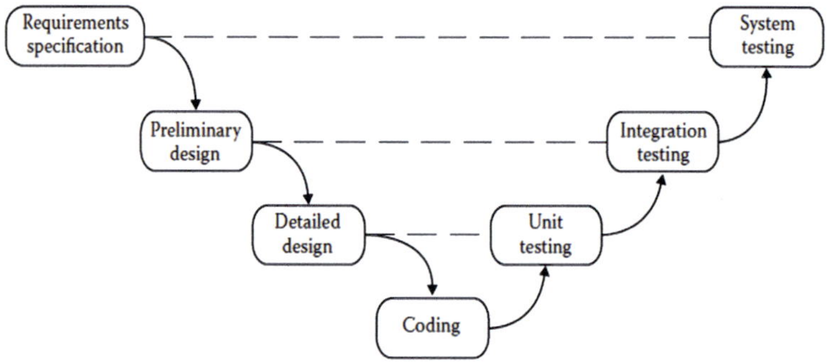

Figure 4.2. The waterfall life cycle as the V-Model.

Source: Wikipedia. Org, creative commons license.

Two points to note: first, there is an unmistakable assumption that functional testing is being performed here, second, an inferred bottom-up testing sequence is being applied. In this context, "bottom-up" refers to the order of testing levels: unit testing comes first, followed by integration testing, and then system testing (Adenowo & Adenowo, 2013).

Unit testing is the most straightforward and easily comprehended of the three primary types of testing: integration testing, system testing, and unit testing. Testing at the system level is better understood than testing at the integration level, but both require clarification (Sumrell, 2007). The bottom–up technique provides some illumination by testing the individual components first, followed by the integration of those components into subsystems, and then testing the overall system. System testing is something that the client (or user) should be aware of, and it frequently overlaps with customer acceptability testing. In most cases, functional testing is performed rather than structural testing; the primary reason for this is that there are not many higher-level structural notations (George & Williams, 2004).

Remember

The Waterfall methodology — also known as the Waterfall model — is a sequential development process that flows like a waterfall through all project phases (analysis, design, development, and testing, for example), with each phase completely wrapping up before the next phase begins.

4.1.1. Waterfall Testing

The waterfall paradigm is intimately connected to top-down development and the design of products by functional decomposition. The functional decomposition of entire unit into tree-like framework of functional components is the final result of the preliminary design phase of the system's development (Petersen et al., 2009). Top–down integration would start with the main program in such a decomposition, examining the next-level units calls, and continuing in this manner till the leaves of the biodegradation tree were reached. At each phase, lower-level units are substituted by stubs, which are essentially throwaway pieces of code that reproduce the behavior of the lower-level units when they are invoked. Integration from the bottom up follows the reverse order, beginning with leaf units and progressing all the way up to the main program. Bottom–up integration involves the replacement of units at greater levels with drivers, which are an additional kind of throwaway code (Elghondakly et al., 2015). These drivers replicate the procedure calls. The "big bang" method consists of simply putting all the units together at the same time, without using any stubs or drivers. In classic integration testing, the objective is to merge previously tested components in relation to a functional decomposition tree. This objective is the same regardless of the approach that is employed. Despite the fact that integration testing is described here as a procedure, discussions of this type offer very little information regarding the various methodologies and procedures (Hernando et al., 2022).

TIPS

Waterfall methodology

1.Analysis.

2.Design.

3.Implementation.

4.Testing.

5.Maintenance.

4.1.2. Pros and Cons of the Waterfall Model

Waterfall model has a long and illustrious history, and ever from its initial publication in 1968, it has been subjected to a great deal of scrutiny and examination. The first comprehensive work was written by Agresti in 1986, and it continues to be a reliable source (Sharma, 2017).

Agresti makes the following observation:

i. Hierarchical management systems are a good fit for the framework.
ii. The steps have clearly outlined end products, also known as exit criteria, which makes it easier to manage the project (Gwinn & Vallyathan, 2006).
iii. The comprehensive design phase denotes the beginning of the point where individuals who are accountable for units can begin working in parallel, which ultimately results in a reduction in the total amount of time required for the development of the project. But what's more noteworthy is that Agresti identifies significant shortcomings in the waterfall model. In the following, we will demonstrate how the generated life cycle models provide solutions to these restrictions. He makes the observation that there is very prolonged feedback cycle between the requirements formulation and the system testing, yet the customer is not present throughout this time (Patisaul & Jefferson, 2010).

iv. The model places a strong emphasis on analysis almost to the exclusion of syntheses, which comes into play for the first time during the integration testing phase.

v. Given the constraints imposed by staffing levels, massive parallel development at unit level might not be viable (Chandra, 2015).

vi. Most importantly, "perfect foresight" is necessary since any errors or omissions that occur at requirements level will spread throughout the rest of the life cycle stages (Loc & Abedon, 2011).

The "omission" component was something that gave the initial waterfall developers a lot of trouble. As a direct consequence of this, nearly all the papers that specified the requirements urged that they be consistent, comprehensive, and clear.

The majority of the methodologies for needs definition make it impossible to establish consistency (decision trees are an exception to this rule), therefore the necessity of clarity is self-evident. The aspect of completeness is particularly intriguing, given that all the successor life cycles begin with the presumption of incompleteness and rely on some kind of iteration to eventually arrive at "completeness" (Liu et al., 2011).

4.2. TESTING IN ITERATIVE LIFE CYCLES

In reaction to the limitations of the standard waterfall paradigm that was described before, practitioners have been coming up with alternate approaches since the early 1980s. The transition away from functional decomposition and towards a concentration on iteration is something that is shared by all of these different options. However, decomposition relies on one of the major flaws of waterfall development that was identified by Agresti (1986), which is the requirement for "perfect foresight."

Although decomposition is a perfect fit for both the top-down waterfall model evolution and the bottom-up testing order, this is one of the major flaws of waterfall development. Functional breakdown can only be done effectively if the system in question has been fully comprehended, and because of this, it encourages analysis almost to the exclusion of synthesis (Tsai et al., 1997).

Because of this, there is a significant gap in time between the requirements specification and the finished system, and during this time, there is no opportunity for the customer to provide feedback on the progress of the project.

Whereas Composition is more analogous to the way individuals actually operate because it involves beginning with something that is already recognized and comprehended, then progressively adding to it, and possibly removing parts of it that are not desired (Bhuvaneswari & Prabaharan, 2013).

The similarities between positive and negative sculpting make for a really interesting analogy. In negative sculpting, work is accomplished by removing undesirable material. This is analogous to the way a mathematician could envision Michelangelo making David: beginning with a block of marble, they would chisel away anything that wasn't David. When creating a positive sculpture, it is common practice to use a substance that is malleable, such as wax. After approximating the central shape, wax is worked into it by either adding to it or scraping it away till the final shape is achieved. After that, the original wax model is cast in plaster (Larman & Basili, 2003). After the plaster has had time to set, the wax is removed by melting it, and the "negative" of the plaster is then utilized to cast molten bronze. Consider the repercussions of making a mistake: in negative sculpting, the entire piece must be discarded and started over from the beginning. A monument in Florence, Italy, houses a half dozen different versions of the David that were rejected at an earlier stage. In the process of positive sculpture, the flawed component is typically extracted and replaced with a new one. As we will see, this is the fundamental characteristic that distinguishes the life cycle models of agile. The fact that composition plays such an important role in the possible alternatives has significant repercussions for integration testing (Shylesh, 2017).

4.2.1. Waterfall Spin-Offs

The waterfall paradigm has three principal derivatives: the spiral model, incremental development and evolutionary development. Incremental development is the most common (Boehm, 1988). In each of these cases, there is a progression of additions or increases, as depicted in Figure 4.3.

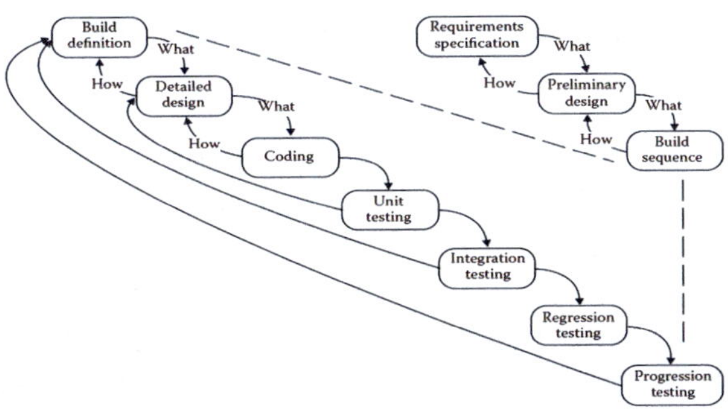

Figure 4.3. Iterative development.

Source: Wikipedia. Org, Creative Commons License.

It is crucial to maintain the design concept as an integral step rather than attempting to amortize such high-level design over a succession of constructions (Tsai et al., 1999). This is because preliminary design contributes significantly to the overall success of the project. In most cases, doing so leads to unfavorable outcomes as a result of design decisions made during the earlier iterations, which are lamented during the later builds. Under both the evolutionary and the spiral models, this one stage of the design process is impossible. This is another significant disadvantage of the bottom-up agile methodologies (Iazzolino et al., 2020).

The typical waterfall phases, from design phase through testing, are carried out within a build; however, there is one significant change: the testing phase of the system is divided into two steps: regression testing and progression testing. The regression testing purpose is to verify that features that were functional in a prior build will continue to do so with the implementation of any newly introduced code. It is possible for regression testing to take place either before or after integrated testing, or even in both locations simultaneously (Putra, 2020). The completion of effective regression testing is a precondition for progression testing, which then determines whether or not the newly added functionality can be validated. We would like to believe that the insertion of new code signals progress, rather than a retreat. Due to the well-known ripple impact that takes place when changes are made to an existing system, performing testing process is essential in any series of builds. In the average manufacturing environment, one change in every five results in the introduction of a new fault (Giddings, 1999).

Iterative, client-focused development is the most effective way to summarize evolutionary design. A stripped-down version of the original product is distributed to users, who are then asked to provide feedback on potential new additions (Lee et al., 2021). This is especially important in applications in where minimizing the amount of time it takes to get a product to market is a top goal. If the initial version is successful in penetrating a portion of target market, then that portion of the market will be "locked in" to any subsequent evolutionary versions. Customers are more likely to feel invested in the development of a product when they see that their feedback is being considered and taken into account (Strand, 2009).

The spiral model proposed by Barry Boehm shares some characteristics with the evolutionary model. The most notable distinction is that increments are established more on the risk factor than they are on the base of suggestions made by customers (Reitzig, 2022). The spiral is placed, with upper left quadrant within the x–y coordinate plane making reference to the method for identifying aims, upper right to the process of risk analyzation, the lower right to the process of development (and testing), and the lower left to the process of planning the subsequent iteration. These four stages—determine objectives, analyze risk, create and test, and plan the next iteration—are iterated in an incremental fashion. The spiral grows larger with each succeeding stage of evolution (Lizcano, 2013).

The first approach to regression testing is to repeat the tests from previous iteration. The second approach to regression testing is to develop a smaller collection of test cases that are explicitly focused on discovering affected flaws. Both approaches are valid approaches to regression testing. In an environment that relies more on manual testing, it is not desired to repeat a whole set of preceding integration tests, however in an environment that relies more on automation, this is acceptable (Cook et al., 2011). When compared to the test case failure expectation during progression testing, the test case failure expectation during regression testing should be (or is) lower. As a general rule, regression tests should fail no more than 5% of the time when they are run after advancement tests. When it comes to advancement testing, this percentage could go up to 20%. Soap Opera Tests are a fascinating name for particular kinds of regression tests that are performed manually. This name comes from the name of a popular soap opera. The plan is to have lengthy regression tests that are difficult to understand, much like the intricate storylines found in soap operas of television. In contrast, a progressive test case might fail due to a select few causes, while a test case of soap opera may fail for a variety of different reasons. If a test case for a soap opera fails, it is obvious that additional targeted testing is needed to pinpoint where the error is.

The naming conventions for the builds are what cause the variances in appearance between the three spin-off models. Incremental development is the rationale for distinct builds is typically to reduce the staff profile. This is because incremental development works best with small teams. The phases of pure waterfall development, from thorough design all the way to unit testing, can require a significant increase in the number of people working on the project. As a result of the fact that many firms are unable to manage such frequent staff fluctuations, the system is segmented into versions that can be serviced by the workforce that is already in place. Even if the presumption of a build sequence is created during evolutionary development, only the very first construction is actually determined. On this basis later builds are determined; often, this is carried out due to priorities stated by the customer/user; as a result, the system changes to match the changing requirements of the user. This hints at the customer-focused principle that underpins the agile methodology (Yuksek et al., 2006).

A build is specified first in terms of quick prototyping, and then it is evaluated to a go/no-go choice based on technology-related risk factors in the spiral model, which is a blend of fast prototyping and evolutionary development. As a result of this, we can see that it is impossible to maintain preliminary design like an essential stage using the evolutionary model or the spiral model. Integration testing is badly impacted to the degree that it cannot be kept as an integral activity. The testing of the system is unaffected. One advantage that is shared by all of these spin-off models is the way they offer early synthesis. This is due to the fact that a build is a collection of deliverable end-user functionality. Also, this results in earlier feedback from customers, which helps to offset two of the drawbacks associated with waterfall development. In the following section, two different strategies for solving the "perfect foresight" problem are discussed (Curcio et al., 2018).

4.2.2. Specification-Based Life Cycle Models

Functional decomposition is risky business at best when neither the customer nor the developer has a complete understanding of the system they are working on. While describing the customer who says, "I don't know what I'm looking for, but I'll recognize it when I see it," Barry Boehm makes light of the situation by telling a joke. The "look and feel" of a system is something that can be provided via the fast prototyping life cycle, as can be seen in Figure 4.4. The end result of this is that customers are able to "see" what they recognize. In turn, this results in very early synthesis, which substantially decreases the size of the feedback loop between the client and the specification (Moreira & Ferreira, 2016). Instead of building the final version of the system, a "fast and dirty" prototype is constructed and then utilized to get input from customers. Further cycles of prototyping may take place depending on the input received. The developer will proceed to build the product according to the correct specification if they and the customer have reached an agreement that a prototype accurately reflects the system that is desired. At this stage, any of these waterfall spin-offs may also be utilized if desired. The ultimate version of this pattern is known as the agile life cycle (Richardson et al., 1989).

Figure 4.4. Rapid prototyping life cycle.

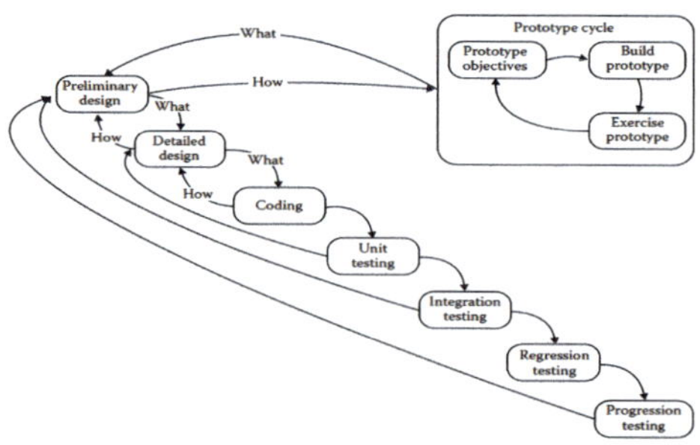

Source: Itsar Bolo Rangka, creative commons license.

The rapid prototyping process does not have any novel repercussions for integration testing; although, it does have some extremely intriguing repercussions for system testing. Where exactly can I find the requirements? Is the standard represented by the most recent prototype? How many individual system test cases be linked to the original prototype? Use of the prototype cycles as information-gathering activities, followed by the production of a requirements specification using a more traditional approach, is one approach that might be useful in responding to concerns such as these (Stocks & Carrington, 1996). Another alternative is to record what the client does when using the prototypes, then to characterize these actions as significant customer scenarios, and finally to use these actions as system test cases. They can be considered the ancestors of the user stories that are used in agile life cycles. The operational (or behavioral) viewpoint may be brought into the specifications phase thanks to fast prototyping, which is the primary contribution of this technique (Au & Paul, 1994). In most cases, system's structure is prioritized over the behavior of the system when it comes to requirements definition methodologies. It is unfortunate that this is the case because the vast majority of consumers need not to care about structure, yet they care about behavior (Pandey & Mehtre, 2014).

The idea of quick prototyping has been expanded upon with the implementation of executable specifications (Figure 4.5). The requirements are described in a format that is readable by the computer (such as petri nets, finite state machines or StateCharts). After that, the client puts the specification into action to observe how the system is supposed to behave and then provides feedback, similar to the rapid prototyping paradigm. Complexity is either inherent to or can be introduced into the executable models. As compared to the fully-fledged version of StateCharts, this is a significant understatement. Creating an executable model needs skill, and implementing it demands an engine (Berzins & Yehudai, 1993). The executable specification approach works particularly well for event-driven systems, in particular those in which the events might arrive in a variety of ordering.

David Harel, the author of StateCharts, calls these kinds of systems "reactive" (Harel, 1988) due to the fact that they respond to happenings in the outside world. In the same vein as rapid prototyping, the goal of an executable specifications is to provide the client with the opportunity to experience different behaviors that were intended for them. Further similarity is that client input could need executable models to be modified before they can be used. A decent engine for an operational model will facilitate the capture of "interesting" system transactions, and the process of converting them into genuine system test cases is frequently very close to being a completely mechanical one. This is one of the ancillary benefits. When this is done in a careful manner, it is possible to track system testing all the way back to the requirements (Gandhi & Robertson, 1992).

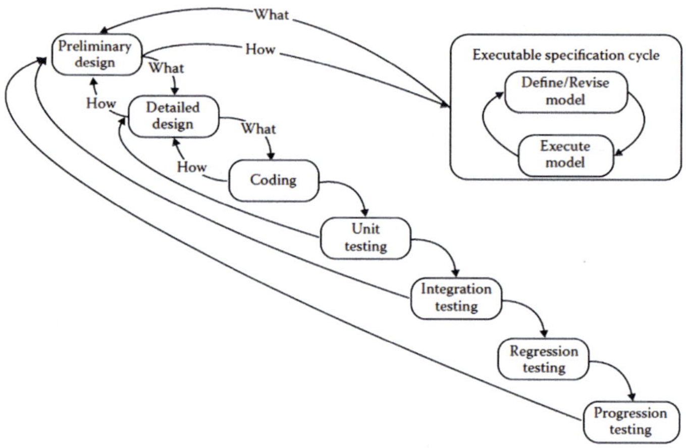

Figure 4.5. Executable specification.

Source: Mathswork, creative commons license.

Once more, this life cycle does not have any bearing on the integration testing that occurs. The fact that the specifications document is more explicit than a prototype is one of the most significant distinctions between the two. More importantly, the generation of system test cases out of an executable specification is frequently a process that can be described as mechanical. Although there will be an increase in work needed to construct a workable specification, this will be partially compensated for by a decrease in the amount of work required to produce system test cases. An additional key difference is presented below:

An intriguing sort at the system level of structural testing can be carried out when system testing is dependent on an executable specification. Last but not least, the stage of executable definition can be integrated into iterative life cycle models, as we saw when we looked at rapid prototyping (Heimdahl & Thompson, 2000).

4.3. AGILE TESTING

In February of 2001, independent consultants came together to form the Agile Alliance and write the Agile Manifesto. The book was translated into a total of 42 different languages and has had a significant impact on the field of software development. The following are some of the fundamental qualities shared by all agile life cycles (Hametner et al., 2012):

1. Customer-driven
2. Bottom–up development

3. Flexibility with respect to changing requirements (Stolberg, 2009).
4. Early delivery of fully functional components (Hellmann et al., 2013).

They are depicted in Figure 4.6 in a sketch form. The criteria for really small iterations of design–code–test are obtained from the expectations that are expressed by the customers in the form of user stories. When does an agile project end? When there aren't any more user stories for the consumer to use (Razak & Fahrurazi, 2011). When we take a look on iterative models from the beginning, we can identify the ancestors of agility, particularly in Barry Boehm's spiral model. On different sources, you'll find anywhere from three to forty different iterations of the agile software development methodology listed. In this section, we analyze three of the more prominent ones and concentrate on how they approach testing (Puleio, 2006).

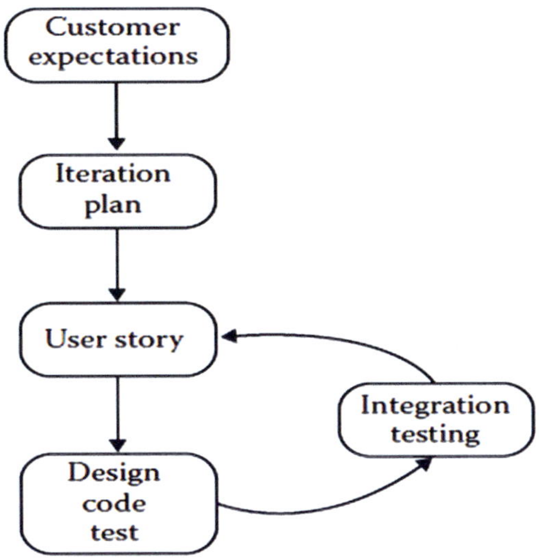

Figure 4.6. Generic agile life cycle.

Source: Laura M. Castro, creative commons license.

4.3.1. Extreme Programming

Extreme Programming (XP), sometimes known as XP, was initially implemented on a project in 1996 by Kent Beck, who was working at the time for Chrysler Corporation. Its implementation was documented. The obvious achievement of the project served as the impetus for his book, despite the fact that it was a modification of an earlier edition (Beck, 2004). The essential elements of XP are presented in Figure 4.7. The fact that user stories are in charge of driving either a system testing and release plan demonstrates that it is patently oriented towards the needs of the client. The release plan outlines a series of iterations, which are all supposed to result in the delivery of a functionally limited component (Beck, 1999). One of the things that sets XP apart from other methodologies is its paired programming emphasis, in which two programmers collaborate closely and frequently use the same development machine and keyboard.

Figure 4.7. The extreme programming life cycle.

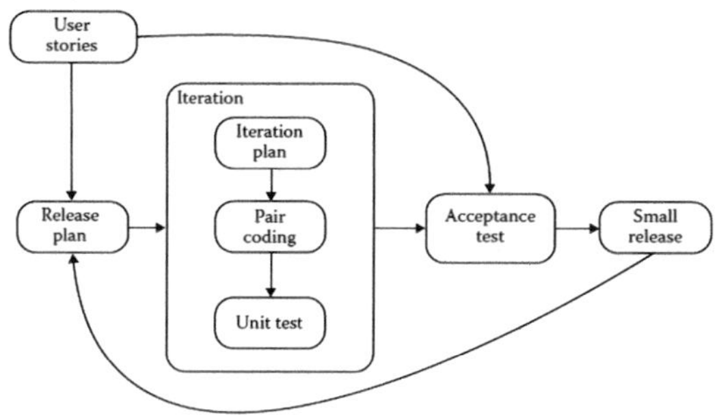

Source: Laura M. Castro, creative commons license.

One person works directly with the code, while the other maintains a perspective that is a little bit higher. The two individuals are, in a way, carrying out an ongoing review. There are a number of parallels can be seen with the fundamental repetitive life cycle depicted in Figure 4.7. The absence of an overarching preliminary design step is a key distinction between the two approaches. Why? Due to the fact that (Kircher et al., 2001). Entails working from the ground up. It is difficult to conceive of what might take place within release plan phase if XP were in fact driven by a series of user stories (Paulk, 2001).

Figure 4.8. Test-driven development life cycle.

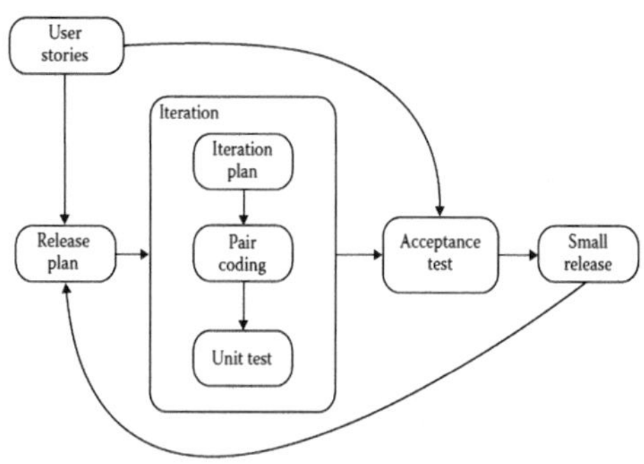

Source: Grata software, creative commons license.

4.3.2. Test-Driven Development

The most extreme kind of agility is test-driven development (also known as TDD). As can be seen in Figure 4.8, its progression is determined by a series of user tales. Each client story can be broken down into multiple tasks, which is where the most significant distinction can be found. The developer must first determine how the task will be tested before beginning to write any code for the task. The specifications are ultimately determined by the testing. Curiously, the next stage involves running the tests on code that does not yet exist. Inevitably, they will fail, but this will lead to the most beneficial aspect of TDD, which is a significantly easier fault separation (Maximilien & Williams, 2003). The tests are performed, and if they fail, the programmer adds almost enough code to let the test pass, and then the tests are run again. If any of the tests are unsuccessful, the developer will return to code and add any necessary adjustments. The subsequent user story is executed once all of the tests are successful (Desai et al., 2008).

Sometimes the developer will make the decision to refactor the code that is already there. After the code has been cleaned up, it is put through the complete suite of tests already in place, which is an approach that is very similar to the concept of regression testing. In order for TDD to be useful, it needs to be carried out in an atmosphere that allows for automated testing. The nUnit family for automated test environments is a good choice for this purpose (George & Williams, 2003).

Testing with TDD is a fascinating process. TDD employs a form of testing known as specification-based testing but since story-level test cases are what drive the code and hence ARE the specification. Yet, given that the code is designed to be as similar to the test cases as is humanly possible, one may make the case that it's also code-based testing. The TDD methodology has two major shortcomings.

The first is something that is consistent across all flavors of agile: the bottom-up methodology does not allow for a single high-level design stage (Williams et al., 2003). It's possible that user stories that emerge later in the sequence will render previous design decisions unnecessary. In that case, refactoring needs to take place not only at the level of the code, but also at the level of the design (Kaufmann & Janzen, 2003). The agile community has a lot of strong feelings concerning the assertion that consistent refactoring would eventually lead to an elegant design. Refactoring across the design levels and codes appears to be the only method to achieve an elegant design provided one of the fundamental premise of agile development, which is that the customer is unsure of what is needed or, alternatively, that the requirements are always shifting. This is an unavoidable barrier that must be overcome for bottom-up development (Turhan et al., 2010).

The second issue is that every single developer is prone to making errors, which is a significant part of the reason why we test in first place. But, take into consideration the following: what gives us reason to believe that TDD (Nagappan et al., 2008) developer is flawless at conceiving of test cases which drive the development? What's even worse is the possibility that later user stories won't match up with earlier ones. TDD has one further drawback that there's no spot in the entire lifecycle for a cross-check to be performed at the user story level (Zhang, 2004).

4.4. SCRUM

The agile life cycle known as Scrum is likely the one that is utilized the most frequently. An overarching focus is placed on the individuals who make up the team as well as their collaboration. The title comes from a tactic used in rugby in which two opposing teams lock arms and try to "hook" the football back onto their own side of the field. As a result of the need for well-coordinated cooperation, the software development process is called a scrum (Schwaber, 1997).

A first glance reveals that Scrum, which stands for "the development life cycle," is primarily comprised of "new names for old ideas." This is especially true in regard to the jargon that is commonly used in Scrum. Roles, ceremonies, and artifacts are three examples of these types of things (Srivastava et al., 2017). Commonly, when people talk about Scrum roles, they are referring to the people who are participating in the project; ceremonies are simply meetings, and artifacts are work products. Scrum initiatives are led by people who behave like traditional supervisors with less administrative power known as (Scrum masters) (Deemer et al., 2010). The Scrum team functions as a development team, while product owners take the place of traditional clients. This diagram was taken from the "official" Scrum literature, which is published by the Scrum Alliance. Consider the various undertakings in light of the repetitive life cycle depicted in Figure 4.9. The conventional iterations are renamed "sprints," and their duration ranges from two to four weeks (Sutherland, 2001). An everyday stand-up meeting is held by the Scrum team each day during a sprint. The purpose of these meetings is to focus on what occurred the previous day and what tasks need to be completed the following day. After that, there is a quick sprint of design, coding, and testing, which is continued through an integration of work completed by the team at end of the day. This is the part about being agile; an everyday build that adds to the sprint-level product of work in a relatively short amount of time. The most notable aspects of the Scrum methodology that stand in contrast to the conventional approach to iterative development are indeed the distinctive terminology and the length of the iterations (Cristal et al., 2008).

Scrum life cycle testing happens at two different levels: Unit level at the conclusion of each day, as well as the integration order of minor releasing at the end of each sprint. The product owner, often known as the customer, is responsible for selecting a Sprint backlog from the product backlog (Sharma & Hasteer, 2016). This action generally correlates to a step in the requirements process. Since this is the moment at which the Scrum team specifies the contents and sequence of particular sprints, the process of sprint definition is quite similar to the conceptual design phase (Streule et al., 2016). The bare essentials?

Unit testing and integration/system testing are the two main layers of testing that are used in Scrum. Why do we talk about integrating systems? Because of minor release that is a deliverables product that can be used by a product owner, it is evidently a work product that is on the system-level. On the other hand, this is the stage in which the entire development work is combined together for the very first time (Ereiz & Mušić, 2019).

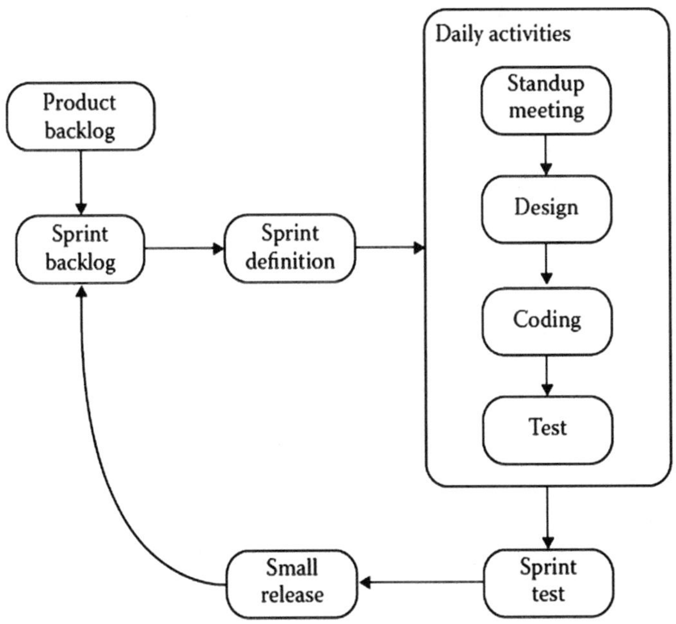

Figure 4.9. The scrum life cycle.

Source: Grata Software, creative commons license.

My good friend Georg is from Germany, and in addition to having a PhD in mathematics, he is also a software engineer and a Go player. We communicated about agile software development via email back and forth for a good portion of a year. Within one point, Georg inquired as to whether or not I am familiar with the eastern board game Go. I don't know, but he said that in order to be a good Go player, it only needs to have a good strategy as well as good tactics (Ambler, 2003). A player of Go would be at a disadvantage if they lacked one of these skills. In the context of software development, he views strategy as equivalent to an overarching design, whereas tactics are defined as development at the unit level (Zhang & Patel, 2010). His perspective on the many forms of agile software development is that there is a gap in the strategy component, which forces us to find a middle ground between both the agile world and the more conventional approaches to software development. First, we take a look at Agile Model-Driven Development, sometimes known as AMDD. This methodology was made famous by Scott Ambler. After this comes my slight reorganization of Ambler's work, which will be referred to from here on out as (MDAD) Model- Driven Agile Development (Alfraihi et al., 2018).

4.6. AGILE MODEL-DRIVEN DEVELOPMENT

The modeling step is where the agile aspects of AMDD come into play. The recommendation given by Ambler is to model only as much as is necessary for the present user narrative, and then to build it using TDD. There is a specific design step in AMDD, which is not present within agile life cycles (Ambler, 2003). This is the primary distinction between the two. (The agilists typically convey their dislike or scorn for modeling by referring to it as the "Big Design Up Front," which they then abbreviate to simply the BDUF) (Ambler, 2006). Figure 4.10. The recognition which design does, in fact, get a position in agile development is Ambler's contribution to the field of agile development. During the time that this article was being produced, there was a lengthy conversation taking place on LinkedIn.

Figure 4.10. The agile model-driven development life cycle.

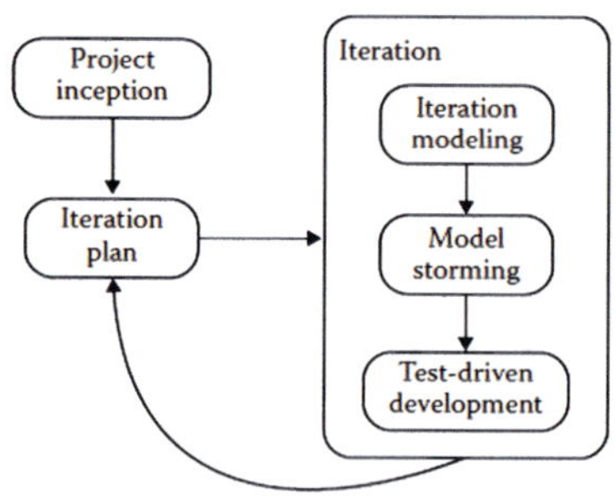

Source: Sheikh Umar Farooq et al., creative commons license.

The topic of discussion was "Is there any room for design in agile software development?" The majority of the responses to this question affirm the necessity of layout in almost any of agile cycle. In spite of all of this, it would appear that AMDD has no capacity for integration or system testing (Alfraihi et al., 2018).

ACTIVITY 2.1:

What is the difference between waterfall testing and agile? Give a detail presentation.

4.6.1. Model-Driven Agile Development

My suggestion for a middle ground between the agile development and traditional worlds is called model-driven agile development, or MDAD for short. It is spurred by Georg's belief that it is necessary to have both tactics and strategy, which is why the compromise is necessary (Kulkarni et al., 2011). What are the key differences between iterative development and MDAD? TDD is the strategy that MDAD suggests using, and it employs Ambler's notion of working in small iterations (Ambler, 2006). The emphasis placed on such an overall model within the strategy, which in turn provides support for MBT, is referred to as the "strategic component." The MDAD testing methodology incorporates all three levels of testing—unit, integration, and system (Matinnejad, 2011).

SUMMARY

In software development, testing is an essential part of the development process to ensure that the software meets the required specifications and functions correctly. Unit testing is the most fundamental type of testing that checks the smallest testable parts of the software, usually individual functions or methods. However, more than unit testing is needed to ensure the overall quality of the software. Testing beyond unit testing involves a broader range of testing techniques, including integration testing, system testing, acceptance testing, and performance testing. Integration testing checks the interaction between different modules or components of the software, ensuring that they work together seamlessly. System testing tests the entire system to ensure all components work together as expected. Acceptance testing involves testing the software against the user's requirements to ensure it meets their needs. Performance testing checks the software's performance under various conditions, including high load and stress. Testing beyond unit testing is essential to ensure that the software functions correctly as a whole and meets the user's requirements. While unit testing is crucial, it should be complemented by other testing techniques to ensure the overall quality of the software.

REVIEW QUESTIONS

1. What are the main types of software testing discussed in this chapter, and how do they differ from one another?
2. What common challenges or pitfalls are associated with software testing, and how does the chapter recommend addressing them?
3. How does the chapter approach the issue of test coverage, and what strategies are recommended for ensuring comprehensive testing?
4. What role does automation play in software testing, and how can it be effectively integrated into the testing process?
5. How does the chapter address the issue of testing in complex or distributed systems, and what strategies are recommended for ensuring reliable and accurate testing in these environments?
6. What are the best practices recommended for managing the testing process and ensuring testing is integrated effectively into the software development lifecycle?

MULTIPLE CHOICE QUESTIONS

1. Which of the following is not a type of software testing technique?

a. Black box testing
b. White box testing
c. Gray box testing
d. Blue box testing

2. What is equivalence partitioning?

a. A technique that involves dividing a range of input values into smaller partitions

b. A technique that involves testing all possible input values

c. A technique that involves testing a single input value

d. A technique that involves testing the boundaries of input values

3. What is boundary value analysis?

a. A technique that involves testing all possible input values

b. A technique that involves testing a single input value

c. A technique that involves testing the boundaries of input values

d. A technique that involves testing input values that are outside the specified range

4. What is the purpose of regression testing?

a. To test new features that have been added to the software

b. To test the software in different environments

c. To ensure that changes to the software have not introduced new defects

d. To test the performance of the software

5. Which of the following is not a common software testing tool?

a. Load testing tool

b. Code coverage tool

c. Bug tracking tool

d. Project management tool

Answers to Multiple Choice Questions

1. (d); 2. (a); 3. (c); 4. (c); 5. (d)

REFERENCES

1. Adenowo, A. A., & Adenowo, B. A., (2013). Software engineering methodologies: A review of the waterfall model and object-oriented approach. *International Journal of Scientific & Engineering Research, 4*(7), 427–434.
2. Alfraihi, H., Lano, K., Kolahdouz-Rahimi, S., Sharbaf, M., & Haughton, H., (2018). The impact of integrating agile software development and model-driven development: A comparative case study. In: *System Analysis and Modeling – Languages, Methods, and Tools for Systems Engineering: 10th International Conference, SAM 2018, Copenhagen, Denmark, October 15–16, 2018, Proceedings 10* (pp. 229–245).
3. Ambler, S. W., (2003). Agile model driven development is good enough. *IEEE Software, 20*(5), 71–73.

4. Ambler, S. W., (2006). Agile model driven development (AMDD). In: *Xootic Symposium* (Vol. 2006, p. 13).
5. Au, G., & Paul, R. J., (1994). Graphical simulation model specification based on activity cycle diagrams. *Computers & Industrial Engineering, 26*(2), 295–306.
6. Barr, E. T., Harman, M., McMinn, P., Shahbaz, M., & Yoo, S., (2014). The oracle problem in software testing: A survey. *IEEE Transactions on Software Engineering, 41*(5), 507–525.
7. Basili, V. R., & Selby, R. W., (1987). Comparing the effectiveness of software testing strategies. *IEEE Transactions on Software Engineering*, (12), 1278–1296.
8. Beck, K., (1999). Embracing change with extreme programming. *Computer, 32*(10), 70–77.
9. Berzins, V., & Yehudai, A., (1993). Using transformations in specification-based prototyping. *IEEE Transactions on Software Engineering, 19*(5), 436–452.
10. Bhuvaneswari, T., & Prabaharan, S., (2013). A survey on software development life cycle models. *International Journal of Computer Science and Mobile Computing, 2*(5), 262–267.
11. Chandra, V., (2015). Comparison between various software development methodologies. *International Journal of Computer Applications, 131*(9), 7–10.
12. Chikh, A., & Aldayel, M., (2012). A new traceable software requirements specification based on IEEE 830. In: *2012 International Conference on Computer Systems and Industrial Informatics* (pp. 1–6).
13. Cook, G. A., Pandit, N. R., & Beaverstock, J. V., (2011). Cultural and economic complementarities of spatial agglomeration in the British television broadcasting industry: Some explorations. *Environment and Planning A, 43*(12), 2918–2933.
14. Cristal, M., Wildt, D., & Prikladnicki, R., (2008). Usage of scrum practices within a global company. In: *2008 IEEE International Conference on Global Software Engineering* (pp. 222–226).
15. Curcio, K., Navarro, T., Malucelli, A., & Reinehr, S., (2018). Requirements engineering: A systematic mapping study in agile software development. *Journal of Systems and Software, 139*, 32–50.
16. Desai, C., Janzen, D., & Savage, K., (2008). A survey of evidence for test-driven development in academia. *ACM SIGCSE Bulletin, 40*(2), 97–101.
17. Elghondakly, R., Moussa, S., & Badr, N., (2015). Waterfall and agile requirements-based model for automated test cases generation. In: *2015 IEEE Seventh International Conference on Intelligent Computing and Information Systems (ICICIS)* (pp. 607–612).
18. Ereiz, Z., & Mušić, D., (2019). Scrum without a scrum master. In: *2019 IEEE International Conference on Computer Science and Educational Informatization (CSEI)* (pp. 325–328).
19. Gandhi, M., & Robertson, E. L., (1992). A specification-based data model. In: *Entity-Relationship Approach—ER'92: 11th International Conference on the Entity-Relationship*

Approach Karlsruhe, Germany, October 1992 Proceedings 11 (pp. 194–209).

20. George, B., & Williams, L., (2003). An initial investigation of test driven development in industry. In: *Proceedings of the 2003 ACM Symposium on Applied Computing* (pp. 1135–1139).
21. George, B., & Williams, L., (2004). A structured experiment of test-driven development. *Information and Software Technology, 46*(5), 337–342.
22. Giddings, S., (1999). The circle of life: Nature and representation in Disney's the lion king. *Third Text, 13*(49), 83–92.
23. Gwinn, M. R., & Vallyathan, V., (2006). Nanoparticles: Health effects—Pros and cons. *Environmental Health Perspectives, 114*(12), 1818–1825.
24. Hametner, R., Winkler, D., & Zoitl, A., (2012). Agile testing concepts based on keyword-driven testing for industrial automation systems. In: *IECON 2012–38th Annual Conference on IEEE Industrial Electronics Society* (pp. 3727–3732).
25. Heimdahl, M. P., & Thompson, J. M., (2000). Specification based prototyping of control systems. In: *19th DASC: 19th Digital Avionics Systems Conference. Proceedings (Cat. No. 00CH37126)* (Vol. 1, pp. 1D3–1). IEEE.
26. Hellmann, T. D., Chokshi, A., Abad, Z. S. H., Pratte, S., & Maurer, F., (2013). Agile testing: A systematic mapping across three conferences: Understanding agile testing in the XP/agile universe, agile, and XP conferences. In: *2013 Agile Conference* (pp. 32–41).
27. Hernando, K., Waite, L., Bairagdar, N., Manigaba, K., Teelucksingh, K., Dunn, R., & Casiano-Colon, A., (2022). A waterfall of susceptibility results: Impact of microbiology testing cascade for MDROs. *Diagnostic Microbiology and Infectious Disease, 104*(1), 115731.
28. Iazzolino, G., Greco, D., Verteramo, S., Attanasio, A. L., Carravetta, G., & Granato, T., (2020). An integrated methodology for supporting the development and the performance evaluation of academic spin-offs. *Measuring Business Excellence, 24*(1), 69–89.
29. Jamil, M. A., Arif, M., Abubakar, N. S. A., & Ahmad, A., (2016). Software testing techniques: A literature review. In: *2016 6th International Conference on Information and Communication Technology for the Muslim World (ICT4M)* (pp. 177–182).
30. Kaufmann, R., & Janzen, D., (2003). Implications of test-driven development: A pilot study. In: *Companion of the 18th Annual ACM SIGPLAN Conference on Object-Oriented Programming, Systems, Languages, and Applications* (pp. 298, 299).
31. Kircher, M., Jain, P., Corsaro, A., & Levine, D., (2001). Distributed extreme programming. *Extreme Programming and Flexible Processes in Software Engineering* (pp. 66–71). Italy.
32. Kulkarni, V., Barat, S., & Ramteerthkar, U., (2011). Early experience with agile methodology in a model-driven approach. In: *Model Driven Engineering Languages and Systems: 14th International Conference, MODELS 2011, Wellington, New Zealand, October 16–21, 2011; Proceedings 14* (pp. 578–590).

33. Larman, C., & Basili, V. R., (2003). Iterative and incremental developments: A brief history. *Computer, 36*(6), 47–56.

34. LEE, C. S., & LEE, K. W., (2021). The effectiveness of object-oriented-QR monopoly in enhancing ice-breaking and education UX: A preliminary study. In: *29th International Conference on Computers in Education (ICCE)* (pp. 403–409).

35. Liu, W., Du, Z., Xiao, Y., Bader, D. A., & Xu, C., (2011). A waterfall model to achieve energy efficient tasks mapping for large scale GPU clusters. In: *2011 IEEE International Symposium on Parallel and Distributed Processing Workshops and PHD Forum* (pp. 82–92). IEEE.

36. Lizcano, A. S., (2013). Merging computational science and urban planning in the information age: The use of location-based social media for urban analysis. In: *2013 13th International Conference on Computational Science and its Applications* (pp. 200–203).

37. Loc-Carrillo, C., & Abedon, S. T., (2011). Pros and cons of phage therapy. *Bacteriophage, 1*(2), 111–114.

38. Luo, L., (2001). *Software Testing Techniques* (Vol. 15232, No. 1–19, p. 19). Institute for software research international Carnegie Mellon university Pittsburgh, PA.

39. Matinnejad, R., (2011). Agile model driven development: An intelligent compromise. In: *2011 Ninth International Conference on Software Engineering Research, Management and Applications* (pp. 197–202).

40. Maximilien, E. M., & Williams, L., (2003). Assessing test-driven development at IBM. In: *25th International Conference on Software Engineering, 2003; Proceedings* (pp. 564–569).

41. Moreira, F., & Ferreira, M. J., (2016). Teaching and learning modeling and specification based on mobile devices and cloud. In: *2016 11th Iberian Conference on Information Systems and Technologies (CISTI)* (pp. 1–6).

42. Nagappan, N., Maximilien, E. M., Bhat, T., & Williams, L., (2008). Realizing quality improvement through test driven development: Results and experiences of four industrial teams. *Empirical Software Engineering, 13*, 289–302.

43. Pandey, S. K., & Mehtre, B. M., (2014). A lifecycle-based approach for malware analysis. In: *2014 Fourth International Conference on Communication Systems and Network Technologies* (pp. 767–771).

44. Patisaul, H. B., & Jefferson, W., (2010). The pros and cons of phytoestrogens. *Frontiers in Neuroendocrinology, 31*(4), 400–419.

45. Paulk, M. C., (2001). Extreme programming from a CMM perspective. *IEEE Software, 18*(6), 19–26.

46. Petersen, K., Wohlin, C., & Baca, D., (2009). The waterfall model in large-scale development. In: *Product-Focused Software Process Improvement: 10th International Conference, PROFES 2009, Oulu, Finland, June 15–17, 2009; Proceedings 10* (pp. 386–400).

47. Puleio, M., (2006). How not to do agile testing. In: *AGILE 2006 (AGILE'06)* (p. 7).

48. Putra, J., (2020). Data management system for thesis monitoring at STMIK IBBI using B-model. In: *2020 3rd International Conference on Mechanical, Electronics, Computer, and Industrial Technology (MECnIT)* (pp. 365–369).

49. Razak, R. A., & Fahrurazi, F. R., (2011). Agile testing with selenium. In: *2011 Malaysian Conference in Software Engineering* (pp. 217–219).

50. Reitzig, M., (2022). Flat fads or more? From a as in "agile" to z as in "Zi Zhu Jing Ying Ti" In: *Get Better at Flatter: A Guide to Shaping and Leading Organizations with Less Hierarchy* (pp. 173–193).

51. Richardson, D., O'Malley, O., & Tittle, C., (1989). Approaches to specification-based testing. In: *Proceedings of the ACM SIGSOFT'89 Third Symposium on Software Testing, Analysis, and Verification* (pp. 86–96).

52. Sawant, A. A., Bari, P. H., & Chawan, P. M., (2012). Software testing techniques and strategies. *International Journal of Engineering Research and Applications (IJERA), 2*(3), 980–986.

53. Schwaber, K., (1997). Scrum development process. In: *Business Object Design and Implementation: OOPSLA'95 Workshop Proceedings 16 October 1995, Austin, Texas* (pp. 117–134).

54. Sharma, G., (2017). Pros and cons of different sampling techniques. *International Journal of Applied Research, 3*(7), 749–752.

55. Sharma, S., & Hasteer, N., (2016). A comprehensive study on state of scrum development. In: *2016 International Conference on Computing, Communication and Automation (ICCCA)* (pp. 867–872).

56. Shylesh, S., (2017). A study of software development life cycle process models. In: *National Conference on Reinventing Opportunities in Management, IT, and Social Sciences* (pp. 534–541).

57. Sinha, A., & Das, P., (2021). Agile methodology Vs. traditional waterfall SDLC: A case study on quality assurance process in software industry. In: *2021 5th International Conference on Electronics, Materials Engineering & Nano-Technology (IEMENTech)* (pp. 1–4).

58. Srivastava, A., Bhardwaj, S., & Saraswat, S., (2017). SCRUM model for agile methodology. In: *2017 International Conference on Computing, Communication and Automation (ICCCA)* (pp. 864–869).

59. Stocks, P., & Carrington, D., (1996). A framework for specification-based testing. *IEEE Transactions on Software Engineering, 22*(11), 777–793.

60. Stolberg, S., (2009). Enabling agile testing through continuous integration. In: *2009 Agile Conference* (pp. 369–374).

61. Strand, R., (2009). Corporate responsibility in Scandinavian supply chains. *Journal of Business Ethics, 85*, 179–185.

62. Streule, T., Miserini, N., Bartlomé, O., Klippel, M., & De Soto, B. G., (2016). Implementation of scrum in the construction industry. *Procedia Engineering, 164*, 269–276.

63. Sumrell, M., (2007). From waterfall to agile-how does a QA team transition? In: *Agile 2007 (AGILE 2007)* (pp. 291–295).

64. Sutherland, J., (2001). Inventing and reinventing scrum in five companies. *Cutter IT Journal, 14*(21), 5–11.

65. Thummadi, B. V., Shiv, O., & Lyytinen, K., (2011). Enacted routines in agile and waterfall processes. In: *2011 Agile Conference* (pp. 67–76).

66. Tsai, B. Y., Stobart, S., Parrington, N., & Thompson, B., (1997). Iterative design and testing within the software development life cycle. *Software Quality Journal, 6*, 295–310.

67. Tsai, W. T., Vishnuvajjala, R., & Zhang, D., (1999). Verification and validation of knowledge-based systems. *IEEE Transactions on Knowledge and Data Engineering, 11*(1), 202–212.

68. Turhan, B., Layman, L., Diep, M., Erdogmus, H., & Shull, F., (2010). How effective is test-driven development. *Making Software: What Really Works, and Why We Believe it*, 207–217.

69. Williams, L., Maximilien, E. M., & Vouk, M., (2003). Test-driven development as a defect-reduction practice. In: *14th International Symposium on Software Reliability Engineering, 2003; ISSRE 2003* (pp. 34–45).

70. Yuksek, O., Komurcu, M. I., Yuksel, I., & Kaygusuz, K., (2006). The role of hydropower in meeting Turkey's electric energy demand. *Energy Policy, 34*(17), 3093–3103.

71. Zhang, Y., & Patel, S., (2010). Agile model-driven development in practice. *IEEE Software, 28*(2), 84–91.

72. Zhang, Y., (2004). Test-driven modeling for model-driven development. *IEEE Software, 21*(5), 80–86.

CHAPTER 5

USER EXPERIENCE

UNIT INTRODUCTION

Despite our importance on usability, only a minority of products deliver on this front. There are various factors at play, including but not limited to history, culture, organization, finances, and others, but exploring all of them would be too lengthy for this book. The good news is that there are established and trustworthy techniques for determining which aspects of a product's design improve its usability, and which ones need to be tweaked for the product to compete successfully in the market (Hassenzahl & Tractinsky, 2006). Because usability is only an issue when missing or absent, it can be difficult to determine what makes something usable. One example of a paradigm shift in usability that has been shown to boost sales is Apple's iPod. Pretend a customer is attempting to purchase from your company's online store. Possible thoughts they're having in response to the site: I haven't located the info I need. Okay, I think I've sought what I'm looking for, but the price tag is a mystery. Is there any left? Is it possible to have it sent to where I currently am? Should I expect free shipping if I spend this much? Most online shoppers have run into problems like these at some point (Datig, 2015).

It's simple to criticize websites because there are so many, but there are countless other situations in which people are forced to deal with inconvenient products and services. When it comes to your alarm clock, phone, and DVR, how well-versed are you? How simple is it to navigate the voice-activated menu of available options when contacting a company (Fronemann & Peissner, 2014)?

Learning Objectives

At the end of this chapter, readers will be able to:

- Understand the concept of usability testing
- Learn the benefits of usability testing
- Understand the types of usability testing
- Learn the steps involved in conducting usability testing
- Understand the usability metrics

Key Terms

- Characteristics of Organizations
- Emulation and Measurement of Product
- Iterative Design
- Usability Testing
- Usable Meaning
- Usable Product

5.1. USABLE MEANING

The absence of usability issues is a major factor in whether something is useful. This book relies on the following definition of usability to outline the process and methodology for conducting usability testing: "when a product or service is truly usable, the user can do what he or she wants to do the way he or she supposes to be able to do it, without interruption, reluctance, or queries.

Let's spend some time discussing what usability is and what it entails before diving into the definition and exploration of usability testing. A product or service's usability increases if it satisfies the user's needs, is easy to use, gains access, and learns about it. Whether or not a product is useful depends on whether or not the user is willing to use it to accomplish his or her goals. All other efforts are pointless without that drive, as the product will remain unsold. Even if a user is willing to use a system for free, it will not be adopted if it does not fulfill their needs. Practicality is probably the factor that gets the least attention during laboratory investigations (Voskobojnikov et al., 2021).

The marketing team is responsible for identifying the features of the product or system that are most important and desired before any other usability aspects are considered. Without it, the development team will have to make educated guesses or even bad, use themselves as the user model.

It is where a system-oriented approach to the design typically takes root. Efficiency is the rate at which a given task can be completed to the user's satisfaction in terms of both accuracy and completeness. For usability testing, you might establish the goal that "95% of all users will be able to load the software within 10 minutes" (Mashapa & van Greunen, 2010).

The effectiveness of a product is measured by how well it fulfills its intended purpose and how easily its intended audience can use it. The error rate is the standard quantitative indicator of this. Like efficiency, the effectiveness of your usability test should be measured in terms of a fraction of the total user base. The standard could read: "95% of all users will be able to load the software correctly on the first attempt."

The effectiveness of a system includes its learnability or the degree to which a user can master its controls with a set amount of instruction over a set time. Infrequent users' ability to re-learn the system after long periods of inactivity also falls under this umbrella. What we mean by "satisfaction" is the information gleaned from interviews with customers, both written and verbal, about their experiences with the product. Users will do better on a product if it caters to their requirements and makes them happy. Users are frequently asked to provide feedback on the products they test, which can help pinpoint issues and their root causes (Javahery et al., 2009). Usability goals and objectives are typically defined in measurable terms of one or more of these traits. However, we must stress that the ability to generate numbers about practice and satisfaction is never the sole determinant of a product's usability. Data can tell us whether a product "works," but a qualitative component of something's usability is also difficult to quantify. The interpretation of the data is crucial for finding a solution to a problem, as behavioral data reveals the root cause of the issue. Blood pressure and pulse rate are two vitals that any doctor can measure. The real value of a doctor comes from the time they spend analyzing a patient's data and coming up with individualized treatment plans. To effectively treat a design problem, looking at the bigger picture and evaluating the likelihood of various potential causes is often necessary rather than relying solely on a few isolated data points. Small nuances exist that the untrained eye misses (Matz, 2013).

Usability and accessibility are like twins. Regarding accessibility, we usually mean the ease with which people can access the resources they need to complete a task. What we mean by "accessibility" in this book, however, is how easy it is for people with physical impairments to use a given product. Making a product accessible to those with disabilities or those using it in unique situations almost always benefits the general public. Designing with accessibility for people with disabilities in mind can clarify and simplify things for people with situational or temporary impairments. Luckily, you can get help from various resources when creating accessible designs. The book's accompanying website features links to useful accessibility-related resources (Baird, 2015).

To incorporate usability testing and other forms of user feedback into your company's user-centered design (UCD) process, you should learn about accessibility best practices. The larger field of UCD includes many methods and techniques we will discuss in this chapter to make things more usable and accessible. Experience design is a broader, more all-encompassing concept that builds on the foundation of UCD. Even if a customer can complete their purchase on your website, they may have questions about the logistics of product delivery, upkeep, service, and possible return. How does your company aid in pre-purchase investigation and selection? Experience design takes all of these into account, so we must consider practicality again (Liu et al., 2013).

Real usability is unnoticeable. When things are going well, you don't pay attention to them. Assuming everyone is at a satisfactory temperature, there will be no complaints. On the other hand, product usability occurs on a scale. That being said, how practical is your offering? Although users can achieve their goals, is there a way to make it even easier to use? Is there any point in trying to enhance it? Usability experts typically focus on fixing existing designs to reduce user frustration. You've set yourself a worthy objective (Tractinsky et al., 2000). Achieving this goal for each customer can be challenging, though. And the portion of the user's experience it impacts while trying to achieve a goal is minimal. It is impossible to quantify something like usability, even though there are quantitative methods for evaluating products' usability. You can only quantify how unusable something is by counting the number of complaints about it, detailing those complaints, and explaining why they are valid.

Incorporating evaluation strategies like usability testing throughout an iterative design process allows for the creation of products and services that are practical, easy to use, and satisfying for the user (Jacobs & McDaniel, 2022).

Remember

User experience also considers the business goals and objectives of the group managing the project.

5.2. WHAT MAKES SOMETHING LESS USABLE? WHY ARE SO MANY HIGH-TECH PRODUCTS SO HARD TO USE?

5.2.1. Five Reasons Why Products Are Hard to Use

In this section, we searched this question, deliberated why the situation exists, and observed the overall antidote to this problem. User guides, on-screen instructions, and error messages are just some of the embedded forms of help discussed in this book's many practical examples of consumer hardware, software, and websites. The techniques described in this book apply to various electronic devices. Even products, such as the control panel for an ultrasound machine or the user manual for a digital camera, fall within the range of this book (Preece et al., 2004).

Those of you who currently work as engineers, user-interface designers, technical communicators, training specialists, or managers in these fields may find several reasons for developing difficult-to-use products and systems all too familiar.

1. During development, the system or machine is the primary focus.
2. Audiences are fluid and evolve.
3. Designing products that people will want to use is challenging.
4. Specialized team members don't always coordinate their efforts.
5. Fifth, there is often incompatibility between the two (Ter Bogt & Engels, 2005).

Figure 5.1.
Bailey's human performance model.

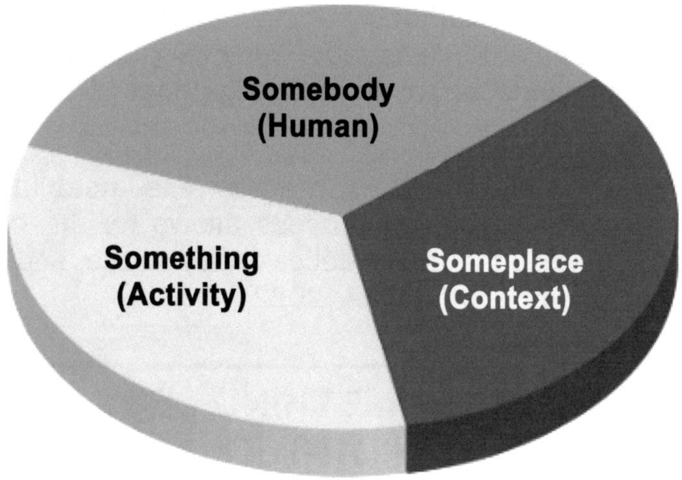

Source: Mohd Azlis Sani Md Jalil et al., creative commons license.

1. Reason 1: Development Focuses on the Machine or System

It's neglected during the product's design and development in favor of the machine or system. Figure 5.1 is a general model of human performance that illustrates this.

Bailey's Human Performance Model demonstrates three crucial factors to consider in any human performance setting.

i. Human;
ii. Activity; and
iii. Context.

Because any system or product design aims to enhance human performance, designers need to keep these three factors in mind as they work on their creations. Performance outcomes for humans are influenced by all three of these factors. Unfortunately, designers, engineers, and programmers have traditionally prioritized the activity component while giving much less weight to the human and the context components. The interdependence of the three parts is another aspect that has been overlooked. This imbalanced strategy has several causes (Wan et al., 2019):

i. An unspoken belief holds that humans can more easily adapt to machines than machines can to humans.
ii. Historically, developers have been more at ease dealing with the "black and white," scientific, concrete issues related to systems than the grey, chaotic, ambiguous issues related to people.

iii. Developers have traditionally been hired and compensated less for their interpersonal "people" skills and more for their technical prowess when tackling complex problems.

iv. The fact that designers historically catered to similar consumers is a major contributor to the neglect of human needs. There was no point in taking the time to investigate such a well-known coworker. Thus, we arrive at our next topic (Woods, 1985).

2. **Reason 2: Target Audiences Enlargement and Adaptation**

Because of how far technology has come into the hands of the average consumer, the demographics of the intended users have shifted significantly. Organizations working on development have been slow to respond to this change. Lovers (also known as early adopters) were the first people to use computer-based products. These people had extensive experience with computers and other mechanical devices, a penchant for learning new things, a penchant for tinkering, and a sense of pride in their ability to diagnose and fix problems. Those responsible for creating these items had a lot in common. Users and creators of these systems were essentially the same people. Because of the similarities, the team used a "next bench" design technique, which involves creating products with the end user in mind, even if they are only physically separated by one bench. As expected, this method was well-received, and users reported few problems (Gengshen, 2003).

To what end would they whine? An integral part of the product's appeal for enthusiast users was the challenge of getting it to work, and they took great pride in their abilities to get products of this complexity up and running. As a result, a "machine-oriented" or "system-oriented" approach to development was generally accepted and became the norm (Braun, 2007).

However, all of that is different now in significant ways. Users typically possess limited expertise with computers and mechanical devices, have little tolerance for tinkering with their brand-new purchase, and have very different expectations from those of the designer.

Even more importantly, modern users are not analogous to designers regarding skill, aptitude, expectation, or any other factor that might be considered during the design process. Companies that previously would have found Ph.D. chemists using their products are now more likely to find high school graduates in those roles. When the gap between the designer and the user is wide, it is clear that the "next-bench" design approach fails as a viable strategy, and businesses that use this approach, even unintentionally, will continue to make products that are difficult to use (Petrovčič et al., 2018).

Nowadays, designers are typically trained professionals with degrees in fields such as human-computer interaction, industrial design, human factors engineering, computer science, or a combination of these. The days when the average person didn't use some electronic or computer-based product at work or home are long gone. Whether it's a cell phone, DVR, website, or high-tech testing equipment, most are designed with the less technically savvy user in mind. The modern user seeks a practical solution, not a new pastime (Adriaens & Biltereyst, 2012).

3. Reason 3: Designing Usable Products Is Difficult

While many businesses act as if "common sense" is all required when designing usable systems, the reality is that it's a challenging, unpredictable endeavor.

Though many have attempted to define usability, the concept continues to elude those lacking behavioral or social science training. Usability is both an art and a science, and everyone seems to have an opinion about what constitutes good usability and how to achieve it—until it comes time to evaluate the usability of a product, that is (which requires an operational definition and precise measurement).

This dismissal of usability concerns is more difficult than if product designers admitted that user experience design was not their forte and sought new product creation approaches. It's not what we don't know that gets us into trouble; it's what we think we know that isn't so, as Will Rogers put it. Usability engineering is often treated as "common sense" by many businesses (Sokol, 1994).

In 1994, when this book first came out, most people working in systems design and development knew nothing about UCD. If they aren't already familiar with UCD principles, most designers today have at least heard of them. But there are still voids in our understanding and ability to practice it. There is still a great requirement for education, assistance, and a systematic approach in applying so-called "common sense" to the design process to internalize usability principles fully (Taati et al., 2013).

4. Reason 4: Team Specialists Don't Always Work in Integrated Ways

A common problem in product and system development is that organizations use highly specialized teams and methods but fail to coordinate their efforts. Many businesses now have product development processes to increase their productivity is broken down into modular, independently developed system components.

The software's user interface, help system, and documentation are all examples of product components. Different people or groups of people usually work on each of these parts. There is, of course, nothing wrong with focusing on a narrow area of expertise. The problem appears when there is insufficient coordination and integration between the various development teams working on the various parts of the system (Bryman, 2007).

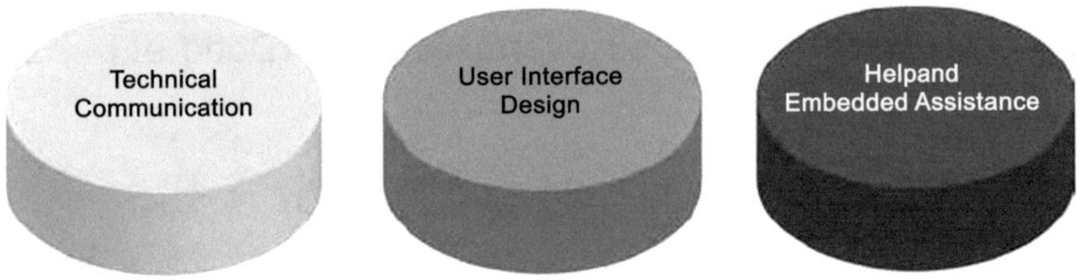

Figure 5.2. Nonintegrated approach to product development.

Source: Semantic Scholar, creative commons license.

It's common practice for product development to occur in silos. If you were an outsider looking at this development, you would see something like Figure 5.2.

The final product reflects the development teams' siloed, autonomous work style. There will be insufficient support for the user interface, or the help center will be poorly organized compared to the interface. A lack of referencing will lead to redundant user guides and support materials. Otherwise, the current UI will not be reflected in the written instructions. I think you get the point.

After the product is introduced to the market, issues arise. Looking at Figure 5.3, you can see how the consumer will perceive and use this new product: as a unified whole. Each of the three parts is expected to function in tandem with and in support of the others without any noticeable differences being noticed by the person. When the product does not function this way, it causes friction between the user and the product, and any benefits from specialization are nullified (Hjelle et al., 2016).

Interestingly, this lack of integration is often made worse by usability testing each component independently, something that many organizations do without realizing the negative impact they are having. The interface is tested independently from the documentation, and the documentation is tested independently from the interface. Ultimately, it doesn't matter if the individual parts work because the whole is useless without them. The product will be considered usable and successful in meeting user needs if all its parts function smoothly.

Recent years have seen improvements in application development methodologies that place a premium on iterative design and interdisciplinary teams. Also, cutting-edge products and services like Netflix, eBay, Yahoo!, the iPod and iPhone, and the newest appliances from Whirlpool are all excellent examples of products and services that have been designed around usability advantages and have become market leaders. Their ability to integrate parts successfully is crucial to their overall success (Dodd et al., 2022).

Figure 5.3. Integrated approach to product development.

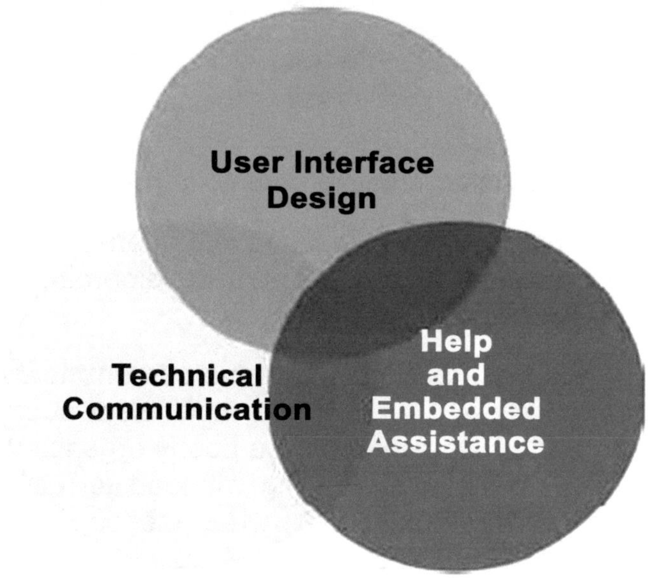

Source: Semantic Scholar, creative commons license.

5. **Reason 5: Design and Implementation Don't Always Match**

There is a large skill gap between user interface design and technical implementation disciplines. While many engineers are well-equipped to handle technical implementation, today focus on design abilities.

In this context, design refers to the product's mode of communication, while implementation describes how the product performs. This difference between planning and carrying out a project has hitherto been largely ignored. Professionals in engineering and design were recruited for their technical abilities (such as programming and machine-oriented analysis) rather than their aesthetic ones (e.g., communication, and human-oriented analysis). It makes sense because the primary difficulty in using earlier computer languages was doing the product work. It would be a bonus if it conveyed its message gracefully, but this was not the primary directive (Harmancioglu et al., 2007).

New generation programming languages and tools to automatically develop program code have made the technical implementation challenge easier. However, design is more difficult than ever because of the growing number of less-tech-savvy users and their increasingly high standards for usability. To use a computer metaphor, we have shifted our attention from the system's inner workings to the environment in which the program is used (how it communicates). This shift in emphasis has necessitated a reorientation in the abilities sought after by designers. In the future, more importance will be placed on conceptualization and less on actual implementation. Perhaps one day, coding expertise will not be required at all stages of user interface design (Balogh, 2001).

The five reasons listed above are only the tip of the iceberg when explaining the success of useless products and systems. What's more crucial is the underlying theme shared by these issues and misconceptions: namely, that too much focus has been placed on the product itself and not enough on the product's results. It is not astonishing that the user remains to receive too little consideration and consideration, especially in the heat of an increasingly rushed and shortened development process. Designers often lose sight of the fact that they are shaping the interaction between a product and a person rather than the product itself. More importantly, designers of this relationship must ensure that the human is free to concentrate on the task at hand and achieving the goal rather than how the task is accomplished. They are also responsible for designing how each part of the product interacts with the others. It necessitates a high level of coordination between the various groups responsible for the product's design and the people who will be using the product in their day-to-day lives or at their places of employment. Nothing from the past can be used with today's user base and technology (Reynolds et al., 2005).

Methods and techniques that help designers shift their perspective and how they design products, such as user-centered design (UCD), which starts with the user's wants and needs and moves inward to the product's actual implementation (UCD). Let's delve deeper into the concept of UCD, as it is only within this framework that usability testing makes sense and thrives (Rosenblum & Ousterhout, 1992).

5.3. WHAT MAKES PRODUCTS MORE USABLE?

Human factors engineering, ergonomics, and usability engineering describe aspects of UCD. Still, these fields have been around for much longer than the term "user-centered design" (UCD) has been in use. The terms "human factors engineering" and "ergonomics" can be used interchangeably; the main distinction between the two has more to do with terminology than with substantive differences in methodology. Human factors engineering is the more common term in the US, while ergonomics is more common in other parts of the world, especially Europe. UCD is the philosophy that prioritizes the user over everything else when designing a product or system. It also encompasses the processes, methods, and procedures necessary to design usable products and systems (Caputo et al., 2016).

Even though the design team has to consider the product's technology (can we build what we have in mind?) and features (will it do what we want it to do?), they must also consider the user's experience. UCD is an approach to product creation that places the user front and center while still considering the capabilities and limitations of any underlying technology and any features the business plans to implement.

Instead of making people alter their routines to fit a product, UCD encourages designers to accommodate how their intended audience performs their tasks. As defined by ISO standard 13407, UCD "is characterized by: the active contribution of users and a clear thoughtful of user and task requirements; an appropriate allocation of function between users and technology; iterative design solutions; multi-disciplinary design" (Sasse et al., 2001).

As a next step beyond UCD, we must consider the user's journey throughout the product's lifecycle. The entire customer interaction, from the first point of sales and marketing contact to the point at which an upgrade is made to the current product or another product is purchased, should ideally be incorporated into a user-centered approach. As a result, businesses would broaden their focus to incorporate customer interactions before and after a purchase. But let's take it slowly and methodically and stay with the design procedure.

UCD has been the subject of countless books and articles. However, the reader needs to grasp the fundamentals of UCD to appreciate the setting of usability testing. Despite its name, usability testing is not the sole method to ensure a good UCD. Specifically, we'd like to stress the following UCD basics:

i. The initial emphasis on end-users and their activities
ii. Product usage evaluation and measurement
iii. Iterative design (Pirolli et al., 1996).

5.3.1. An Early Emphasis on Users and Tasks

Instead of just classifying users, we suggest keeping them in constant contact with the design team as they work. Your team requires training and coaching on handling these kinds of interactions. As you learn more and gain more experience, you'll be ready to take on this responsibility (Karat & Karat, 2003).

The goal of establishing regular contact with customers is commendable; however, doing so for the sake of ticking a box on a performance review form is not a good reason to engage in such contact. Users' information needs to be gathered in a systematic, organized fashion. Before a data collection session, designers must receive expert interviewers' training. If this isn't done, the findings may be highly inaccurate (Herlocker & Konstan, 2001).

5.3.2. Evaluation and Measurement of Product Usage

Here, early in the design process, prototypes are developed and tested with real users to gauge their ability to learn and use (Oliver & Bearden, 1985).

5.3.3. Iterative Design and Testing

There has been a lot said about how crucial iteration is in design. It isn't merely some final touches added at the end of the development process, though. Instead, the iterative design allows for early testing of conceptual models and design ideas, which can lead to a complete rethinking of the original design. Without proper preparation, the impact of iterative design is trivial and superficial. The ultimate goal of iterative design is to "shape the product" through prototyping, testing, redesign, and retesting (Tsai et al., 1997).

5.4. CHARACTERISTICS OF ORGANIZATIONS THAT TRAIN UCD PRACTICES

Putting the user first necessitates a shift in perspective for most businesses regarding strategy, product creation, and customer focus. Although there is not yet a foolproof method for success, there are some things that all businesses that employ UCD have in common. To give one illustration:

i. User-involved phases
ii. Collaborative efforts spanning multiple disciplines
iii. Conscientious, enlightened management;
iv. A "learn as you go" attitude;
v. Defined usability goals and objectives (Jokela, 2002).

5.4.1. Stages That Include User Input

In contrast to the standard phases used in more conventional development methodologies, a user-centered approach relies on gathering feedback from actual users at every stage of the development before moving on to the next. Methods like usability testing are just one option for accomplishing this. Usability engineering and human factors are now standard processes in the product development cycles of most large corporations that create technological products or systems. Doubts crop up during that procedure. Figure 5.4 depicts these inquiries along with some potential solutions (Leontief, 1970). Many different usability engineering tasks will be performed during each stage. Although this lifecycle is written from the perspective of the human factors specialist's activities, it's important to remember that there are many points throughout the process where team members must work together. It brings us to the next characteristic of UCD-aware businesses (Timmer et al., 2015).

5.4.2. A Multidisciplinary Team Approach

Design can no longer be the purview of a single individual or even an isolated field. One designer may be held ultimately responsible for a product's design, but that designer does not possess all the answers. Designing highly complex products for less technically savvy end users is daunting (Tanaka, 2003).

The UCD calls for a wide range of expertise and, most importantly, insight into the end user and their needs. Engineers, marketers, trainers, UI designers, HCI researchers, multimedia producers, and other specialists from various disciplines are increasingly working together on projects. Furthermore, many of these specialists have education and experience in related fields, making interdisciplinary collaboration simpler and more exciting (Morton et al., 2018).

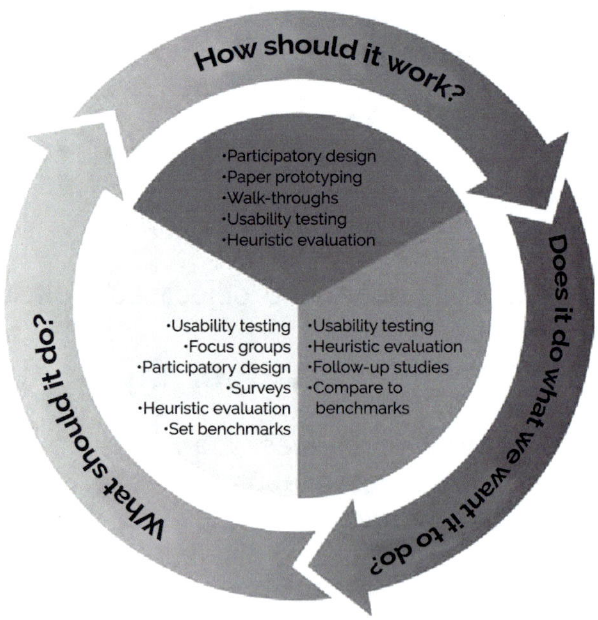

Figure 5.4. Questions and methods for answering them.

Source: Geeksforgeeks, creative commons license.

5.4.3. Apprehensive, Progressive Management

The dedication of upper management to the company's lifecycle and the implementation of the guidelines' teeth through the enforcement of accountability on the design team are usually good indicators of how seriously a company takes usability. The upper echelons of management know the financial benefits of usability and the importance of capturing a sizable portion of the market (Rose, 2013).

5.4.4. A "Learn as You Go" Perspective

Universal Design for Learning (UCD) is an iterative process that molds the final result. It calls for designers to believe that the best design is uncovered gradually through experimentation and iteration. Before evaluating with the end user, any conventions about proceeding remain just that: assumptions. The effectiveness and preferences of the final user determine all design choices (Eidt, 1992).

5.4.5. Defined Usability Goals and Objectives

If a product's design process will result in something people will actually want to use, it needs to be well-organized and methodical, starting with broad goals and working down to finer details. No objective, usability or otherwise, can be realized if it is not clear and well-defined. The term "usability" needs to be defined internally.

i. Usefulness
ii. Efficiency
iii. Effectiveness
iv. Satisfaction
v. Accessibility

Those mentioned above are all factors that contribute to a product's usability. As a result, we are back to where we started explaining what makes a product practical. What follows is a short summary of some of the most important approaches a usability expert uses to guarantee a thoughtfully crafted design with the end user in mind (Butler, 1985).

5.5. WHAT ARE TECHNIQUES FOR BUILDING IN USABILITY?

As a collection of tools, methods, and practices, UCD is used at various stages of the product creation process. Usability testing is one of these techniques;

reviewing the major methods will give you a better idea of their place. It is important to remember that the techniques presented here would typically be used in the order presented during different stages of a product's development lifecycle (Smith et al., 2006).

5.5.1. Ethnographic Research

Research methods from the anthropological sciences are frequently used in ethnographic studies. Users are observed in their natural environments (at work, at home, in a coffee shop, etc.) to learn more about the people you're designing for, the problems they face, the solutions they need, and the surroundings in which they complete those problems. User profiles, personas (archetype users), scenarios, and task descriptions can be derived from qualitative research and used to inform design decisions at every development lifecycle stage (Gusterson, 2008).

5.5.2. Participatory Design

Participatory design incorporates a representative user or users into the design process, making it less of a technique and more of a manifestation of UCD. Typically employed in creating proprietary systems, this method places the end user squarely in the center of the design process from the very outset of the project, drawing on the user's expertise, experience, and even emotional responses to the design (Kensing et al., 1998). The users who are meant to represent the whole run the risk of becoming too close to the design team. People start to act and think like those around them or stop raising important issues or criticisms for fear of being reprimanded by their coworkers (Robertson & Simonsen, 2012). Short, individualized workshops where users, designers, and developers collaborate on a specific design aspect are another variant of this method. For instance, the best product dimensions are developed through collaborative efforts between users, designers, and engineers using functional prototypes (Scariot et al., 2012).

5.5.3. Focus Group Research

Focus group research is useful in the early stages of a project because it allows you to get feedback from a cross-section of potential end-users on your rough ideas. To some extent, this constitutes a "proof of concept" evaluation. In other cases, it's used to confirm the identity of the representative user and establish the characteristics that best describe them. One of the most distinguishing features of focus group research is that it always involves more than one participant at a time (Edmunds, 1999).

Concepts presented in these group sessions may be as simple as sketches on paper or as complex as interactive digital prototypes or physical models. The goal is to figure out how well-received the ideas are, where they fall short, and how they can be improved to be more widely accepted and put to good use. The power of the focus group lies in its capacity to delve deeply into the opinions of a small sample of people to gain insight into the perspectives of actual end users (Breen, 2006). Focus groups are not a replacement for usability testing and are, in fact, very different from these. If you want to learn about specific performance issues or actual behaviors, a focus group is not the best way. Remember that focus group participants will tell you whatever they feel like sharing with you, which will likely differ from their actions. Usability tests are most useful for observing user behavior, measuring performance issues, and possibly collecting qualitative data (Onwuegbuzie et al., 2009).

5.5.4. Surveys

Many people's opinions can be gathered about a product's current or potential features by conducting surveys. In contrast to the focus group, which can dig deep into respondents' motivations and attitudes, surveys can use statistical extrapolation from larger samples to conclude the population as a whole. One of the most well-known ongoing surveys, the Nielsen ratings, is used to inform multimillion-dollar business decisions for the entire country based on the opinions of about 1500 individuals (Marsh, 1984). While surveys have a place at any stage of the user lifecycle, they are most commonly used in the beginning to gain insight into the user base. Surveys require crystal-clear language everyone can read and comprehend, which is difficult without extensive testing and planning. Again, observing users in action during a usability test is preferable to asking them about what they do or have done (Jamsen & Corley, 2007).

5.5.5. Walk-Throughs

By visualizing a user's path through an early concept or prototype of the product, walk-throughs are used to investigate how a user might fare with the product once you have a good idea of who your target users are and the task goals they have. Typically, the designer in charge of the project leads the team through simulated user tasks (sometimes even acting as the user). In contrast, a second team member takes notes on any issues or concerns that arise (Aliaga & Carlbom, 2001). IBM pioneered structured walk-throughs for code reviews, wherein participants take on defined roles (such as moderator and recorder) and adhere to strict rules (such as a maximum walk-through duration of two hours). If possible, it's better to have a real user, perhaps from a preferred client, participate in the design process as a stand-in for the designer (Smith-Jackson, 2004).

5.5.6. Open and Closed Card Sorting

Create "findability" of content or features using card sorting in the design process. It is a low-cost approach to collecting user feedback on the UI's content structure, terminology, and labeling. One method is to provide participants with cards depicting content without titles or categories, allowing users to name the content themselves (an open card sort), while another is to provide participants with preliminary or preexisting categories, requesting that they sort content or functions into those (a closed sort) (Paul, 2008).

5.5.7. Paper Prototyping

Users are shown a paper version of a product feature and then asked questions or given other opportunities to provide feedback. Mocking up pages with paper and pencil on graph paper, or creating line drawings or wireframe drawings of screens, pages, or panels, with a version of the page for each state, can help you learn if the flow of screens or pages you've planned meets users' expectations. If the prototype is for an e-commerce website's shopping cart, you could demonstrate the cart pre-loaded with items, the cart in action as items are added and removed, and the cart with shipping and taxes calculated (Sefelin et al., 2003).

By exposing the top-level navigation, you can find out if the labels aid users in knowing what to expect next and if the categories you've planned reflect how users think and talk about tasks. When a user selects a primary option, you display the submenu for that option in real-time. This process will continue until the user has explored the depths of the navigation you envisioned and planned for them. Alternatively, you could ask people who use your prototype what they think of it. Questions can concern anything from specifics like organization and layout to more general ones like how to locate certain menu items or specific pieces of data (Signer & Norrie, 2007).

Critical information can be gathered rapidly and cheaply with the help of a paper prototype or a paper-and-pencil evaluation. Before writing any code, it is possible to identify which features and functions are intuitive and which are not. In addition, technical writers can use the method before they write a single word of text to gauge how intuitive their table of contents will be. This method requires little continued investment and can be used repeatedly (Li et al., 2010).

5.5.8. Expert Evaluations

A neutral party (such as a usability expert or human factors consultant) examines a product or system in an expert evaluation. The expert evaluates generally accepted usability principles (heuristics) from research, human factors literature, and practical experience. The perspective is from the end-user group the product is intended for them (Smith et al., 2002).

Expertise in both the domain area (such as healthcare, financial services, and so on, depending on the application) and the specific technology employed by the product (a "double" specialist) can be more effective than either expertise alone (Bashynska, 2015).

ACTIVITY 5.1:

What are the characteristics of organizations that train UCD practices? Give a detail presentation.

SUMMARY

This chapter provides an introduction to usability testing, which is the process of evaluating how user-friendly a product or service is by observing how users interact with it. It covers the benefits of usability testing, including improved user satisfaction, increased efficiency, and reduced development costs. It also discusses the different types of usability testing, such as heuristic evaluation, cognitive walkthroughs, and user testing, as well as the various methods for collecting data during usability testing, including surveys, interviews, and observation. It also highlights the importance of usability testing throughout the product development process and the need for ongoing testing and evaluation to ensure continued usability and user satisfaction.

REVIEW QUESTIONS

1. What is usability testing, and why is it important in developing digital products?
2. Describe the difference between formative and summative usability testing. When is each type of testing most appropriate?
3. What are some common methods for collecting and analyzing data during usability testing? How do you decide which methods to use?
4. Explain the concept of "think-aloud" protocols. How do they help researchers understand user behavior?
5. What are common usability metrics used to evaluate user performance and satisfaction? What are the strengths and weaknesses of each type of metric?
6. How do you recruit participants for a usability testing study? What are some common challenges in participant recruitment, and how can they be addressed?

MULTIPLE CHOICE QUESTIONS

1. What is the primary goal of usability testing?

a. To find all possible defects in the product
b. To measure the user satisfaction with the product
c. To identify areas of improvement in the product
d. To evaluate the aesthetics of the product

2. Which of the following is NOT a common method of usability testing?

a. Paper prototyping
b. A/B testing
c. Eye tracking
d. Online surveys

3. What is the difference between formative and summative usability testing?

a. Formative testing is conducted after the product is launched, while summative testing is conducted before the launch.

b. Formative testing is conducted with a small group of users, while summative testing is conducted with a larger group.

c. Formative testing focuses on identifying areas of improvement, while summative testing evaluates the overall usability of the product.

d. Formative testing is conducted by the development team, while a third-party usability testing company conducts summative testing.

4. Which of the following is NOT a common usability metric?

a. Time on task

b. Number of clicks

c. Task success rate

d. User demographics

5. Which of the following is a common challenge in usability testing?

a. Finding enough participants for the study

b. Getting participants to follow the study protocol

c. Ensuring that the study environment is comfortable for the participants

d. All of the above

Answers to Multiple Choice Questions

1. (c); 2. (d); 3. (c); 4. (d); 5. (d)

REFERENCES

1. Adriaens, F., & Biltereyst, D., (2012). Glocalized telenovelas and national identities: A "textual cum production" analysis of the "telenovelle" Sara, the Flemish adaptation of Yo soy Betty, la fea. *Television & New Media, 13*(6), 551–567.
2. Aliaga, D. G., & Carlbom, I., (2001). Plenoptic stitching: A scalable method for reconstructing 3D interactive walk throughs. In: *Proceedings of the 28th Annual Conference on Computer Graphics and Interactive Techniques* (Vol. 1, pp. 443–450).
3. Baird, C., (2015). *Useful, Usable, Desirable: Applying User Experience Design to Your Library: Aaron Schmidt and Amanda Etches 2014* (Vol. 168). Chicago, IL: ALA Techsource, ISBN: 978-0-8389-1226-3.
4. Balogh, L., (2001). Design and application guide for high speed MOSFET gate drive circuits. In: *Power Supply Design Seminar SEM-1400, Topic* (Vol. 2, pp. 1–9).

5. Bashynska, I. O., (2015). Using the method of expert evaluation in economic calculations. *Aktual'ni Problemy Ekonomiky= Actual Problems in Economics*, (169), 408.
6. Braun, S., (2007). Interpreting in small-group bilingual videoconferences: Challenges and adaptation processes. *Interpreting, 9*(1), 21–46.
7. Breen, R. L., (2006). A practical guide to focus-group research. *Journal of Geography in Higher Education, 30*(3), 463–475.
8. Bryman, A., (2007). Barriers to integrating quantitative and qualitative research. *Journal of Mixed Methods Research, 1*(1), 8–22.
9. Butler, K. A., (1985). Connecting theory and practice: A case study of achieving usability goals. *ACM SIGCHI Bulletin, 16*(4), 85–88.
10. Caputo, D. D., Pfleeger, S. L., Sasse, M. A., Ammann, P., Offutt, J., & Deng, L., (2016). Barriers to usable security? Three organizational case studies. *IEEE Security & Privacy, 14*(5), 22–32.
11. Datig, I., (2015). Walking in your users' shoes: An introduction to user experience research as a tool for developing user-centered libraries. *College & Undergraduate Libraries, 22*(3, 4), 234–246.
12. Dodd, A., Guerin, S., Delaney, S., & Dodd, P., (2022). How can we know what we don't know? An exploration of professionals' engagement with complicated grief. *Patient Education and Counseling, 105*(5), 1329–1337.
13. Edmunds, H., (1999). The focus group research handbook. *The Bottom Line, 12*(3), 46–46.
14. Eidt, Jr. C. M., (1992). Quality in R&D: Applying quality to R&D means 'learn-as-you-go.' *Research-Technology Management, 35*(4), 24–31.
15. Fronemann, N., & Peissner, M., (2014). User experience concept exploration: User needs as a source for innovation. In: *Proceedings of the 8th Nordic Conference on Human-Computer Interaction: Fun, Fast, Foundational* (Vol. 1, pp. 727–736).
16. Gengshen, H., (2003). Translation as adaptation and selection. *Perspectives: Studies in Translatology, 11*(4), 283–291.
17. Gusterson, H., (2008). Ethnographic research. *Qualitative Methods in International Relations: A Pluralist Guide, 1*(3), 93–113.
18. Harmancioglu, N., McNally, R. C., Calantone, R. J., & Durmusoglu, S. S., (2007). Your new product development (NPD) is only as good as your process: An exploratory analysis of new NPD process design and implementation. *R&D Management, 37*(5), 399–424.
19. Hassenzahl, M., & Tractinsky, N., (2006). User experience-a research agenda. *Behavior & Information Technology, 25*(2), 91–97.
20. Herlocker, J. L., & Konstan, J. A., (2001). Content-independent task-focused recommendation. *IEEE Internet Computing, 5*(6), 40–47.

21. Hjelle, K. M., Skutle, O., Førland, O., & Alvsvåg, H., (2016). The reablement team's voice: A qualitative study of how an integrated multidisciplinary team experiences participation in reablement. *Journal of Multidisciplinary Healthcare, 1*, 575–585.
22. Jacobs, D., & McDaniel, T., (2022). A survey of user experience in usable security and privacy research. In: *HCI for Cybersecurity, Privacy and Trust: 4th International Conference, HCI-CPT 2022, Held as Part of the 24th HCI International Conference, HCII 2022, Virtual Event, June 26–July 1, 2022, Proceedings* (Vol. 1, pp. 154–172). Cham: Springer International Publishing.
23. Jamsen, J., & Corley, K., (2007). E-survey methodology. In: *Handbook of Research on Electronic Surveys and Measurements* (Vol. 1, pp. 1–8). IGI Global.
24. Javahery, H., Deichman, A., Seffah, A., & Taleb, M., (2009). A user-centered framework for deriving a conceptual design from user experiences: Leveraging personas and patterns to create usable designs. *Human-Centered Software Engineering: Software Engineering Models, Patterns and Architectures for HCI, 1*(2), 53–81.
25. Jokela, T., (2002). Making user-centered design common sense: Striving for an unambiguous and communicative UCD process model. In: *Proceedings of the Second Nordic Conference on Human-Computer Interaction* (Vol. 1, pp. 19–26).
26. Karat, J., & Karat, C. M., (2003). The evolution of user-centered focus in the human-computer interaction field. *IBM Systems Journal, 42*(4), 532–541.
27. Kensing, F., Simonsen, J., & Bodker, K., (1998). MUST: A method for participatory design. *Human-Computer Interaction, 13*(2), 167–198.
28. Leontief, W., (1970). Environmental repercussions and the economic structure: An input-output approach. *The Review of Economics and Statistics, 1*, 262–271.
29. Li, Y., Cao, X., Everitt, K., Dixon, M., & Landay, J. A., (2010). FrameWire: A tool for automatically extracting interaction logic from paper prototyping tests. In: *Proceedings of the SIGCHI Conference on Human Factors in Computing Systems* (Vol. 1, pp. 503–512).
30. Liu, S., Zheng, X. S., Liu, G., Jian, J., & Peng, K., (2013). Beautiful, usable, and popular: Good experience of interactive products for Chinese users. *Science China Information Sciences, 56*, 1–14.
31. Marsh, C., (1984). Problems with surveys: Method or epistemology? *Sociological Research Methods: An Introduction, 1*, 82–102.
32. Mashapa, J., & Van, G. D., (2010). User experience evaluation metrics for usable accounting tools. In: *Proceedings of the 2010 Annual Research Conference of the South African Institute of Computer Scientists and Information Technologists* (Vol. 1, pp. 170–181).
33. Matz, K., (2013). *Designing Usable Apps: An Agile Approach to User Experience Design* (Vol. 1, pp. 1–10). Winchelsea Press (Winchelsea Systems Ltd).
34. Morton, G., Masters, J., & Cowburn, P. J., (2018). Multidisciplinary team approach to heart failure management. *Heart, 104*(16), 1376–1382.

35. Oliver, R. L., & Bearden, W. O., (1985). Disconfirmation processes and consumer evaluations in product usage. *Journal of Business Research, 13*(3), 235–246.

36. Onwuegbuzie, A. J., Dickinson, W. B., Leech, N. L., & Zoran, A. G., (2009). A qualitative framework for collecting and analyzing data in focus group research. *International Journal of Qualitative Methods, 8*(3), 1–21.

37. Paul, C. L., (2008). A modified Delphi approach to a new card sorting methodology. *Journal of Usability Studies, 4*(1), 7–30.

38. Petrovčič, A., Rogelj, A., & Dolničar, V., (2018). Smart but not adapted enough: Heuristic evaluation of smartphone launchers with an adapted interface and assistive technologies for older adults. *Computers in Human Behavior, 79*, 123–136.

39. Pirolli, P., Pitkow, J., & Rao, R., (1996). Silk from a sow's ear: Extracting usable structures from the web. In: *Proceedings of the SIGCHI Conference on Human Factors in Computing Systems* (Vol. 1, pp. 118–125).

40. Preece, J., Nonnecke, B., & Andrews, D., (2004). The top five reasons for lurking: Improving community experiences for everyone. *Computers in Human Behavior, 20*(2), 201–223.

41. Reynolds, P., Bosma, N., Autio, E., Hunt, S., De Bono, N., Servais, I., & Chin, N., (2005). Global entrepreneurship monitor: Data collection design and implementation 1998–2003. *Small Business Economics, 24*, 205–231.

42. Robertson, T., & Simonsen, J., (2012). Challenges and opportunities in contemporary participatory design. *Design Issues, 28*(3), 3–9.

43. Rose, S. P., (2013). Making progress amid transition: Apprehension is reasonable during times of change, but we've got to keep moving forward. *Healthcare Financial Management, 67*(10), 26–27.

44. Rosenblum, M., & Ousterhout, J. K., (1992). The design and implementation of a log-structured file system. *ACM Transactions on Computer Systems (TOCS), 10*(1), 26–52.

45. Sasse, M. A., Brostoff, S., & Weirich, D., (2001). Transforming the 'weakest link'—A human/computer interaction approach to usable and effective security. *BT Technology Journal, 19*(3), 122–131.

46. Scariot, C. A., Heemann, A., & Padovani, S., (2012). Understanding the collaborative-participatory design. *Work, 41*(Supplement 1), 2701–2705.

47. Sefelin, R., Tscheligi, M., & Giller, V., (2003). Paper prototyping-what is it good for? A comparison of paper-and computer-based low-fidelity prototyping. In: *CHI'03 Extended Abstracts on Human Factors in Computing Systems* (Vol. 1, pp. 778, 779).

48. Signer, B., & Norrie, M. C., (2007). PaperPoint: A paper-based presentation and interactive paper prototyping tool. In: *Proceedings of the 1st International Conference on Tangible and Embedded Interaction* (Vol. 1, pp. 57–64).

49. Smith, A., Gulliksen, J., & Bannon, L., (2006). Building usability in India: Reflections from the Indo-European systems usability partnership. In: *People and Computers*

XIX—The Bigger Picture: Proceedings of HCI 2005 (Vol. 1, pp. 219–232). Springer London.

50. Smith, J. A., Hayes, C. E., Yolton, R. L., Rutledge, D. A., & Citek, K., (2002). Drug recognition expert evaluations made using limited data. *Forensic Science International, 130*(2, 3), 167–173.
51. Smith-Jackson, T. L., (2004). Cognitive walk-through method (CWM). In: *Handbook of Human Factors and Ergonomics Methods* (Vol. 1, pp. 785–793). CRC Press.
52. Sokol, M. B., (1994). Adaptation to difficult designs: Facilitating use of new technology. *Journal of Business and Psychology, 8*, 277–296.
53. Taati, B., Snoek, J., & Mihailidis, A., (2013). Video analysis for identifying human operation difficulties and faucet usability assessment. *Neurocomputing, 100*, 163–169.
54. Tanaka, M., (2003). Multidisciplinary team approach for elderly patients. *Geriatrics & Gerontology International, 3*(2), 69–72.
55. Ter Bogt, T. F. M., & Engels, R. C. M. E., (2005). "Partying" hard: Party style, motives for and effects of MDMA use at rave parties. *Substance Use & Misuse, 40*(9, 10), 1479–1502.
56. Timmer, M. P., Dietzenbacher, E., Los, B., Stehrer, R., & De Vries, G. J., (2015). An illustrated user guide to the world input–output database: The case of global automotive production. *Review of International Economics, 23*(3), 575–605.
57. Tractinsky, N., Katz, A. S., & Ikar, D., (2000). What is beautiful is usable. *Interacting with Computers, 13*(2), 127–145.
58. Tsai, B. Y., Stobart, S., Parrington, N., & Thompson, B., (1997). Iterative design and testing within the software development life cycle. *Software Quality Journal, 6*, 295–310.
59. Voskobojnikov, A., Wiese, O., Mehrabi, K. M., Roth, V., & Beznosov, K., (2021). The U in crypto stands for usable: An empirical study of user experience with mobile cryptocurrency wallets. In: *Proceedings of the 2021 CHI Conference on Human Factors in Computing Systems* (Vol. 1, pp. 1–14).
60. Wan, Z., Xia, X., Lo, D., & Murphy, G. C., (2019). How does machine learning change software development practices? *IEEE Transactions on Software Engineering, 47*(9), 1857–1871.
61. Woods, D. D., (1985). Cognitive technologies: The design of joint human-machine cognitive systems. *AI Magazine, 6*(4), 86–87.

CHAPTER 6

USABILITY TESTING

UNIT INTRODUCTION

Usability testing is a term that is frequently and sometimes arbitrarily used to describe any method used to assess a system or product. Frequently, it is clear from the speaker's context that they are referring to one of the other strategies (Lindgaard & Chattratichart, 2007).

In this book, the phrase "usability testing" refers to a procedure that uses standardized questionnaires that are reflective of the intended market to assess how well a product satisfies specified usability requirements. By including actual users, procedures like expert evaluations, walkthroughs, and the like that don't involve actual users in the process are no longer classified as usability testing (Sonderegger et al., 2016).

Usability testing is a method of inquiry that has its origins in the traditional experimental approach. One can perform a wide variety of tests, from formal, classical experiments with enormous sample sizes and intricate test designs to very casual, qualitative investigations with just one subject (Wichansky, 2000). Each testing strategy has unique goals and needs various amounts of time and resources. To get results quickly in commercial product development environments, this book focuses on more casual, less sophisticated tests (Markopoulos & Bekker, 2003).

Learning Objectives

At the end of this lesson, students will be able to:

- Understand the importance of usability testing in the design and development process of a product or service.
- Learn about the different types of usability testing methods, including heuristic evaluation, cognitive walkthrough, and user testing.
- Understand how to plan and conduct a usability test, including defining test goals, selecting participants, and creating test scenarios.
- Learn how to collect and analyze usability testing data, including identifying common usability issues and prioritizing them for resolution.
- Understand how to use usability testing results to inform design decisions and improve the overall user experience of a product or service.

Key Terms

- Dynamic Characteristic
- Formative Study
- Goals of Testing
- Reliability
- Usability Testing

6.1. WHY TEST? GOALS OF TESTING

According to some businesses, usability testing is a component of a bigger initiative to increase product profitability. There are several advantages to doing this, which ultimately also benefit greatly consumers: design decisions are driven by data acquired from actual users to uncover design faults so they may be fixed, minimizing or eradicating user aggravation (Wharton et al., 1993).

6.1.1. Informing Design

Usability testing's main objective is to acquire data that can be used to identify and address usability issues in products and the supporting documentation before they are released. The goal is to guarantee the production of goods that:

i. Help people be productive and effective at what they want to do,
ii. Are valuable to and useful to the intended audience
iii. Are simple to learn (Bielaczyc, 2013).
iv. Are enjoyable to use (perhaps even pleasant).

6.1.2. Eliminating Design Problems and Frustration

The simplicity with which consumers may use the product is one aspect of income. By fixing design issues before the product is released, you can also achieve the following objectives for your target audience:

1. Provide the conditions for effective communication between your business and its clients.
2. Create the expectation that the goods your company sells are of a high caliber and are simple to use (Klein et al., 1999).
3. Provide evidence that the company values the objectives and concerns of its clients.
4. Make a product available that consumers find helpful, efficient, effective, and enjoyable (Latten, 1998).

TIPS

Usability testing refers to evaluating a product or service by testing it with representative users.

6.1.3. Improving Profitability

The aims or advantages of testing for your company are:

- **Creating a historical record of usability benchmarks for future releases:** A corporation can make sure that future goods meet or even exceed present usability criteria by keeping track of test results.
- **Minimizing the cost of service and support calls.** Little support requests and service calls from customers will result in a better useable product (Díez et al., 2012).
- **Increasing sales and the probability of repeat sales:** Customers that are satisfied with their purchases will recommend them to other consumers or users. Also, satisfied customers are more likely to continue with the product and future releases than they are to choose a rival brand (Rosenblatt & Lee, 1985).
- **Acquiring a competitive edge because usability has become a market separator for products:** Usability has emerged as one of the key strategies for setting one's product apart from that of a rival in the eyes of the client.
- One only needs to glance through the most recent advertisements to find products characterized in terms like "simple" and "easy," and others. Sadly, when put to the test, this knowledge rarely proves to be accurate (Riyadi, 2017).
- **Minimizing risk:** Indeed, usability testing has been done for years by all businesses and organizations. However, this kind of testing has been known as "product release," and the "testing" involves using the product in the market. Usability testing is done before release can significantly reduce the chance of delivering a product with substantial usability issues. This is a very hazardous technique (AL-Omar & AL-Mutairi, 2008).

6.2. BASICS OF THE METHODOLOGY

The fundamental approach for carrying out a usability test has its roots in the traditional way of carrying out a controlled experiment. By isolating and adjusting variables in a controlled environment, a specific hypothesis is first generated and then evaluated using this formal approach, which is frequently used to undertake fundamental research. The hypothesis is then extensively evaluated, frequently using the proper inferential statistical technique(s), and is either supported by the findings or disproved. These investigations call for the use of a real experimental design and demand that (LeSage & Pace, 2011):

- A hypothesis must be formulated. A hypothesis outlines what you anticipate will happen during testing. For instance, "Help built-in format A will increase experienced users' speed and failure rate more than help provided in format B." The hypothesis must contain as much detail as possible.

- Randomly chosen (using a very systematic method) participants must be assigned to experimental conditions. To choose a meaningful sample from the wider population, one must first comprehend the features that define the target population. It can be challenging to select randomly from a community of existing consumers (Chivanga & Monyai, 2021).
- Tight controls must be employed. Irrespective of whether statistical significance is the aim, experimental controls are essential to ensure the accuracy of the information. Before to and during the test, each individual should have a roughly identical experience. Controlling the degree of engagement with the test moderator is also necessary.
- Control groups must be employed. A control group must be used to verify the outcomes, and this group's management should only differ in concerning to the one variable under investigation.

The sample (of users) must be of sufficient size to measure statistically significant differences between groups. Adequate sample size must be employed to statistically compare differences across groups. A too-small sample size can produce inaccurate results (Mather & Tucker, 1974).

The aforementioned strategy provides the foundation for carrying out traditional experiments, and it is the preferred technique when performing basic research. For the following reasons, it is not the approach recommended in this book, nevertheless (Williams & Rast, 2020).

It is frequently impractical or improper to conduct usability testing using such a technique in the fast-paced, extremely stressful development environment that most readers will experience. The numerous organizational restrictions—both political and non-political—make it impossible. It is incorrect since the goal of usability testing is to make educated design decisions to enhance goods, not necessarily to develop and test certain hypotheses, which is research (Teixeira, 2008). These kinds of research involve extensive background knowledge in experimental methodology and statistics, thus it is best to leave them to a qualified usability or human factors professional. The outcomes of conducting this kind of in-depth study without the necessary knowledge and experience can frequently be quite deceptive and result in a worse scenario than if no inquiry had been done. Because one frequently has limited control over this issue, it is frequently very challenging to implement the idea of randomly allocating participants in the setting where testing occurs most frequently. This is particularly true when it comes to including current consumers as participants (Schwartz et al., 2001). The sample size is yet another justification for a less formal approach. One's sample size is contingent on knowledge of specific information about that community, which is frequently insufficient, in to generate generalizable results for a specified target population (and sometimes the precise reason for the test). Without this knowledge, testing 10 to 12 persons per condition may be necessary to be safe, and testing 40 or more participants may be necessary to establish statistically significant results. The classical technique is designed to acquire quantitative evidence of research hypotheses, such as whether one design is superior to another. This is the final and most crucial point. It is not intended to gather in-depth knowledge on how to solve issues and redesign goods. We anticipate that the majority of readers will be more focused on the latter than the former (Morykwas et al., 1997).

Although experimental rigor is at its foundation, the strategy we recommend is more informal and iterative. To undertake any study, experimental rigor is crucial, as the reader will learn in later chapters of this book. A series of fast, focused studies starting early in the development cycle can accomplish a lot. This book's goal is to teach readers how to conduct this kind of less formal but well-designed test that will pinpoint a product's specific usability flaws, its root cause, and how to fix them. The sections that follow provide an overview of this strategy's fundamentals.

6.3. BASIC ELEMENTS OF USABILITY TESTING

Instead of developing hypotheses, develop research aims and objectives or test goals. The use of an end-user representative sample, which may or may not be selected at random. Demonstration of the workplace as it actually is. Observation of consumers who either use or evaluate a product prototype. The test moderator carefully interrogated and questioning participants, often in depth. Collection of preferences and effectiveness metrics, both quantitative and qualitative. Improvement suggestions for the product's design. In the chapters that follow, we explain the "how-to" of this strategy (Ward & Hiller, 2005).

6.4. WHEN SHOULD YOU TEST?

Figure 6.1. Usability testing throughout the product lifecycle.

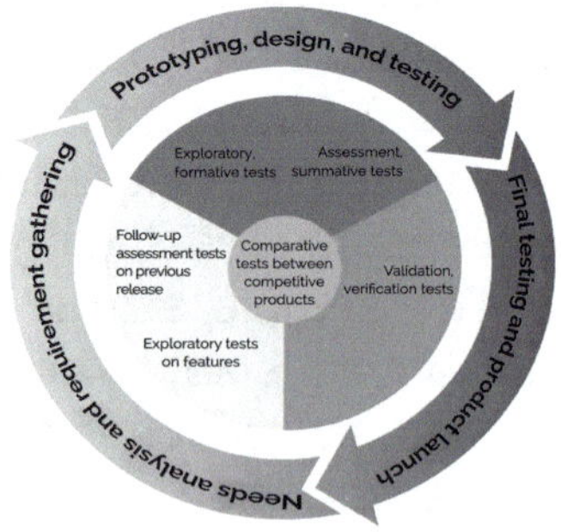

Source: Technology networks, creative commons license.

Every stage of the development lifecycle requires some form of usability testing. The research questions posed, the degree of product completion and the time allotted for implementing fixes to issues discovered during testing serve to differentiate the type of testing. This chapter describes four test kinds that correspond to the general stages of any product development cycle (Figure 6.1) (Kennel et al., 2010).

Remember

During a test, participants will try to complete typical tasks while observers watch, listen, and takes notes.

6.4.1. Our Types of Tests: An Overview

There are many distinct testing procedures in the textbooks, each with a bit distinct goal. Identical testing methods are frequently referred to by many names. This can be very perplexing. The best strategy for selecting which tests to describe and highlight might be to utilize the product lifecycle as a point of reference for outlining various test kinds. You should be able to comprehend the benefits and purpose of a test by connecting it to a certain stage in the lifecycle (Whetzel & McDaniel, 2009).

We provide a high-level overview of three tests: exploratory (also known as formative), assessment (sometimes known as summative), and validation (also known as verification). Each test is discussed with the approximate stage of the product development lifecycle at which it would be used. The comparison test, the fourth type of test, is not connected to any particular lifecycle phase but can be employed as a crucial component of any of the other three tests (Poljak et al., 2020).

Each exam uses a largely consistent core methodology. Each test will have a different emphasis on qualitative versus quantitative metrics as well as a different level of participant-test moderator interaction. However, the tests discussed here were selected with an emphasis on the bottom line and are unquestionably biased towards a setting with constrained resources and tight deadlines (Schöck et al., 2009).

The value of an incremental model is another reason we're providing the test types in the context of the product development lifecycle. Using usability testing as a part of an incremental method of product creation gives it the most impact and effectiveness. This means that the best chance of producing a useful product during the product development lifecycle is during a cycle of design, testing, and measurement, and redesign. Even if significant product faults or deficiencies are overlooked during one test, further testing cycles provide the chance to find these issues (McCann & Ames, 2005).

A project can be advanced steadily and quickly using an incremental design and testing technique, and the product can be "shaped" to match the abilities, aspirations, and capabilities of the final users. We firmly believe that this strategy adds value when resources are scarce and that the best outcomes can be attained by carrying out a succession of brief, focused tests that build on one another (Garousi et al., 2013).

The tests we're about to discuss do, though, lend themselves to an incremental design method, so one need not worry about using the tests at precisely the right time. Instead, think about what you need to know about your product, and let that guide your aims and the proper use of a given test method. Do not be discouraged if you are unable to run several tests, either. One exam is nearly always preferable to none, and it is preferable to concentrate on your strengths rather than your weaknesses (Collins, 2003).

Figure 6.1 displays the first three tests—experimental (or formative), assessment (or comprehensive), and validation (or verification)—alongside the rough lifecycle stages at which they are carried out most successfully. Let's now go over each in turn (Pancerz et al., 2015).

6.5. EXPLORATORY OR FORMATIVE STUDY

6.5.1. When

The exploring study is carried out quite shortly after launch when a product is still being specified and created in its early phases (thus the reason it is occasionally referred to as "formative"). The product's user profile and usage design (or problem identification) should have been established by this stage in the development cycle. The project team is likely struggling with the functional requirements and early product prototypes. Maybe the design stage is about to start once the demands and specifications phase has been finished (Lee, 2011).

6.5.2. Objective

The explorative study's primary goal is to assess the viability of early design proposals. The exploratory study is focused on the elevated feature of a user interface or content, which can be thought of as being differentiated into a more detailed component and another aspect (Qu & Furnas, 2008).

For instance, it would be extremely beneficial for Web application interface designers to know from the outset whether the user intuitively understands the interface's core components. Designers may wish to know, for instance, how effectively the interface:

i. Aids users' efforts towards a goal.

ii. Expresses the desired workflow (Cheng & Foley, 2018).

Enables the user to move between screens and within of screens. Technical writers may also want to investigate the following high-level challenges while creating a task-oriented user guide for a software product.

i. The overall structure of the subject topic;

ii. Using a verbal or visual approach;

iii. How well the recommended format facilitates discoverability;

iv. How to handle reference information; and

v. Expected places of assistance and communications.

These rising problems have repercussions that go beyond the product because you also want to confirm your user-prejudice assumptions. To define the other, you must first comprehend the first. The following are some common consumer questions that an exploratory study might try to address:

i. How do consumers perceive and consider using the product?

ii. Does the product's fundamental functionality offer the consumer any benefit?

iii. How successfully and readily can users navigate?

iv. How quickly can users conclude about how to use this user interface from their prior knowledge?

v. What kind of prerequisite knowledge is required to use the product?

vi. Which product features are "walk up and use" and which are more likely to need assistance or written instructions?

vii. How should the table of contents be set up to accommodate users of all skill levels?

It is impossible to overstate the significance of this kind of preliminary study and research because this is the moment when important design choices are made that affect everything that will come after. The product will almost certainly have usability issues later on if the project starts with incorrect assumptions and flawed premises about the user. Like constructing a home, once the basis for one sort of model is established, it is impossible to build a completely new model without first tearing down the foundation. All that comes after is determined by the underlying structure (Green, 2019).

6.5.3. Overview of the Methodology

For exploratory tests to determine the viability of early design concepts, there must typically be substantial communication between the consumer and test moderator. The creation of early iterations of the product's user interface and/

or its support materials for examination by users interacting is one method of providing answers to extremely fundamental problems, comparable to those stated previously. When it comes to software, this usually entails creating a mockup or prototype simulation of the product that depicts its rising operations, basic layout, and framework. One may use static screen images or even paper draughts of screens before creating a working prototype. Foam core, clay, or plastic models that are two- or three-dimensional can be used to illustrate hardware. One may offer very basic designs for manuals, teaching materials, or help screens as user support items (Robbins, 2003).

It's not necessary to depict every aspect of the product's functioning while creating a prototype. Instead, one simply needs to demonstrate enough functionality to meet the specific test purpose. For instance, you simply need to display the pull-down menus and the top layer of options if you want to examine how the user reacts to them. If the user continues past the first layer, you might display a screen that says, "not yet implemented," or something similar, and inquire as to what they were expecting to see next (LaViolette, 1985).

Figure 6.2. Test monitor and participant exploring the product.

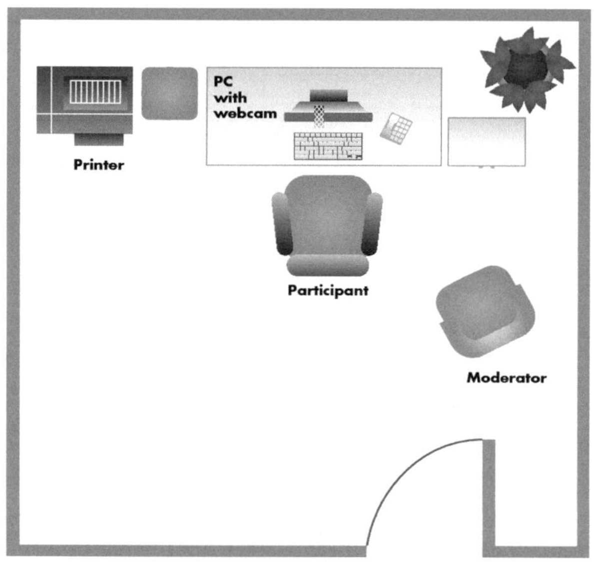

Source: Technology Networks, creative commons license.

A "horizontal representation" is the term used to describe this kind of prototype because the user can only go so far in terms of depth. But, you ought to prototype multiple functions "vertically" so users may move deeper if your test purpose is to assess how well a user can move down numerous menu layers. A horizontal display of all main aspects and a vertical display of two of the functions might help you accomplish both goals. The test of such a prototype would involve the user attempting to do typical chores. Alternatively, if it is too early to execute tasks, the consumer may simply "walk through" or examine the product while being guided by a test moderator as they respond to questions. The user may even be able to accomplish both in some circumstances. The approach relies on where the development cycle is in the process and how sophisticated the mockups are (Vulić et al., 2015).

An experimental test's testing procedure is typically highly casual and resembles a partnership between the test subject and test moderator, with lots of interactions between them. An examination of the user's thought process is essential because so much of the information you need to know is cognitive. Together, the test moderator and participant may examine the product, with the moderator either conducting a nearly continuous interview or urging the participant to "think aloud" as much as possible. The test moderator and participant can sit next to one another, unlike later tests when there is significantly less interaction, as seen in Figure 6.2.

Request suggestions from the audience on how to make unclear parts clearer. In contrast to later tests, when a greater emphasis is placed on quantifying how well the user can do, here you aim to understand why the user behaves as he or she does by gathering qualitative data.

The distinguishing characteristic of the explorative test is its focus on discussion and examination of elevated ideas and thought processes, which helps to shape the final design. This is true regardless of whether you utilize a working prototype, early manuals, and static screens or whether the user executes commands or simply "walks through" a product with the test moderator (Rouquerol et al., 2012).

6.5.4. Example of Exploratory Study

Let's go over how a normal investigation might develop for a product, like a website, as the exploring test's nature is frequently quite abstract. Imagine you are browsing a website's home page with options in the left navigation that, when the user hovers their mouse over them, display more options (Galbreath, 2005).

Suppose that the user interface is still in its very early stages of development and consists only of a single screen with no connections or underlying structure. Nevertheless, the navigation menus work, allowing the user to see the menu choices listed beneath each menu header, as depicted in Figure 6.3 (Holloway & McConigley, 2009).

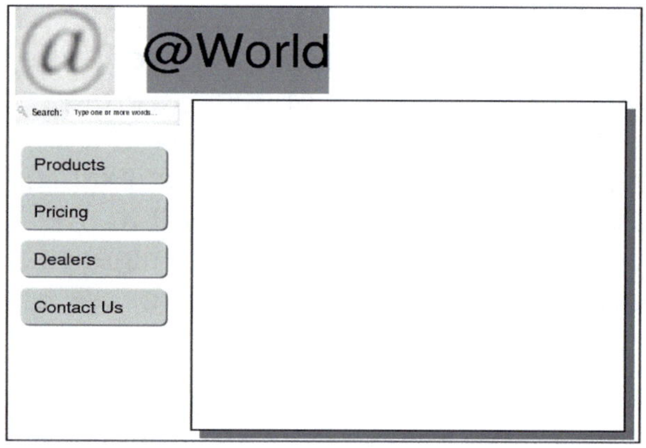

Figure 6.3. Web page navigation interface.

Source: Geeksforgeeks, creative commons license.

You may keep going in this direction by having the user attempt to complete practical tasks while extensively discussing their presumptions and mental processes (Doolen & Hacker, 2005).

Consequently, if the web page is so unfinished that the navigation does not function and you wanted to assess how well the navigation was organized, you could just ask the user to point to the navigation label that corresponds to the task they would expect to complete, similar to a paper-and-pencil evaluation. This strategy would identify the tasks that required more effort and were less intuitive (Hallingberg et al., 2018).

6.6. ASSESSMENT OR SUMMATIVE TEST

6.6.1. When

Perhaps the most prevalent kind of usability test that is undertaken is the assessments test. It is likely the easiest and most uncomplicated test to create and carry out for a beginner usability specialist. Early or midway through the product development cycle, generally, after the foundational or high-level design or organization of the product has been determined, assessment tests are undertaken (Lam, 2013).

6.6.2. Objective

By assessing the usability of more basic functions and features of the product, the assessment test seeks to build on the results of the exploratory test. The assessment test starts by focusing on the meat and the flesh if the exploratory test's goal is to work on the product's framework (Fancsali et al., 2018). This test looks at how well the idea has been executed, assuming that the product's fundamental conceptual model is sound. Instead of just investigating a product's intuitiveness, you want to know how well a user can carry out complete, realistic tasks as well as pinpoint any product usability issues (Setiyana, 2016).

6.6.3. Overview of the Methodology

The approach for an assessment test is a cross between the unstructured investigations of the exploratory test and the more closely regulated measurement of the validation test, and it is frequently referred to as an information-gathering or proof test. In contrast to the exploratory test (Karna & Sahai, 2012):

1. Rather than just browsing and leaving comments on the screens, sites, and other elements, the user will always be engaged in tasks (LaViolette, 1985).
2. Because real activities are more important than thinking processes in the test, the test moderator will interact with the participant less.
3. Data on quantitative metrics will be gathered (Al Kilani & Kobziev, 2016).

6.7. VALIDATION OR VERIFICATION TEST

6.7.1. When

The thoroughly evaluate, also known as the verification test, is typically carried out late in the development cycle and, as the name implies, is intended to assess a product's usability in comparison to industry standards or, in the case of a verification test, to ensure that earlier issues have been fixed and no new ones have been added. The validation test often takes place much closer to the product's delivery than the preceding two tests, which occur during a very active and ongoing design cycle (Mattocks et al., 2010).

6.7.2. Objective

The goal of the validating test is to assess how the product stacks up against a preset benchmark or usability standard, such as a project-related quality standard, an internal corporate standard from the past, or even a performance standard set by a rival company (Monteiro et al., 2009). Before it is released, it will be determined whether or not the product complies with this standard, and if not, what the reason(s) are. The usability targets defined early in the project are typically where the standards come from. They in turn derive from prior usability testing, marketing research, user interviews, or just the development team's best predictions (Wallace & Fujii, 1989).

Usability goals are frequently expressed in terms of quality standards, such as effectiveness and efficiency, which measure how successfully and quickly the user can carry out specific activities and tasks. Alternatively, the goals could be expressed in terms of user preferences, such as obtaining a specific ranking or rating. The flavor of a verification test is slightly different. Here, it's important to make sure that any usability problems that were discovered during earlier tests have been properly addressed and fixed (Balci, 1994).

The validation test itself should then be used to establish company standards for upcoming goods, which makes perfect sense. The same can be done with verification. For instance, future iteration of the product must perform at least as well as the setup procedures for a software package, which should be able to be completed in five minutes with no more than one mistake. Then, products can be created with this standard as a goal, ensuring that usability is maintained as new features are added in subsequent iterations (Balci, 1995). Evaluation of the end-to-end performance of all a product's elements is one of the main goals of the validation test, often for the first time. For instance, all the stages in a procedure or workflow, or the integration of documentation, help, and software/hardware. It is impossible to exaggerate the value of an integrated testing stage. It is not rare for components to not function effectively together because they are frequently built in a manner that is comparatively secluded from one another. An organization would be wise to learn this before releasing anything because, from the user's perspective, it is all one product and is expected to function that way (Nayani & Mollaghasemi, 1998).

Another goal of the testing stage fact, any test carried out very late in the development cycle—has come to be characterized as "disaster or catastrophic insurance" in the business. The possibility of releasing a new product with significant defects or one that would need to be recalled worries the administration the most at this later phase (Grace & Taghipour, 2004). Slipping the timetable may be preferable to recalling the goods or having to mail "fixes" to every user if such a fault is found. If you can foresee a significant flaw in the product, you constantly have an advantage, even if there is no time to fix it before launch. The support personnel can be trained, a solution can be created, and even public relations replies can be created. Despite all these benefits, some businesses would still prefer to remain unaware of product flaws (Sargent, 2010).

6.7.3. Overview of the Methodology

With three key exceptions, the validating test is carried out similarly to the assessment test.

Benchmarks or standards for the test's tasks are either created or discovered before the actual test begins (Bekö et al., 2020). This can be as straightforward as fixing the issues found in earlier experimental tests, or it can involve precise error or time measures. The test moderator interacts with the participants either very little or not at all while they are doing tasks. (And it's unlikely that kids are asked to "think aloud") (Ramos et al., 2013).

ACTIVITY 6.1:

What is usability testing? Give a detailed demonstration.

The main objective is the gathering of statistical data, but the causes of poor performance are also noted. If you are comparing user performance to a standard, you should plan and decide how the standard will be adhered to and what will happen if the product does not reach the standard. For instance, if the requirement for a task is "time to finish," would you contrast the standard to the average score of all participants, or will you require that 70% of participants achieve the requirement? What circumstances will cause the product's timetable to be changed? Would there be enough time for the tasks that failed to satisfy the standard to be retested? All of these issues need to be addressed and settled before the test (Seifrtova et al., 2009).

Since you're making significant quantitative judgments about the product, a testing process places a greater emphasis on experimental rigor and consistency than an assessment test would. Ensure that the design team members contributed to and were on board with the creation of the test standards. They won't feel as though the standards are excessively high or unreachable in this way (Landers et al., 2017).

SUMMARY

Usability testing is a technique used to evaluate a product or service by testing it with representative users. The chapter on usability testing discusses the importance of usability testing in the product development process and how it can be used to identify usability issues and improve user satisfaction. The chapter outlines the steps involved in conducting a usability test, including setting goals, defining tasks, recruiting participants, conducting the test, and analyzing the results. The chapter also guides on choosing the appropriate testing method, such as remote testing or in-person testing, and the importance of considering accessibility and inclusivity in the testing process. The chapter emphasizes the importance of iterating and improving the product based on the feedback obtained from usability testing. Finally, the chapter provides tips on communicating usability testing results to stakeholders and incorporating the findings into the product development process.

REVIEW QUESTIONS

1. What is usability testing, and why is it important in the design process?
2. What are the different types of usability testing methods available, and how do they differ?
3. How do you select participants for usability testing, and what criteria should you use?
4. What common usability issues can arise during testing, and how can they be addressed?
5. How do you analyze and interpret usability testing data, and what are some common metrics used?
6. What are some best practices for conducting effective and efficient usability testing sessions?

MULTIPLE CHOICE QUESTIONS

1. What is the purpose of usability testing?

a. To evaluate the user interface of a product or website
b. To test the performance of the product or website
c. To measure the effectiveness of advertising campaigns
d. To analyze user behavior on social media

2. What is the primary benefit of conducting usability testing?

a. To identify user needs and preferences
b. To increase sales revenue
c. To improve search engine rankings
d. To reduce production costs

3. Which of the following is a key aspect of preparing for a usability test?

a. Determining the target audience

b. Developing the product or website

c. Conducting market research

d. Creating a marketing campaign

4. Which type of usability testing involves observing users as they interact with a product or website in a natural setting?

a. Remote testing

b. Guerrilla testing

c. In-person testing

d. Expert review

5. What is the goal of analyzing the results of a usability test?

a. To identify design flaws and areas for improvement

b. To compare the product or website to competitors

c. To increase brand awareness

d. To generate new leads

Answers to Multiple Choice Questions

1. (a); 2. (a); 3. (a); 4. (b); 5. (a)

REFERENCES

1. Al Kilani, M., & Kobziev, V., (2016). An overview of research methodology in information system (IS). *Open Access Library Journal, 3*(11), 1–9.
2. AL-Omar, H., & AL-Mutairi, A., (2008). Bank-specific determinants of profitability: The case of Kuwait. *Journal of Economic and Administrative Sciences, 24*(2), 20–34.
3. Balci, O., (1994). Validation, verification, and testing techniques throughout the life cycle of a simulation study. In: *Proceedings of Winter Simulation Conference* (pp. 215–220).
4. Balci, O., (1995). Principles and techniques of simulation validation, verification, and testing. In: *Proceedings of the 27th Conference on Winter Simulation* (pp. 147–154).
5. Bekö, G., Wargocki, P., Wang, N., Li, M., Weschler, C. J., Morrison, G., & Williams, J., (2020). The indoor chemical human emissions and reactivity (ICHEAR) project: Overview of experimental methodology and preliminary results. *Indoor Air, 30*(6), 1213–1228.
6. Bielaczyc, K., (2013). Informing design research: Learning from teachers' designs of social infrastructure. *Journal of the Learning Sciences, 22*(2), 258–311.

7. Cheng, M., & Foley, C., (2018). Understanding the distinctiveness of Chinese post-80s tourists through an exploration of their formative experiences. *Current Issues in Tourism, 21*(11), 1312–1328.
8. Chivanga, S. Y., & Monyai, P. B., (2021). Back to basics: Qualitative research methodology for beginners. *Journal of Critical Reviews, 8*(2), 11–17.
9. Collins, D., (2003). Pretesting survey instruments: An overview of cognitive methods. *Quality of Life Research, 12*, 229–238.
10. Díez-Mediavilla, M., Alonso-Tristán, C., Rodríguez-Amigo, M. D. C., García-Calderón, T., & Dieste-Velasco, M. I., (2012). Performance analysis of PV plants: Optimization for improving profitability. *Energy Conversion and Management, 54*(1), 17–23.
11. Doolen, T. L., & Hacker, M. E., (2005). A review of lean assessment in organizations: An exploratory study of lean practices by electronics manufacturers. *Journal of Manufacturing Systems, 24*(1), 55–67.
12. Fancsali, S. E., Zheng, G., Tan, Y., Ritter, S., Berman, S. R., & Galyardt, A., (2018). Using embedded formative assessment to predict state summative test scores. In: *Proceedings of the 8th International Conference on Learning Analytics and Knowledge* (pp. 161–170).
13. Galbreath, J., (2005). Which resources matter the most to firm success? An exploratory study of resource-based theory. *Technovation, 25*(9), 979–987.
14. Garousi, V., Mesbah, A., Betin-Can, A., & Mirshokraie, S., (2013). A systematic mapping study of web application testing. *Information and Software Technology, 55*(8), 1374–1396.
15. Grace, J. R., & Taghipour, F., (2004). Verification and validation of CFD models and dynamic similarity for fluidized beds. *Powder Technology, 139*(2), 99–110.
16. Green, F., (2019). An exploration into the value of formative assessment and the barriers associated with the implementation of formative strategies. In: K. W. M., K. B. A., D. W., & L., (eds.), *Rethinking Teacher Education for the 21st Century: Trends, Challenges and New Directions* (pp. 203–222).
17. Hallingberg, B., Turley, R., Segrott, J., Wight, D., Craig, P., Moore, L., & Moore, G., (2018). Exploratory studies to decide whether and how to proceed with full-scale evaluations of public health interventions: A systematic review of guidance. *Pilot and Feasibility Studies, 4*, 1–12.
18. Holloway, K., & McConigley, R., (2009). Descriptive, exploratory study of the role of nursing assistants in Australian residential aged care facilities: The example of pain management. *Australasian Journal on Ageing, 28*(2), 70–74.
19. Karna, S. K., & Sahai, R., (2012). An overview on Taguchi method. *International Journal of Engineering and Mathematical Sciences, 1*(1), 1–7.
20. Kennel, K. A., Drake, M. T., & Hurley, D. L., (2010). Vitamin D deficiency in adults: When to test and how to treat. In: *Mayo Clinic Proceedings* (Vol. 85, No. 8, pp. 752–758).

21. Klein, J., Moon, Y., & Picard, R. W., (1999). This computer responds to user frustration. In: *CHI'99 Extended Abstracts on Human Factors in Computing Systems* (pp. 242, 243).
22. Lam, R., (2013). Formative use of summative tests: Using test preparation to promote performance and self-regulation. *The Asia-Pacific Education Researcher, 22*, 69–78.
23. Landers, T., Davis, J., Crist, K., & Malik, C., (2017). APIC MegaSurvey: Methodology and overview. *American Journal of Infection Control, 45*(6), 584–588.
24. Latten, J. E., (1998). A scheduling-conflict resolution model: Are you frustrated by scheduling conflicts that take your students away from your performance ensembles? Read on for ways to possibly eliminate these problems. *Music Educators Journal, 84*(6), 22–26.
25. LaViolette, P. A., (1985). An introduction to subquantum kinetics: I. An overview of the methodology. *International Journal of General System, 11*(4), 281–293.
26. Lee, I., (2011). Formative assessment in EFL writing: An exploratory case study. *Changing English, 18*(1), 99–111.
27. LeSage, J. P., & Pace, R. K., (2011). Pitfalls in higher order model extensions of basic spatial regression methodology. *Review of Regional Studies, 41*(1), 13–26.
28. Lindgaard, G., & Chattratichart, J., (2007). Usability testing: What have we overlooked? In: *Proceedings of the SIGCHI Conference on Human Factors in Computing Systems* (pp. 1415–1424).
29. Markopoulos, P., & Bekker, M., (2003). On the assessment of usability testing methods for children. *Interacting with Computers, 15*(2), 227–243.
30. Mather, L. E., & Tucker, G. T., (1974). Meperidine and other basic drugs: General method for their determination in plasma. *Journal of Pharmaceutical Sciences, 63*(2), 306–307.
31. Mattocks, C. J., Morris, M. A., Matthijs, G., Swinnen, E., Corveleyn, A., Dequeker, E., & Wallace, A., (2010). A standardized framework for the validation and verification of clinical molecular genetic tests. *European Journal of Human Genetics, 18*(12), 1276–1288.
32. McCann, J. C., & Ames, B. N., (2005). Is docosahexaenoic acid, an n− 3 long-chain polyunsaturated fatty acid, required for development of normal brain function? An overview of evidence from cognitive and behavioral tests in humans and animals. *The American Journal of Clinical Nutrition, 82*(2), 281–295.
33. Monteiro, P., Machado, R. J., & Kazman, R., (2009). Inception of software validation and verification practices within CMMI Level 2. In: *2009 Fourth International Conference on Software Engineering Advances* (pp. 536–541).
34. Morykwas, M. J., Argenta, L. C., Shelton-Brown, E. I., & McGuirt, W., (1997). Vacuum-assisted closure: A new method for wound control and treatment: Animal studies and basic foundation. *Annals of Plastic Surgery, 38*(6), 553–562.
35. Nayani, N., & Mollaghasemi, M., (1998). Validation and verification of the simulation

model of a photolithography process in semiconductor manufacturing. In: *1998 Winter Simulation Conference, Proceedings (Cat. No. 98CH36274)* (Vol. 2, pp. 1017–1022).

36. Pancerz, K., Mich, O., Burda, A., & Gomuła, J., (2015). A tool for computer-aided diagnosis of psychological disorders based on the MMPI test: An overview. *Applications of Computational Intelligence in Biomedical Technology,* 201–213.
37. Poljak, M., Valenčak, A. O., Domjanič, G. G., Xu, L., & Arbyn, M., (2020). Commercially available molecular tests for human papillomaviruses: A global overview. *Clinical Microbiology and Infection, 26*(9), 1144–1150.
38. Qu, Y., & Furnas, G. W., (2008). Model-driven formative evaluation of exploratory search: A study under a sensemaking framework. *Information Processing & Management, 44*(2), 534–555.
39. Ramos, B., Miller, F. A., Brandão, T. R. S., Teixeira, P., & Silva, C. L. M., (2013). Fresh fruits and vegetables—An overview on applied methodologies to improve its quality and safety. *Innovative Food Science & Emerging Technologies, 20,* 1–15.
40. Riyadi, S., (2017). Financial performance efficiency of Indonesia government banks in improving profitability. *International Journal of Financial Innovation in Banking, 1*(3, 4), 239–252.
41. Robbins, R. J., (2003). Phenolic acids in foods: An overview of analytical methodology. *Journal of Agricultural and Food Chemistry, 51*(10), 2866–2887.
42. Rosenblatt, M. J., & Lee, H. L., (1985). Improving profitability with quantity discounts under fixed demand. *IIE Transactions, 17*(4), 388–395.
43. Rouquerol, J., Baron, G. V., Denoyel, R., Giesche, H., Groen, J., Klobes, P., & Unger, K., (2012). The characterization of macroporous solids: An overview of the methodology. *Microporous and Mesoporous Materials, 154,* 2–6.
44. Sargent, R. G., (2010). Verification and validation of simulation models. In: *Proceedings of the 2010 Winter Simulation Conference* (pp. 166–183).
45. Schöck, M., Els, S., Riddle, R., Skidmore, W., Travouillon, T., Blum, R., & Wang, L., (2009). Thirty meter telescope site testing I: Overview. *Publications of the Astronomical Society of the Pacific, 121*(878), 384.
46. Schwartz, S. H., Melech, G., Lehmann, A., Burgess, S., Harris, M., & Owens, V., (2001). Extending the cross-cultural validity of the theory of basic human values with a different method of measurement. *Journal of Cross-Cultural Psychology, 32*(5), 519–542.
47. Seifrtova, M., Novakova, L., Lino, C., Pena, A., & Solich, P., (2009). An overview of analytical methodologies for the determination of antibiotics in environmental waters. *Analytica Chimica Acta, 649*(2), 158–179.
48. Setiyana, R., (2016). Analysis of summative tests for English. *English Education Journal, 7*(4), 433–447.
49. Sonderegger, A., Schmutz, S., & Sauer, J., (2016). The influence of age in usability testing. *Applied Ergonomics, 52,* 291–300.

50. Teixeira, A., (2008). Basic composition: Rapid methodologies. *Handbook of Muscle Foods Analysis,* 291–314.
51. Vulić, I., De Smet, W., Tang, J., & Moens, M. F., (2015). Probabilistic topic modeling in multilingual settings: An overview of its methodology and applications. *Information Processing & Management, 51*(1), 111–147.
52. Wahl, N. J., (2000). Student-run usability testing. In: *Thirteenth Conference on Software Engineering Education and Training* (pp. 123–131).
53. Wallace, D. R., & Fujii, R. U., (1989). Software verification and validation: An overview. *IEEE Software, 6*(3), 10–17.
54. Ward, J. L., & Hiller, S., (2005). Usability testing, interface design, and portals. *Journal of Library Administration, 43*(1, 2), 155–171.
55. Wharton, C. M., Cheng, P. W., & Wickens, T. D., (1993). Hypothesis-testing strategies: Why two goals are better than one. *The Quarterly Journal of Experimental Psychology, 46*(4), 743–758.
56. Whetzel, D. L., & McDaniel, M. A., (2009). Situational judgment tests: An overview of current research. *Human Resource Management Review, 19*(3), 188–202.
57. Wichansky, A. M., (2000). Usability testing in 2000 and beyond. *Ergonomics, 43*(7), 998–1006.
58. Williams, D. R., & Rast, P., (2020). Back to the basics: Rethinking partial correlation network methodology. *British Journal of Mathematical and Statistical Psychology, 73*(2), 187–212.

CHAPTER 7

THE PROCESS OF CONDUCTING A TESTING

UNIT INTRODUCTION

The design for the test serves as the basis for the entire examination. It covers your usability tests who, when, how, where, and why, and what you are testing. It is possible to fall into the habit of skipping the step of laying out a comprehensive test strategy when working under the often unyielding time constraint imposed by project deadlines. It's possible that you already have a pretty solid concept of what it is you want to put to the test in your head, and because of this, you opt against writing it down. You should not take such a casual approach; it is a mistake that will inevitably come back to haunt you (Pawliuk et al., 2021).

Learning Objectives

At the end of this chapter, readers will be able to:

- Understanding the importance of testing in the software development process and how it contributes to software quality.
- Learning the different types of testing, such as functional, performance, security, etc., and their purposes.
- Understanding the testing life cycle and the different stages involved in the testing process, such as test planning, test design, test execution, and test reporting.

- Learning how to define test objectives, test cases, and test scenarios that align with the software requirements.
- Understanding the importance of test automation and how to automate testing processes using tools and frameworks.
- Learning how to track defects and issues during testing and report them effectively.

Key Terms

- Focal Print
- Major Vehicle
- Test blueprint
- Test Plan
- Test Plan Parts

7.1. WHY CREATE A TEST PLAN?

When you realize that testing will be required, start drafting the test plan. With time when the project progresses, keep improving it, get input and buy-in, etc. There is a limit to flexibility, so you must establish a fair deadline before the test, after which the test plan cannot be altered. This date should also mark when the product cannot be altered until after the test. The test plan may be a sole concrete milestone at that stage in the development cycle, and it serves a vital purpose (Bosse & Gerosa, 2017).

If the deadline has passed, take all the necessary steps to freeze the product design you will evaluate. Further alterations may render the test design, questions, and data collection method invalid. If you are pressured to alter the test after the deadline, ensure that everyone knows the associated dangers. If changes are made so soon after the test date, the test may be nullified and the product may also not work properly (Pissoort & Armstrong, 2016).

Following are some major reasons why it is crucial to establish a complete test plan, & some suggestion for using it as a communication tool within the development team (Mohacsi & Ramler, 2019).

TIPS

Fundamental Test Process

1. Test Planning and Control.
2. Test Analysis and Design.
3. Test Implementation and Execution.
4. Evaluating Exit Criteria and Reporting.
5. Test Closure

7.1.1. It Serves as a Test Blueprint

In a same way that a house's design specifies exactly what will be constructed, the test plan specifies precisely how your product will be tested. In the same way, you wouldn't want your home builder to "wing it," The test plan sets stage for subsequent events. You do not want unresolved issues just before testing your first participant (Pearlman, 2011).

7.1.2. It Serves as Major Vehicle for Communication

The test plan is mainly a primary communication between principal developers & designers, test moderator, and remainder of team. The test plan is a document that each member of the development team who will be participating in the test, as well as management (if it is involved and enthusiastic), should evaluate in order to comprehend how the test will proceed and to determine whether their specific requirements will be met (Al - Bayari & Sadoun, 2005).

You utilize it to obtain buy-in & input from other members so that everyone agrees with what'll happen. Because projects are continually evolving from week to week & day to day, you don't want a candidate to claim after exam that their specific objectives were not addressed (Nettleton et al., 2006):

Everyone directly affected by test results should evaluate plan, especially when your organization initially begins testing. This is both economically and politically sensible (Lin et al., 2018).

7.1.3. It Implies or Defines the Required Resources

The test plan outlines or indicates the internal and external resources required. Once you have outlined precisely what will occur and when predicting what you will need to do on the test is much simpler. The test plan should explicitly or implicitly explain the resources required to complete the test successfully (Lim, 2006).

7.1.4. It Provides Focal Point for Milestone and Test

Without test plan, details become unclear & ambiguous, especially when efficiency is important. The test plan compels a systematic approach to testing and reminds the development team of approaching deadlines. In light of the preceding, it is absolutely appropriate and quite possible that the test plan will be established in stages as you gain a deeper understanding of test objectives & communicate with the individuals who'll be engaged. Projects are dynamic; even best-laid plans will change once testing begins. By establishing the test strategy in phases, modifications can be accommodated (Lim & Gregory, 2006). As your time and budget limits become evident, your test may become less ambitious but more straightforward. Perhaps, you may be unable to recruit as many qualified participants as you anticipated. Maybe not all modules or sections of paper will be completed by the deadline. Perhaps your test goals are too vague and require simplification and concentration. All of these real-world instances necessitate revisions to the test and test strategy (Liu, 2007).

7.2. THE TEST PLAN PARTS

Depending on sort of test and the level of formality your company expects, test plan templates will vary. Still, following are the common sections to include, along with a brief explanation. This chapter concludes with sample test plan.

1. Test's goals, purpose & objectives
2. Characteristics of participants
3. Research questions (Nelson, 2005).

4. Method (test design)
5. List of tasks
6. Test equipment, logistics & environment
7. Role of test moderator
8. Data collection & evaluation measures
9. Report presentation & content (Harter, 1976).

These components are explored in length in following sections, excluding the role of the test moderator, which receives its chapter, Chapter 4, because it needs special consideration (Tseng et al., 2009).

7.2.1. Review Goal & Purpose of Test

i. In this section of document, you must provide an overview of reasons for doing this test at this time. You do not need to specify precise objectives or challenges to be investigated in this section; rather, the primary focus or drive, often from your organization's perspective, should be highlighted. For instance: Attempts the test to handle issues reported by the support desk or call center of company (Dyck 1987).
ii. Have server web usage statistics or logs revealed that your company's website visitors abandon a transaction at a particular stage?
iii. Has a new policy recently been implemented mandating the testing of all products before their release? Does management believe it is crucial for the development team to observe actual users at this time (Krasny et al., 2014).

It is acceptable for the test purpose to remain vague, because the objectives will be reduced to quantitative assertions by the research questions and problem statements. It is important that testing is aligned with the organization's business objectives and is the best effective technique for resolving the issue or opportunity (Lochbaum et al., 2016).

7.2.1.1. When Not to Test

The following are ambiguous and incorrect motives for conducting usability testing on a product. They are rarely written down and are often transmitted verbally. These are not valid testing justifications, and they invariably undermine the effort (Desurvire et al., 1992).

i. You can enhance user convenience (You might be able to test a portion of the customer experience, but not all of the client touchpoints your business has).
ii. Everyone else has program for usability testing (Rochon et al., 2012).

iii. The third week of each month is when the testing meeting rooms are open (so is the cafeteria every evening).

iv. Lou attended most recent ACM SIGCHI conference (Association for Computing Machinery Special Interest Group on Computer-Human Interaction), where he discovered this extremely cool testing method (let Lou first highlight the method's advantages to company).

v. You want to determine whether the market needs this product (backward logic; a focus group or survey is a more appropriate technique early on) (Huberty, 2009).

If you are eager to start usability testing, you might think, I don't care why we test as long as we test. The repercussions can be dealt with later. And none of those mentioned above factors causes problems in the medium run. But,

if you want to test to be a fundamental component of how your company creates products in the long run, you must link testing to product's demands and the organization's overarching business needs. If not, you risk your testing becoming another passing trend or one of the newest techniques that change with the seasons (Mill et al., 1992).

7.2.1.2. Good Reasons to Test

The following list provides some more rational justifications for testing, which should provide positive results and open the door for more testing in the future. You want to see if the two main groups of users equally use the product (Maynard & Marlaire 1999).

If there are known issues with the interface, you want to know if the documentation can make up for them. Many complaints about using the product have been made to you. You are most interested in learning about the precise nature of the issue and your plan for resolving it within this year's development budget (Martin et al., 2007).

7.3. COMMUNICATE RESEARCH QUESTIONS

This component of the test plan is the most crucial since it outlines the problems and questions that must be solved and directs the remaining planning, designing, and testing tasks, as well as the research.

The study questions must be specific, accurate, transparent, and measurably (or observably) feasible. It would help if you still articulated precisely what you expect to discover when conducting exploratory testing in the early stages of designing a product, which is often less regimented (Figure 7.1) (Kubey et al., 1996).

PRODUCT	RESEARCH QUESTIONS
Web sites	How easily do users understand what is clickable?
	How easily and successfully do users find the products or information they are looking for?
	How easily and successfully do users register for the site?
	Where in the site do users go to find Search? Why?
	How easily can users return to the home page?
Small interfaces	How easily do users switch between modes on multi-purpose buttons?
	How well do users understand the symbols and icons?
	Which ones are problematic? Why?
	How easily do users download updates and features?
	How quickly can users perform common tasks?
Hardware	How easily and successfully can users use all buttons on the control panel?
	Can users use the control panel without assistance or training?
	How easily can users find the correct input and output ports?
	How easily can users change settings in the menus?
Online and written documentation	Do users go to online help when they encounter error messages?
	How easily do users find topics they are looking for in the online help? How well do the topic titles reflect what users are looking for?
	How well do they understand the content of the topics they find?
	How helpful is the topic content?
	Which parts of each topic do users pay attention to?
	Can users easily switch between reading the online help and interacting with the interface to complete the task?
Software	How closely does the flow of the software reflect how the user thinks of the work flow?
	How easily and successfully do users find the tools or options they want?
	Do users use the toolbar icons or the standard menus? Why?
	Is the response time a cause of user frustration or errors?
General	What obstacles prevent users from completing installation and set up?
	Can users perform common tasks within established benchmarks?
	What are the major usability flaws that prevent users from completing the most common tasks?
	How does ease-of-use compare in the planned release to the last release?
	How does ease-of-use compare between our product and the competition?
	Is there an appropriate balance of ease of use and ease of learning?

Figure 7.1. An example of research questions from a usability test of a hotel reservations website.

Source: Geeksforgeeks, creative commons license.

You can find yourself in the unfortunate situation of doing a great test but failing to address the main worry of developers on the project team if you don't have a clear, concise research question(s). Instead, you can end up with a test whose creation is hampered by disagreement on what should be tested. Knowing from experience that the test objectives were never written down caused test preparation to go in circles and controversy surrounding the test itself (Smeltzer, 1993).

Following are 2 examples vague & unfocused vague research questions.

EXAMPLE 1. Is the current product usable?

EXAMPLE 2. Is product ready for release, or does it require more work?

Such questions are challenging, not because they don't make sense. Instead, they're ambiguous and insufficient. They neither specify nor indicate how to quantify or measure the outcomes. These claims guarantee a favorable bias in the findings of any test. Why? How do you identify a solution if the parties involved cannot agree on the difficulties or issues that must be resolved? Of course, one won't naturally look for issues in those conditions (Rude, 2009).

An example of numerous more adequately targeted research questions for various product kinds is shown in the table below. Discussions with individual developers or developer's team, marketing staff, technical writers, & so forth should be the starting point for the research question(s). Be prepared if they have trouble articulating the test's objectives and can only explain the broadest questions or goals. This could mean one of the following (Sprague, 1993):

i. They are not yet prepared to take the test.

ii. They require more education and understanding of the purposes, nature, and manner of testing.

iii. They require assistance in turning their goals into quantifiable research questions. Do not be reluctant to pitch in and assist (Carpio et al., 2008).

You might go back to research questions to determine if they are clear or require more clarity if you are having extraordinary trouble creating the test and relevant measures, choosing the right end users, or even designing the data collection form (Smeltzer, 1993).

7.4. SUMMARIZE PARTICIPANT CHARACTERISTICS

In this part of the test plan, you'll detail the characteristics of the target audience for the product/document you'll be evaluating. Determine the features of the intended audience through collaborative efforts with other members of your organization for specific instructions on creating a user profile and recruiting test subjects. Figure 7.2 depicts a sample participant profile for a hotel booking website usability test (Aromataris et al., 2015).

Figure 7.2. Sample participant characteristics and desired mix.

Characteristic	Desired number of participants
Participant type	
pilot	1
regular	12
backup	2
Total number of participants	**14**
Travel frequency	
infrequently: 1-5 trips per year	4
moderately often: 6-12 trips per year	4
very often: 13 or more trips per year	4
Types of travel	
mostly business	6
mostly leisure	6
Booking experience	
book their own trips and accommodations	all
book online most of the time	6
book on the phone or other method	6
Age	
21-30	2-3
31-40	4-5
41-50	4-5
51-60	2-3
Gender	
female	6
male	6

Source: Geeksforgeeks, creative commons license.

Be sure to use the appropriate sample size when describing participant characteristics. The rule of thumb that "you cannot have too many participants" should be considered when deciding how many people to use in a test. It's important to have a large enough sample size to detect statistically significant differences between groups reliably, and a small sample size makes that difficult. Use at least 10–12 subjects per condition for a legitimate experiment. However, studies show that four to five participants who represent one audience cell will expose about 80% of the usability deficiencies of a product for that audience and that this 80% will represent most of the major problems when conducting a less formal usability test. There's no harm in studying more than a handful of people if you have the time and resources. 20% more flaws you find might be significant for your product (Boisvert et al., 2010).

For the most part, our numerous experiments corroborated the hypothesis mentioned above. Jeff identified roughly 80% of the issues in one case with just the first four out of eight subjects. Yet the final participant, number 8, made a colossal mistake on one task that would have necessitated a product service call. With only four people tested, we would have never found this. Hiring more people to test with reduces the risk of missing a crucial issue before you gain experience while also giving you more chances to hone your moderating skills (Ganz et al., 2012).

A "discount" usability testing practice, in which multiple, small, iterative usability tests are conducted over time, may be useful if you have little time and budget. First, run an experiment with four or five participants from a single cell and a single or double set of conditions, then incorporate the results into the interface and run another experiment with the same set of participants and conditions. A large sample size after three or four tests is possible because the development team can make adjustments between each testing round (Rogevich & Perin, 2008).

7.4.1. Description of the Method

In this test plan section, you will explain in great detail how you intend to conduct the research with the participants and how the testing session will progress. It is a brief description of the testing procedure you intend to use. It needs to summarize the entire testing process, beginning with the participants' arrival and ending when they leave. It is so that an observer can know what to expect. If you're wondering why the test plan needs such specifics, the following explanations should help. Others can see the big picture and offer input based on what they anticipate unfolding (Chicheł et al., 2007).

Having a clear idea of what needs to be done and what materials need to be developed before participants arrive allows you, as the test developer, to concentrate on those tasks. The need to inform other resources, such as a receptionist who will greet the participants as they enter a company's lobby, of your plans is highlighted. It ensures that multiple test moderators can consistently administer the test if that is a requirement of the test design (Sandelowski, 2000).

One of the more advanced abilities required of a usability professional is test design, which frequently necessitates familiarity with experimental design and methods as well as fundamental statistical analysis.

When designing a test, it's important to first zero in on and thoroughly comprehend its goals and objectives before settling on a test layout that will most efficiently unearth the desired information. Results can be questioned if they were obtained using a flawed test design or lacking experimental rigor. It hinders the development of usability engineering within the company and can lead to incorrect recommendations.

That's why it's important to consult an expert the first few times you run a usability test to get their input on how to structure the evaluation best (Brown et al., 2008).

Your goals for the test, or what you hope to discover about the product and its users, will heavily inform the design of the test. The extent to which the design is influenced by resources, constraints, and imagination varies from person to person.

Real-world limitations include time, money, management support, development team enthusiasm, and the availability of participants. In what follows, we will look at sample test plans for some of the more typical testing scenarios (Weidner & Eggum, 1966).

Then, we provide some suggestions for maintaining the highest standards of experimentation. One of the simplest ways to test a website is to have multiple users, all of whom belong to the same user group (for example, older adults), carry out a series of representative tasks on various site pages and report their findings to you.

7.4.2. Independent Groups Design

When different groups of people test different aspects of a website, we call this an independent group design. As can be seen in the table below, for our example, this design necessitates 15 participants. It reduces the possibility of transfer of learning effects brought on by performing one set of tasks before performing other similar tasks. In other words, if you're having trouble with the usability of Task B, you might find that finishing Task A makes it easier to finish Task B. If the tasks will take a very long time and there's a chance the participants will get tired, this design is a good option (Morris & DeShon, 2002).

TASK A SIGN UP TO BECOME A MEMBER	TASK B FIND ONLINE CLASSES TO TAKE	TASK C FIND VOLUNTEER OPPORTUNITIES
Terry	Pat	Tracy
Lesley	Michael	Dana
Lisa	Andrea	Duane
Kim	Erin	Aaron
Blair	Paula	Janet

7.4.3. Within-Subjects Design

Maybe it would be too expensive to test more than 15 people. As shown in the table below, if each participant completes all three modules, you only need five participants instead of fifteen. A within-subjects design describes such an arrangement. Although, you still need to think about the transmission of learning effects. To reduce these consequences, the order in which tasks are performed should be shuffled around or balanced using counterbalancing. By changing the order of the presentation of tasks, you can bind the effects of teach transfer (Greenwald, 1976). To counteract this, you have each participant present the modules in a different order, as shown in the table below. By randomizing the order of the modules, you minimize the transfer effects while requiring only four participants. Indeed, there are still some problems to fix. It's a big call if the modules you need to set up your hardware typically go in a specific order, as they would in real life (Yik et al., 2013). Does it matter more to provide a random order of tasks (possible in the lab), risk confusing and alienating the participant, and provide a realistic task order for users and possibly mask some usability problems on later tasks? Most people would argue that you should keep things in their original order. Even if you decide against it, you'll still need to deal with the possibility of transfer effects, perhaps by giving all participants some pre-performance training. In addition, it's a good idea to incorporate rest breaks into each session (Poulton, 1982).

PARTICIPANT	TASK SEQUENCE
Terry	A, B, C
Lesley	B, C, A
Lisa	C, A, B
Kim	B, A, C
Blair	C, B, A

7.5. TESTING MULTIPLE PRODUCT VERSIONS

Let's examine yet another everyday example. Let's say you have two products in development—Version A and Version B—and you want to see which has more potential as the final design. (These varying states are referred to as "conditions"). You're interested in comparing the two user groups (supervisors and technicians) to determine any performance differences. It will produce the following table, which depicts a 2× × 2-matrix layout (Anand et al., 2022).

GROUP	VERSION A	VERSION B
Supervisors	4	4
Technicians	4	4

It takes 16 people to meet the four criteria in an independent group design. Each cell in the table describing the test's setup is populated by a different group of participants. Four managers, four workers, four workers, etc., will use Version A. But let's say you're limited to a sample size of 8. A simple solution would be to have just two people fill out each cell, but that raises the possibility that no meaningful conclusions can be drawn from the data collected from any given group. Instead, as shown in the table below, have both the supervisors and the technicians try each version. Like in the previous illustration, the version tested last may have an unfair advantage because the participant may have learned how to complete the tasks while using the first version. On the other hand, this could have the opposite effect, making it more challenging for the participant to learn the second version because of how drastically it differs from the first. In either case, you run the risk of getting skewed results (Saraf et al., 2022).

SUPERVISORS	VERSION	TECHNICIANS	VERSION
Ginny	A, B	Laurie	A, B
Stephanie	B, A	Janice	B, A
Ken	A, B	Arnold	A, B
James	B, A	Andrew	B, A

As before, you'll rebalance the order in which the versions are presented to account for these potential differences. Based on the data in the table above, some of the eight participants will start with Version A, and others will start with Version B. The equal number of iterations of each version in both the first and last positions nullifies the potential for bias (Singh et al., 2017).

7.6. TESTING MULTIPLE USER GROUPS

Let's examine a situation that's slightly more involved but still plausible. Let's pretend your product's target market consists of two distinct types of people—

managers and clerks. During your testing, you should look for discrepancies in product mastery between and among various user demographics. You're looking for newcomers and seasoned veterans to each group and any differences between them. So, you'll need to have a range of job types and levels within each. Again, you will use a matrix layout (like the one below) (Lee & Lee, 2018). Different people will fill out the four conditions in the above table. There should be at least 16 people involved if you want to recruit at the shown rate of 4 people per cell. However, a within-subjects design cannot be used if there are too many subjects (about four subjects per group is the minimum needed to evaluate group differences). Instead, you'll need to conduct a simpler study with fewer participants per cell or fewer participants overall. Remember that if fewer than four people are in a cell, it will be difficult to draw meaningful conclusions about the whole. You'll likely have to ignore potential group differences to make your research manageable (McHugh, 2011).

7.7. LIST THE TASKS

The task list includes all the activities the test takers will require. This list should include reading the instructions, installing the software, and using the product. These activities are being developed in two phases. Only project team members, not potential test takers, will be provided with the detailed task list description during the early stages of test creation. Only provide as much information as necessary for test plan reviewers to determine whether the intended tasks are being adequately tested (Weitzner & Calamia, 2020). Later, you'll present the participants with more involved scenarios that expand upon the initial tasks. The test takers will be able to complete the tasks with minimal guidance from the moderator, thanks to the authenticity of the details and settings provided by the scenarios (Bellotti et al., 2004).

7.8. PARTS OF A TASK FOR THE TEST PLAN

The test plan only needs to discuss four aspects of each activity being tested briefly:

Incorporate only the minimum information necessary to convey the task to the project team. Usually, just one sentence will do to describe something (Goetz et al., 2007).

7.8.1. The Materials and Machine States Required to Perform the Task

When conducting usability tests, the surrounding environment is crucial. Depending on how early in development the product is, you may find yourself only if these materials or simulating the machine state yourself as the test moderator. For instance, if you were conducting user testing for a website before the screens were coded or prototyped, you might have given out printed wireframe drawings of the pages. Alternatively, you (or the participant) could open the file on the screen at the appropriate time if the page was already on the computer but not yet connected as part of a working prototype (Nakajima et al., 2018).

Some tests may be documented while others aren't, or vice versa. Tests of wireless network installation instructions should account for the fact that some steps—such as assigning drives to computers on the new network—will not require written instructions. When applicable and helpful, your task list may include product components being put through their paces for this endeavor. For instance, if a task requires the user to enter a customer name into a web form, you may want to outline the sequence of screens or web pages the user must visit to complete the task. This information makes indicating whether or not the entire system is being used easier (Wang et al., 2020).

7.8.2. A Description of Successful Completion of the Task

In what ways will you know when you've succeeded? It's incredible how much debate there will be over this issue and how frequently developers have different views on what constitutes a completed task. Specificity in measurement and clarity in understanding is improved when successful completion criteria (SCC) are included in the task description. In addition to outlining your work's scope, SCC guides how points will be awarded during an examination. A lack of clarity in determining the SCC indicates that the product's design is causing problems for the development team. For this reason, creating and recording the SCC is beneficial (Mann et al., 2007).

Success criteria can be set in several ways, such as when the participant reaches a predetermined point in the task or screen flow, when they reach the desired endpoint (even if they make mistakes getting there), or when they reach the specified number of errors or wrong turns (Butler & Cartier, 2004).

7.9. TIMING OR OTHER BENCHMARKS

You may use the amount of time that has passed as a measure of a benchmark or as a success. If you decide to use time-based benchmarks, it is strongly recommended that you do so only after giving it a lot of careful thought and only when the conditions are just right. For example, time spent on task is a useful metric for validating and Summarizing test results, but it is almost never suitable for formative testing or early exploratory (Saavedra & Smith, 1996). It is not a good idea to monitor time-on-task if you are also going to ask participants to think openly, because doing so usually slows down performance on the task. But, it is also not advisable not to measure time-on-task. Please refer to Benchmark Timings sidebar for further information regarding benchmark timings. You might use error rates as a benchmark instead of time if you prefer not to employ time as a measurement; for instance, finishing a task with really no mistakes of any sort (Murray et al., 2015).

7.10. TIPS FOR DEVELOPING THE TASK LIST

Even while it can appear simple at first glance, this is actually a pretty nuanced process. Having participants carry out activities that make use of the components of product in question is the key to uncovering usability faults in a roundabout manner. What you are actually evaluating is how your product interacts with the customer who ultimately buys it. Your product and the documentation that goes along with it are, from the perspective of the end user, merely a means to an end they are either utilized to resolve an issue or to provide a service (Davis et al., 2022).

The tasks that you construct for the test need to represent this relationship and, to the greatest extent feasible, permit the test to disclose the points where the product becomes more of a barrier than a benefit for performing a task. It is your responsibility to ensure that this happens. Let's take a look at a basic illustration of a work that has to be completed in order to meet a test objective, and while we're at it, let's go over some of the potential stumbling blocks (Rai, 2016).

7.10.1. Example Task: Navigation Tab on a Website

Imagine that one of the goals of your exam is to determine how simple it is to comprehend the label of a tab that is displayed on an online image-sharing platform that is utilized by both amateur and expert photographers. The purpose of the test is stated as follows:

"Determine whether or not users are able to comprehend the significance of the XYZ label." On the website, there are a total of 6 tabs containing text labels; nevertheless, the XYZ title is the one that causes the most trouble. It is referred to as Organize (Mead et al., 1997).

In the version of the website that is now live, users anticipate that they will be able to use the function to rearrange the sequence in which their photographs show on the viewing pages; however, the feature's intended use is to organize images into categories. If you merely take the aim at face value, which is "Establish if users can grasp the significance of the XYZ label," you can decide to create a job which involves having the test moderator answer questions about the users' ability to comprehend the label: "Have the participants explain the significance of the XYZ label to you once you've shown them the label."

To put it another way, the moderator of the exam will receive feedback regarding the label. Because of labeling is the component of the product that is in question here, this appears to be a straightforward and simple solution. On the other hand, this view simplifies the circumstance too much. You can determine the fact that there are basically 3 separate processes related with applying the basic label in the appropriate manner if you carry out a simple study (Goldberg et al., 2002).

i. Noticing the label
ii. Reading the label
iii. Processing the information and responding correctly

In addition, all three procedures take place within the extremely particular context of making use of the website in order to upload photos to the internet:

i. If all you do is show the participant the label, then the only processes you're addressing are the second and third ones. You will have no way of knowing whether or not the participants observe the label, which comes before the other behaviors. You will also make the entirety of the context irrelevant. During the course of browsing the website, the participants will be required to carry out a specific task or tasks at the time when they are meant to be reading the label. Instead of having someone draw their attention to the label and inquire about their thoughts, they will be performing the task themselves. This "context" is essential since it has a significant impact on the individuals' capabilities to process the information (Buscher et al., 2009).
ii. You should also examine how the position of label on website page impacts things. If it is located amongst 5 other labels and other activities, you should evaluate how well the participants do despite the presence of these possible distractions.

After conducting research into the application, environment, and location of labels, you are aware that it is not sufficient to only ask the participants to describe the meaning of the label. Instead, you need to give them a task in which they're expected to utilize the label, and then you need to determine whether or not they notice the label, read it, and use it in the correct manner (Czaja et al., 2013).

7.10.2. Ways to Prioritize Tasks

After going over a working example of establishing a task, the following step is to determine which other activities absolutely have to be incorporated into the plan. Because of time restrictions, it is quite rare that you really test all of the many tasks that make up a whole documentation, interface or both together at the same time. Unless you are ready to spend an excessive amount of resources, it is not viable to perform testing sessions that extend for days at a time. Instead, you will often be put in a position where you need to test a sample that is representative of the product's functionalities (Lehtola et al., 2004).

It is vital that while selecting this sample of activities, you work out as a lot of the most critical elements of the item as is reasonably practical and make sure to cover all of the test goals. Your work list should be filtered or reduced to something more manageable but at the same time you should make it a priority to record as many usability problems as feasible. The following is a summary of some typical strategies that you can use to prioritize the tasks on your list or cut down on it without having to make any unnecessary sacrifices (Burns & Naikar, 2016).

Prioritize by Frequency: Choose the activities that are representative of the ones that are carried out the most regularly by your end population of users. When utilizing the product, the most common activities are those that are carried out on a daily basis by the regular end user and may account for as much as seventy-five to 80% of total usage time.

When you were assessing a word processing package, you would like to make sure that the final user could easily complete the following tasks until you worried about the more obscure tasks, such as "how to cover up a comment that doesn't print out." For instance, when you're evaluating a word processor package, you might want to make sure that end user can easily carry out the following tasks (Claassen et al., 2014).

i. Open a file.
ii. Save a file.
iii. Edit a file.
iv. Print a file.

The majority of the time, tests consist of a series of arcane tasks that only around five percent of the user needs population would ever find, let alone use. Why? Because they are typically on the cutting edge of the product, we hypothesis that development team views those "five percenters" as the activities that present the most opportunity for intellectual growth and professional challenge. Sadly, the general end user doesn't really share the priority or enthusiasm that the developer has for these obscure duties.

If, after applying the "75% usage recommendation," there's still time to test extra tasks, including tasks that at least 25% of your end user group performs consistently. If there's still the opportunity to evaluate more tasks after applying the "75% usage guideline," Including the duties that are completed less frequently only after you have verified that your most common responsibilities have been attended to (Xuan et al., 2012).

Prioritize by Criticality: When a task results in a support call, data loss, product damage, or user injury, it is considered to be a critical task. Critical tasks are ones that, if performed poorly or ignored, could have major repercussions for the end user, the product, or the company's reputation. In essence, you want to be sure that the tasks that cause the most suffering and maybe negative press are caught.

Prioritize by Vulnerability: In this context, the term "vulnerability" refers to those responsibilities that you have the sneaking suspicion, well before evaluation, will be difficult to carry out or that have recognized weaknesses in their design.

Most frequently, the project team will have a strong grasp on this and, when questioned, will voice their concerns regarding a new feature, procedure, interface design, portion of a document, etc. In that case, the examination should contain questions and activities that cover these primary subject areas.

Sometimes, in the spirit of "being neutral," developers will pretend that all functions operate as poorly (or well), and that none of them are particularly problematic. This is done to avoid the appearance of prejudice. They don't want their known flaws to be revealed during the test for whatever reason, whether it be a good intention or something less admirable. As a result, activities that are manifestly difficult to do and that represent entire chunks, components or web pages of a document are omitted from the test. These omissions later turn out to be albatrosses if there's no time to fix them since the test was completed too quickly.

To prevent this from happening, apply your best critical judgment to determine which features or tasks are not quite finished, are new or have never been tested before, or have been challenging for in-house people to complete. In the event that you are uncertain, a human performance specialist can assist you in determining the weak points of the products by carrying out an assessment. An expert assessment can also assist you in refining the scope of your overall test objectives (Conaghan et al., 2001).

Prioritize by Readiness: If you leave testing till a very late phase of the development cycle, you might have no choice except to stick with features that are already ready to be tested or completely forego testing.

Even if this is not the best option, there are occasions when you have no other choice. There is no guarantee that you will always get the opportunity to wait for each and every screen, component and user guide section to be finished. Always keep in mind that it is preferable to test something rather than nothing.

7.11. DESCRIBE THE TEST ENVIRONMENT, EQUIPMENT, AND LOGISTICS

This portion of a test plan covers the environment that you will strive to mimic during the test as well as the equipment that the participants will need to have in order to successfully complete the exam. You might, for instance, desire to act out the setting of a sales department for an item that is utilized by insurance brokers. Alternately, chemists might employ your item in a laboratory that studies the environment. Now, let's say you only have a desire to evaluate the item in an extremely noisy office that is also quite packed and in which the phones are continuously ringing. Do as much as possible to recreate the real-world situations, regardless of the regular working atmosphere. This does not only make it easier for the participant to take on the position of actual end consumers, but it also ensures that the test findings will be a more accurate indicator of how the product will operate in the environment in which it is typically utilized.

The only equipment that is going to be used by the participants is the equipment that is being discussed here. Phones, laptops, printers, and other electronic devices are all examples of equipment. It is not required to detail the data gathering equipment or the cameras that you will be employing in order to monitor the test (Marquez et al., 2022).

7.11.1. EXPLAIN WHAT THE MODERATOR WILL DO

This section serves to define what you will be doing as a test moderator, which is especially crucial when there will be spectators of a test who are not familiar with the process of testing. Indicate when the moderator of the exam will engage in an activity that deviates from the norm and has the potential to cause confusion. For instance, it is not always evident why and in what conditions the person who is moderating the examination is asking probing questions and intervening. This is especially the case in situations in which the test administrator might be role-playing or purposely performing devil's advocacy with a participant who is extremely compliant (Wilson et al., 1989).

7.11.2. List the Data You Will Collect

This part of the testing phase provides a summary of the several sorts of metrics that will collect even during test, including data on performance as well as preferences. Error rates, the number of times the support was accessed by task, the amount of time it took to complete a task, and so on are all examples of performance data, which represent measurements of participant behavior. Included in participant rankings, responses to questions, and other similar

ACTIVITY 7.1:

What are the processes of conducting a test? Give a detail presentation.

information are all examples of preference data, which represent measures of user opinion or thought process. Your research questions should serve as the foundation for the data collection. Sometimes a reference to these measurements will already be present in an earlier part of the test plan, like the methodology section. Measures of performance and preferences might be utilized statistically or qualitatively, based on the aims of the test (Szabo et al., 2010). If you include the evaluation metrics that you want to use during the test, any parties that have an interest in doing so will have a much easier time examining the test plan. It'll also ensure that they receive the kind of data which they anticipate getting from the test, which will be beneficial to them (Wang & Strong, 1996). Following is a selection of the various kinds of measurements that might be gathered throughout the course of a normal test.

7.11.3. Sample Performance Measures

1. The quantity and proportion of tasks correctly done with and without
2. Guidance or prompts
3. The quantity and kind of prompts used
4. The quantity and % of assignments that were wrongly performed
5. The total number of wrong choices (errors)
6. The number of omission errors
7. Number of improper menu selections
8. Number of wrong icons chosen
9. The total number of assistance desk calls.
10. Number of accesses to the user manual
11. Amount of index visits
12. The number of times the contents page has been accessed
13. The total number of "negative remarks or mannerisms"
14. Length of time needed to access the manual's information
15. Length of time needed to get online help information
16. Time required to correct mistakes (s)
17. The amount of duration spent reading a particular handbook section
18. Talking to the help desk takes time.
19. Duration of each assignment (Azeroual et al., 2018).

SUMMARY

The process of conducting testing involves various stages to ensure that a product or system meets the required standards of quality and functionality. The process starts with planning, where the testing team determines the objectives, scope, and approach for testing. This stage also includes creating test plans, test cases, and test scripts. The next stage is the preparation phase, where the testing team sets up the testing environment, including hardware and software, and prepares the test data. This stage also involves identifying and allocating resources, such as testers and testing tools. The execution phase is where the actual testing takes place, and the testing team executes the test cases and scripts to detect defects and ensure the system's functionality. During this stage, the team may also perform regression, performance, and security tests. Once the testing is complete, the testing team analyzes the results to identify defects and issues. The team then reports the defects to the development team, who will fix the issues and re-test the system. The final stage is the closure phase, where the testing team documents the testing results and produces a final report. This report provides a summary of the testing process, including the objectives, scope, approach, test cases, and results.

MULTIPLE CHOICE QUESTIONS

1. **What is the first step in the testing process?**
   a. Test planning
   b. Test execution
   c. Test analysis
   d. Test design
2. **Which of the following is not a type of testing?**
   a. Unit testing
   b. Integration testing
   c. Regression testing
   d. Debugging testing
3. **What is the purpose of test execution?**
   a. To identify defects
   b. To design test cases
   c. To plan testing activities
   d. To analyze test results
4. **Which of the following is not a commonly used test design technique?**
   a. Equivalence partitioning
   b. Boundary value analysis

c. Decision table testing

d. Random testing

5. What is the goal of test analysis?

a. To identify defects

b. To design test cases

c. To plan testing activities

d. To analyze test results

Answers to Multiple Choice Questions

1. (a) 2. (d) 3. (a) 4. (d) 5. (d)

REFERENCES

1. Al - Bayari, O., & Sadoun, B., (2005). New centralized automatic vehicle location communications software system under GIS environment. *International Journal of Communication Systems, 18*(9), 833–846.
2. Anand, A., Das, S., Singh, O., & Kumar, V., (2022). Testing resource allocation for software with multiple versions. *International Journal of Applied Management Science, 14*(1), 23–37.
3. Aromataris, E., Fernandez, R., Godfrey, C. M., Holly, C., Khalil, H., & Tungpunkom, P., (2015). Summarizing systematic reviews: Methodological development, conduct and reporting of an umbrella review approach. *JBI Evidence Implementation, 13*(3), 132–140.
4. Azeroual, O., Saake, G., & Schallehn, E., (2018). Analyzing data quality issues in research information systems via data profiling. *International Journal of Information Management, 41*, 50–56.
5. Bellotti, V., Dalal, B., Good, N., Flynn, P., Bobrow, D. G., & Ducheneaut, N., (2004). What a to-do: Studies of task management towards the design of a personal task list manager. In: *Proceedings of the SIGCHI Conference on Human Factors in Computing Systems* (pp. 735–742).
6. Boisvert, M., Lang, R., Andrianopoulos, M., & Boscardin, M. L., (2010). Telepractice in the assessment and treatment of individuals with autism spectrum disorders: A systematic review. *Developmental Neurorehabilitation, 13*(6), 423–432.
7. Bosse, Y., & Gerosa, M. A., (2017). Why is programming so difficult to learn? Patterns of difficulties related to programming learning mid-stage. *ACM SIGSOFT Software Engineering Notes, 41*(6), 1–6.
8. Brown, C. H., Holman, E. W., Wichmann, S., & Velupillai, V., (2008). Automated classification of the world's languages: A description of the method and preliminary results. *Language Typology and Universals, 61*(4), 285–308.

9. Burns, C. M., & Naikar, N., (2016). Prioritization: A double-edged sword? *Journal of Cognitive Engineering and Decision Making, 10*(1), 105–108.
10. Buscher, G., Cutrell, E., & Morris, M. R., (2009). What do you see when you're surfing? Using eye tracking to predict salient regions of web pages. In: *Proceedings of the SIGCHI Conference on Human Factors in Computing Systems* (pp. 21–30).
11. Butler, D. L., & Cartier, S. C., (2004). Promoting effective task interpretation as an important work habit: A key to successful teaching and learning. *Teachers College Record, 106*(9), 1729–1758.
12. Carpio, L., Hall, P., Lingard, L., & Schryer, C. F., (2008). Interprofessional communication and medical error: A reframing of research questions and approaches. *Academic Medicine, 83*(10), S76–S81.
13. Chicheł, A., Skowronek, J., Kubaszewska, M., & Kanikowski, M., (2007). Hyperthermia–description of a method and a review of clinical applications. *Reports of Practical Oncology & Radiotherapy, 12*(5), 267–275.
14. Claassen, C. A., Pearson, J. L., Khodyakov, D., Satow, P. M., Gebbia, R., Berman, A. L., & Insel, T. R., (2014). Reducing the burden of suicide in the US: The aspirational research goals of the national action alliance for suicide prevention research prioritization task force. *American Journal of Preventive Medicine, 47*(3), 309–314.
15. Conaghan, P., Edmonds, J., Emery, P. A. U. L., Genant, H. A. R. R. Y., Gibbon, W. A. Y. N. E., Klarlund, M., & Ostergaard, M., (2001). Magnetic resonance imaging in rheumatoid arthritis: Summary of OMERACT activities, current status, and plans. *The Journal of Rheumatology, 28*(5), 1158–1162.
16. Czaja, S. J., Sharit, J., Lee, C. C., Nair, S. N., Hernández, M. A., Arana, N., & Fu, S. H., (2013). Factors influencing use of an e-health website in a community sample of older adults. *Journal of the American Medical Informatics Association, 20*(2), 277–284.
17. Davis, K., Lo, H. Y., Lichliter, R., Wallin, K., Elegores, G., Jacobson, S., & Doughty, C., (2022). Twelve tips for creating an escape room activity for medical education. *Medical Teacher, 44*(4), 366–371.
18. Desurvire, H., Kondziela, J., & Atwood, M. E., (1992). What is gained and lost when using methods other than empirical testing. In: *Posters and Short Talks of the 1992 SIGCHI Conference on Human Factors in Computing Systems* (pp. 125, 126).
19. Dyck, M. J., (1987). Assessing logotherapeutic constructs: Conceptual and psychometric status of the purpose in life and seeking of noetic goals tests. *Clinical Psychology Review, 7*(4), 439–447.
20. Fenech, M., (1993). The cytokinesis-block micronucleus technique: A detailed description of the method and its application to genotoxicity studies in human populations. *Mutation Research/Fundamental and Molecular Mechanisms of Mutagenesis, 285*(1), 35–44.

21. Ganz, J. B., Davis, J. L., Lund, E. M., Goodwyn, F. D., & Simpson, R. L., (2012). Meta-analysis of PECS with individuals with ASD: Investigation of targeted versus non-targeted outcomes, participant characteristics, and implementation phase. *Research in Developmental Disabilities, 33*(2), 406–418.
22. Goetz, C. G., Fahn, S., Martinez - Martin, P., Poewe, W., Sampaio, C., Stebbins, G. T., & LaPelle, N., (2007). Movement disorder society - sponsored revision of the unified Parkinson's disease rating scale (MDS - UPDRS): Process, format, and clinimetric testing plan. *Movement Disorders, 22*(1), 41–47.
23. Goldberg, J. H., Stimson, M. J., Lewenstein, M., Scott, N., & Wichansky, A. M., (2002). Eye tracking in web search tasks: Design implications. In: *Proceedings of the 2002 Symposium on Eye Tracking Research & Applications* (pp. 51–58).
24. Greenwald, A. G., (1976). Within-subjects designs: To use or not to use? *Psychological Bulletin, 83*(2), 314.
25. Harter, H. L., & Moore, A. H., (1976). An evaluation of exponential and Weibull test plans. *IEEE Transactions on Reliability, 25*(2), 100–104.
26. Huberty, T. J., (2009). Test and performance anxiety. *Principal Leadership, 10*(1), 12–16.
27. Krasny-Pacini, A., Chevignard, M., & Evans, J., (2014). Goal management training for rehabilitation of executive functions: A systematic review of effectiveness in patients with acquired brain injury. *Disability and Rehabilitation, 36*(2), 105–116.
28. Kubey, R., Larson, R., & Csikszentmihalyi, M., (1996). Experience sampling method applications to communication research questions. *Journal of Communication, 46*(2), 99–120.
29. Lee, S., & Lee, D. K., (2018). What is the proper way to apply the multiple comparison test? *Korean Journal of Anesthesiology, 71*(5), 353–360.
30. Lehtola, L., Kauppinen, M., & Kujala, S., (2004). Requirements prioritization challenges in practice. In: *Product Focused Software Process Improvement: 5th International Conference, PROFES 2004, Kansai Science City, Japan, April 5–8, 2004. Proceedings 5* (pp. 497–508).
31. Lim, L. P., Garnsey, E., & Gregory, M., (2006). Product and process innovation in biopharmaceuticals: A new perspective on development. *R&D Management, 36*(1), 27–36.
32. Lin, X., Yajnanarayana, V., Muruganathan, S. D., Gao, S., Asplund, H., Maattanen, H. L., & Wang, Y. P. E., (2018). The sky is not the limit: LTE for unmanned aerial vehicles. *IEEE Communications Magazine, 56*(4), 204–210.
33. Liu, L., Wang, L., Sun, J., Zhou, Y., Zhong, X., Yan, A., & Xu, N., (2007). An integrated test-bed for PAT testing and verification of inter-satellite lasercom terminals. In: *Free-Space Laser Communications VII* (Vol. 6709, pp. 34–38).
34. Lochbaum, M., Zişan, K. Ç., Kara-Aretha, G., Taylor, W., & Ricardo, Z., (2016). "Task and ego goal orientations in competitive sport: A quantitative review of the

literature from 1989 to 2016." *Kinesiology, 48*(1), 3–29.

35. Mann, D. L., Ho, N. Y., De Souza, N. J., Watson, D. R., & Taylor, S. J., (2007). Is optimal vision required for the successful execution of an interceptive task? *Human Movement Science, 26*(3), 343–356.
36. Marquez-Barja, J. M., Naudts, D., Maglogiannis, V., Hadiwardoyo, S. A., Moerman, I., Klepper, M., & Vandenbossche, J., (2022). Designing a 5G architecture to overcome the challenges of the teleoperated transport and logistics. In: *2022 IEEE 19th Annual Consumer Communications & Networking Conference (CCNC)* (pp. 264–267).
37. Martin, D., Rooksby, J., Rouncefield, M., & Sommerville, I., (2007). 'Good' organizational reasons for 'bad' software testing: An ethnographic study of testing in a small software company. In: *29th International Conference on Software Engineering (ICSE'07)* (pp. 602–611).
38. Maynard, D., & Marlaire, C., (1999). Good reasons for bad testing performance: The interactional substrate of educational testing. *Constructing (In) Competence: Disabling Evaluations in Clinical and Social Interaction*, 171–196.
39. McHugh, M. L., (2011). Multiple comparison analysis testing in ANOVA. *Biochemia Medica, 21*(3), 203–209.
40. Mead, S. E., Spaulding, V. A., Sit, R. A., Meyer, B., & Walker, N., (1997). Effects of age and training on world wide web navigation strategies. In: *Proceedings of the Human Factors and Ergonomics Society Annual Meeting* (Vol. 41, No. 1, pp. 152–156).
41. Miller, K. W., Morell, L. J., Noonan, R. E., Park, S. K., Nicol, D. M., Murrill, B. W., & Voas, M., (1992). Estimating the probability of failure when testing reveals no failures. *IEEE Transactions on Software Engineering, 18*(1), 33.
42. Mohacsi, S., & Ramler, R., (2019). Why software testing fails: Common pitfalls observed in a critical smart metering project. In: *Software Quality: The Complexity and Challenges of Software Engineering and Software Quality in the Cloud: 11th International Conference, SWQD 2019, Vienna, Austria, January 15–18, 2019, Proceedings 11* (pp. 73–92).
43. Morris, S. B., & DeShon, R. P., (2002). Combining effect size estimates in meta-analysis with repeated measures and independent-groups designs. *Psychological Methods, 7*(1), 105.
44. Murray, K. E., Whitty, S., Liu, S., Luu, J., & Betz, V., (2015). Timing-driven titan: Enabling large benchmarks and exploring the gap between academic and commercial CAD. *ACM Transactions on Reconfigurable Technology and Systems (TRETS), 8*(2), 1–18.
45. Nakajima, K., Hauser, H., Li, T., & Pfeifer, R., (2018). Exploiting the dynamics of soft materials for machine learning. *Soft Robotics, 5*(3), 339–347.
46. Nelson, W. B., (2005). A bibliography of accelerated test plans part II-references. *IEEE Transactions on Reliability, 54*(3), 370–373.

47. Nettleton, E., Thrun, S., Durrant-Whyte, H., & Sukkarieh, S., (2006). Decentralized SLAM with low-bandwidth communication for teams of vehicles. In: *Field and Service Robotics* (Vol. 24, pp. 179–188).

48. Pawliuk, C., Brown, H. L., Widger, K., Dewan, T., Hermansen, A. M., Grégoire, M. C., & Siden, H. H., (2021). Optimizing the process for conducting scoping reviews. *BMJ Evidence-Based Medicine, 26*(6), 312.

49. Pearlman, M., (2011). Finalizing the test blueprint. In: *Building a Validity Argument for the Test of English as a Foreign Language™* (pp. 241–272).

50. Pissoort, D., & Armstrong, K., (2016). Why is the IEEE developing a standard on managing risks due to EM disturbances? In: *2016 IEEE International Symposium on Electromagnetic Compatibility (EMC)* (pp. 78–83).

51. Poulton, E. C., (1982). Influential companions: Effects of one strategy on another in the within-subjects designs of cognitive psychology. *Psychological Bulletin, 91*(3), 673.

52. Rai, R., (2016). Tips to organize a conference: Experiences from DERMACON 2016, Coimbatore. *Indian Dermatology Online Journal, 7*(5), 424.

53. Rochon, J., Gondan, M., & Kieser, M., (2012). To test or not to test: Preliminary assessment of normality when comparing two independent samples. *BMC Medical Research Methodology, 12*(1), 1–11.

54. Roemer, J. E. (1986). Equality of resources implies equality of welfare. The Quarterly Journal of Economics, 101(4), 751-784.

55. Rogevich, M. E., & Perin, D., (2008). Effects on science summarization of a reading comprehension intervention for adolescents with behavior and attention disorders. *Exceptional Children, 74*(2), 135–154.

56. Rude, C. D., (2009). Mapping the research questions in technical communication. *Journal of Business and Technical Communication, 23*(2), 174–215.

57. Saavedra, R. H., & Smith, A. J., (1996). Analysis of benchmark characteristics and benchmark performance prediction. *ACM Transactions on Computer Systems (TOCS), 14*(4), 344–384.

58. Sandelowski, M., (2000). Whatever happened to qualitative description? *Research in Nursing & Health, 23*(4), 334–340.

59. Saraf, I., Iqbal, J., Shrivastava, A. K., & Khurshid, S., (2022). Modelling reliability growth for multi - version open source software considering varied testing and debugging factors. *Quality and Reliability Engineering International, 38*(4), 1814–1825.

60. Singh, V. B., Sharma, M., & Pham, H., (2017). Entropy based software reliability analysis of multi-version open source software. *IEEE Transactions on Software Engineering, 44*(12), 1207–1223.

61. Smeltzer, L. R., (1993). Emerging questions and research paradigms in business communication research. *The Journal of Business Communication (1973), 30*(2), 181–198.

62. Sprague, J., (1993). Retrieving the research agenda for communication education: Asking the pedagogical questions that are "embarrassments to theory." *Communication Education, 42*(2), 106–122.
63. Szabo, J. K., Vesk, P. A., Baxter, P. W., & Possingham, H. P., (2010). Regional avian species declines estimated from volunteer - collected long - term data using list length analysis. *Ecological Applications, 20*(8), 2157–2169.
64. Tseng, S. T., Balakrishnan, N., & Tsai, C. C., (2009). Optimal step-stress accelerated degradation test plan for gamma degradation processes. *IEEE Transactions on Reliability, 58*(4), 611–618.
65. Wang, A. Y. T., Murdock, R. J., Kauwe, S. K., Oliynyk, A. O., Gurlo, A., Brgoch, J., & Sparks, T. D., (2020). Machine learning for materials scientists: An introductory guide toward best practices. *Chemistry of Materials, 32*(12), 4954–4965.
66. Wang, R. Y., & Strong, D. M., (1996). Beyond accuracy: What data quality means to data consumers. *Journal of Management Information Systems, 12*(4), 5–33.
67. Weidner, K., & Eggum, B. O., (1966). Protein hydrolysis: A description of the method used at the department of animal physiology in Copenhagen. *Acta Agriculturae Scandinavica, 16*(3, 4), 115–119.
68. Weitzner, D. S., & Calamia, M., (2020). Serial position effects on list learning tasks in mild cognitive impairment and Alzheimer's disease. *Neuropsychology, 34*(4), 467.
69. Wilson, T. D., Kraft, D., & Dunn, D. S., (1989). The disruptive effects of explaining attitudes: The moderating effect of knowledge about the attitude object. *Journal of Experimental Social Psychology, 25*(5), 379–400.
70. Xuan, J., Jiang, H., Ren, Z., & Zou, W., (2012). Developer prioritization in bug repositories. In: *2012 34th International Conference on Software Engineering (ICSE)* (pp. 25–35).
71. Yik, M., Widen, S. C., & Russell, J. A., (2013). The within-subjects design in the study of facial expressions. *Cognition & Emotion, 27*(6), 1062–1072.

CHAPTER 8

EXPANDING FROM USABILITY TESTING TO DESIGNING THE USER EXPERIENCE

UNIT INTRODUCTION

Up until this point, the details regarding the scientific components of drafting, developing, carrying out, and presenting the findings of a usability test, have been discussed. Testing for usability has also been presented within the perspective of a user-centered method for creating products by a company. This chapter provides a broader perspective on increasing the impact that user-centered design (UCD) and user experience design have on a company. These propositions are directed largely toward an individual who has been made responsible for usability within his or her business (or who would wish to take on this role) but who has received little to no professional training in UCD (Redish, 2007).

A phased program is used to underscore how important it is to construct such a program in stages over several years. According to the phased diagram, when it comes to product development, companies that have not previously adopted such a program face a significant challenge when attempting to implement a user-centered approach (Meloncon, 2017). This undertaking is full of same challenges, risks, and political interests that come with any significant shift in the corporate culture. It needs a great deal of planning and paying close attention to the "human" concerns within the firm. Nevertheless, depending on the level of management support and the number of resources that have been allocated to usability, an organization might want to move more quickly or more slowly, Put these ideas into action in a different order, or steer clear of those that do not make sense (Ellis & Kurniawan, 2000). The critical thing is to recognize and take into consideration the dynamics that are at play within a specific business. The process of establishing a program follows a path that is more spontaneous than it is structured or planned by speaking with those who have been through the process before (El Bassiti & Ajhoun, 2013). No foolproof method can be applied in a "cookie cutter" fashion to each and every company, and any effort to do so will put a program in jeopardy. This chapter is a reflection of the collective experiences of many people and groups that have put usability into action, UCD, and experience design in both big and small start-ups and established businesses. These individuals and groups have all been involved in implementing these practices at some point (Benoît et al., 2010).

Learning Objectives

At the end of this chapter, readers will be able to:

- Understanding the difference between usability testing and user experience design
- Understanding the importance of user experience in product design
- Understanding the user-centered design process
- Learning how to design for user experience
- Learning how to evaluate user experience
- Understanding the role of usability testing in user experience design

Key Terms

- Shealth Mode
- Usability Related Activities
- Usability Testing
- User Experience

8.1. STEALTH MODE: ESTABLISH VALUE

A usability specialist can be in this stage right now—silently carrying out usability tests and other user-centered design (UCD) operations to highlight the benefits of these initiatives—while trying to make friends rather than intimidating or frightening people. This phase is referred to as "stealth mode" because, although there may be a usability champion in management, there is likely limited funding for regular studies and limited access to real users (Philippidis, 2022).

Evaluate the current situation in your company and look for ways to make a meaningful contribution. Initially, the aim is to steadily make progress while educating the company about the advantages of usability and UCD (Van Hout & Bingham, 2013).

8.1.1. Pick the First Project Carefully

When selecting or executing an initial "kick-off" project, opt for one with moderate to high visibility within the company and a high likelihood of progress. Having a champion(s) and the slightest hindrance from executing a test will make success more attainable. A champion is a management figure with influence who is devoted to the concept of usability and has a personal stake in seeing the program thrive (Lewis, 2005).

A documentation project can be an ideal kick-off since it may appear less intimidating to others in the company. Start with achievable goals, such as testing only a segment of a manual. A midway assessment test is likely the easiest and most effortless test for a novice usability specialist to conduct (Auger, 2013). For instance, an early stage of a product could be tested, such as the activation guidelines for a cell phone. Earlier involvement in the project is recommended for the greatest impact on the product, although later involvement may be more politically suitable and less intimidating at first. Once the project is finished, emphasize, and publicize the initial success widely within the organization (Cooper et al., 2000). The reader may be preparing or conducting their first usability test when reading this. However, there is no need to worry as the current usability testing project was likely opted for valid reasons. The results can still be useful regardless of how carefully or casually chosen. The important thing is that a usability test is being carried out, which is a positive development (Jiang et al., 1996).

8.2. START SLOWLY AND CONSERVATIVELY, GET BUY-IN

As indicated previously, UCD is a difficult project within an enterprise, and there is a risk in just "jumping on the usability bandwagon." It's crucial to establish a usability program gradually, building on each achievement rather than attempting to transform the company all at once completely. Similar to quality, usability cannot be merely dictated from above. Instead of existing as some flimsy "user-friendly" flag that everyone waves but gets very little results, it requires the backing of every member of the organization to get into the organization's lifeblood (Brody et al., 2019).

Rather than just attacking usability issues head-on, think about gradually infiltrating the company. Beginning too optimistically can jeopardize a long-term initiative, as was indicated in an earlier tale about the premature installation of a furnished usability lab. Initially, folks you want to assist could view usability as a danger and a loss of control. On the other hand, once they realize that the user-centered approach makes sense as a rational method of doing business and that it is not a danger, usability's most vocal opponents will frequently become its most enthusiastic champions (Grundlingh, 2008).

8.2.1. Volunteer Your Services

To proceed gradually, one should not be a shrinking violet. Usability is currently in high demand, presenting an opportunity to assert oneself. Opportunities should be sought to leverage one's efforts. For instance, if assigned to test product documentation, this is a chance to affect the user interface positively (Sfikas, 1999). When reporting on the test, problems from sources other than those directly tested should be included as a "courtesy" if they arise, such as inaccurate end-user characterizations or software interfaces. Personal expansion on these findings and assistance in overcoming them should be offered (Nesbit & Brudney, 2010).

Even if a usability project occurs very late in the life cycle and has only a few advantages, one should take it on. Although a test conducted very late may not have a significant impact on the current product release, it will affect the subsequent release some weeks later. Hence, one should keep the long-term vision in mind. Even for small projects, a professional, well-thought-out report should be created to be acceptable and usable within one's organization. Others seeking to learn about "usability" will scrutinize one's methodology and approach (Harper & Allen, 1997).

8.2.2. Create a Strategy and Business Case

To establish expectations and an overall philosophy that will determine ultimate success, one should begin strategically. Even if one is new to usability issues, a long-term perspective should be adopted from the outset. A usability plan should be developed that spans a two to three-year period. Management should be engaged to discuss the organization's long-term vision for usability (Bruce,

1998). This will include identifying where the organization is headed, the UCD techniques and methods to be employed, hiring requirements, modifications, and additions to the product life cycle, usability tests and evaluations, internal awareness-building, educational opportunities, and external services required, such as recruiting or market research firms and usability consultants. Guidelines for projects, including usability checkpoints in the life cycle, usability objectives, and test types, may also be included in the plan (Schaltegger et al., 2012).

The plan may be developed for personal use or shared with others, depending on one's position and level of responsibility within the organization. Emphasis is placed on a plan at such an early stage because, without it, usability may falter. As the company becomes more committed to implementing a usability program, it will need to address the issues in the plan. Even if starting from scratch, the techniques implemented should be successful, with people wanting more. Being one jump ahead and ready for success is essential (Versteeg & Bouwman, 2006). The plan should consider the organization's political realities and management's level of commitment. The right balance should be kept between stretching the organization and proposing impossible tasks. It's important to remember that any plan is subject to revision as circumstances change. It's a living document (Welch et al., 2023).

8.2.3. Build on Successes

It's important to avoid going for the home run and instead focus on making steady, incremental progress with singles and doubles. This applies to both specific products and the overall program. Over time, even "minor" revisions can result in significant improvements (Mizrahi & Rosenthal, 2001). Adopting a small-scale approach can help prevent setbacks or resistance, which can create doubts in the early stages of developing a usability program. As the user progresses from project to project, efforts should be directed towards earlier and earlier involvement, as this is where the greatest usability benefits can be demonstrated (Lyall & Fletcher, 2013).

8.2.4. Set Up Long-Term Relationships

A blended top-down and bottom-up approach is advocated for establishing long-term partnerships within the company. This entails working from the bottom up and the top down simultaneously. Usability necessitates dedication from both lower-level staff and the management team. Working from the ground up entails carrying out projects and displaying the results. Working from the top down entails teaching and involving management in the advantages of usability testing and UCD. Of course, soliciting the assistance of usability supporters will be required to undertake such a comprehensive effort (Friedman, 2000).

8.3. SELL YOURSELF AND WHAT YOU ARE DOING

Explain to people what you do and how it benefits the organization, its clients, and users, whether internal, external, or both. You may have thousands of interactions with individuals in the business over the span of a week. Consider these opportunities to sow seeds and teach people about the advantages of UCD. Two or three seeds will eventually sprout; others will approach you for assistance (Gorry et al., 2010).

One must be prepared to sell, sell, and sell at every chance, especially in the beginning. Take advantage of every opportunity to give presentations or arrange brief training sessions for individuals with a vested interest and others who are simply curious.

A presentation containing usability test results is an obvious choice. Such presentations could include video extracts from a test, similar to a "greatest hits" tape, focusing on the most spectacular, cost-saving, and embarrassment-averting incidents. Nothing beats witnessing real customers or representative users struggling to bring home the reality of and need to remedy usability issues. Never act defensively in the face of poor test results. Five "small" inconsistencies can add up to one major annoyance for a user (Grossman, 1991).

Nonetheless, a balance must be established. Professional deception may also play a role in persuading employees to adopt UCD techniques in your firm. Some people may be put off by overt evangelism or door-to-door missionary zeal (Atkinson, 2012).

8.3.1. Strategize: Choose Your Battles Carefully

Initially, achieving usability may prove challenging due to the requirement to break established behavior patterns inside the business. During the course of their work, usability specialists may find themselves in challenging situations, but they should be able to plan for and respond appropriately to whatever challenges they face (Dhamija & Tygar, 2005).

Instead of becoming involved in petty debates, it is best to conserve one's energy for more important matters, such as gaining access to actual clients and running many tests. In order to carry out examinations that need a higher level of objectivity or expertise, a third-party provider may be hired.

A seasoned usability specialist is aware of which concerns are worth the fight for and when it is appropriate to surrender on less significant matters. The budget and the business case for extending into the UCD can be more easily crafted with the help of this knowledge (Hansen et al., 2013).

8.4. FORMALIZE PROCESSES AND PRACTICES

After the initial seeds of UCD yield results and the benefits become apparent, start formalizing the process by creating physical and organizational structures to support it (Lampland, 2010).

8.4.1. Establish a Central Residency for User-Centered Design

Careful consideration must be given to the organizational placement of the support for UCD. Two primary strategies can be applied to this positioning:

i. Usability support may be housed at the project level by employing a dedicated usability professional to work on a single project and report to the same project manager as the rest of the team (Thursky & Mahemoff, 2007).

~ OR ~

ii. Usability can be centralized, and a centralized manager can receive reports from one or more specialists who support various projects. The first method is typically utilized by companies that are considered to be "usability-mature." These companies have many usability specialists on staff, all of whom are dedicated to certain projects and report directly to the managers of those projects (Lucchi & Delera, 2020).

Both techniques have the potential to be fruitful, but, for an organization that is just starting with usability, the centralized approach is mostly advised for two reasons:

1. Usability advocacy can be extremely challenging and solitary, as the usability specialist is sometimes placed in a combative role on a project. It is beneficial to have a boss who has a primary emphasis on usability because the support of others is so important to one's self-confidence, viewpoint, and eventual level of achievement. Having numerous usability specialists report to a single manager rather than several allows for more collaboration, learning from one another's experiences, and the cultivation of a genuine sense of team spirit. This is of utmost significance in companies that are relatively new to UCD (Bendixen et al., 2017).
2. It is simple for a usability specialist to become overly impacted by the objectives of the project team when they report back to a project manager on a particular project. The objectives of the project team may be in direct opposition to the aims of the usability team. If changing the design might result in additional work for the developers, who are your very close colleagues, being truthful about a specific design

could be tough for certain people. This uncertainty eventually puts one's autonomy and their ability to advocate for themselves as a user in jeopardy. Because there is less societal pressure connected with this reporting structure, reporting to a manager who is not directly involved in the project as well as working on numerous projects, can be helpful in maintaining one's autonomy, objectivity, and especially user advocacy. Both of these things can be done while reporting to management who is not directly involved in the project (Walden et al., 2020).

After getting the ball rolling with consistent usability testing and building up some momentum, it is a good idea to either build a permanent location or take over an existing one. It is not always suggested to construct a laboratory that is completely outfitted due to the high costs involved, its relative isolation, and the potential annoyance it could provide to clients. For instance, it may be most efficient to perform usability research for owners of small enterprises at their place of business. Still, consumers with impairments may have a specialized configuration that cannot be successfully recreated in a lab setting (Atkinson et al., 2009). It is important to remember that a laboratory is merely a component of a successful overall program, not the program itself. Establishing a laboratory before it has gained universal recognition of its usefulness or is capable of being utilized consistently may cause management to question the programs worth when circumstances are difficult. It is advisable to have a straightforward or mobile laboratory that may be utilized as required. For businesses with a well-known brand, it is possible to set up a secondary laboratory away from the main location in order to conduct research in complete anonymity. In addition, a physical location should be established to archive recordings and reports. This location should be designated as the "Center for Usability Truths Revealed," It should provide resources for all members of the organization to help them advance the goal of UCD becoming an accepted practice. This should be done regardless of whether testing takes place in the physical location (Gudipati & Sethi, 2017).

8.5. ADD USABILITY-RELATED ACTIVITIES TO THE PRODUCT LIFE CYCLE

To flourish beyond the surface, usability must be integrated into the structure of the organization's development cycle. Finally, it should be regarded as a fully ordinary activity, similar to any other form of development. It must simply be viewed as the proper technique to create and construct a first-rate product (Göransson et al., 2003).

As a result, avoid creating a separate life cycle for development activities and another for usability activities. The more usability is conceived of as apart from other activities, the more vulnerable it is to be undercut. When actions like creating usability targets, officially identifying the user, doing a job analysis, and defining testing checkpoints become second nature, the usability specialist will know usability has arrived and will be tough to destroy (Carter et al., 2005).

8.5.1. Educate Others Within the Organization

This proposal contains various aspects. The following are some particular methods for disseminating usability information, as well as broadening one's personal perspectives:

i. Firstly, employ data derived from usability tests (and other forms of research) as proof to elucidate usability determinations to colleagues on all occasions, such as why a specific design may be superior to another (Guiffrida, 2003). Rather than anticipating that developers will comply with one's position or expertise regarding user preferences when providing suggestions, it is preferable to take the time to explain the suggested changes and their advantages, as well as the potential hazards if such modifications are not implemented. It may be beneficial to enhance the conclusions and suggestions with support from other published research reports that have comparable findings. One should pay attention to their reservations and incorporate them into the proposals (Ashraf, 2012).

ii. Host workshops on the theories, strategies, and practices of UCD. But, be certain that they are pertinent and suitable for the target audience. Some people only need to be aware of the advantages and the right moment to carry out a trial or other research; they don't need to comprehend the specifics of usability testing. The success stories, the steps in the process, and the anticipated costs, benefits, and return on investment must be shared with others. For more credibility and a less exclusive approach, hire experts to deliver brief lectures on a particular topic of interest to the people or management. This might be anything from a brief lunch meeting to a comprehensive presentation (Agarwal et al., 2014).

iii. Create a usability resource area with a collection of usability-related books, articles, and project-specific usability materials. Provide a location where anyone is welcome to go and acquire materials, even if it's just one booth in a larger facility. Test plans and test reports that can be utilized as templates and resources by other testers can be included in the project-related materials. Create a noticeboard and add interesting articles from publications like magazines, journals, newspapers, and blogs, as well as reviews of products. Submit product reviews that identify usability as a major problem, whether they are positive or bad.

Urge everyone to donate interesting items, particularly those that feature success stories. Distribute reports and articles to both supporters and opponents who need to be informed (Jansen, 2004).

iv. Write an article for the internal newsletter of your organization extolling the merits of usability testing and publish it. Even better, describe the outcomes of the most recent experiment, including any consequences for the client or end user. Pay attention to benefits that are not limited to only the product being evaluated but instead have consequences not just for that product but also for other linked items and the whole customer experience. Politics prevent many different organizations from cooperating with one another in their research endeavors, even though many different organizations are made of groups that manufacture similar goods for similar clients (Guthman, 2008).

v. Create and distribute an individual newsletter. The results of a single usability test can be utilized in the development of other products that are conceptually similar (Lane, 2007).

8.5.2. Identify and Cultivate Champions

Who will get benefits from usability testing within the company? Who is itching to get their hands on usability data? Learn the responses to these questions. Use your power to appoint a usability champion to each project team, someone whose responsibility is to look out for the client or user for those projects that don't have formal usability assistance. An advocate would be in charge of, at least, bringing up usability problems at meetings, making sure that usability is covered in all design documentation and specifications, and assisting, even just administratively, with the execution of particular UCD techniques like testing. Without these leaders, development is slower and "business as usual" persists (Howell, 2005). Find a means to bring these champions together when necessary, perhaps by creating a review group or advisory board. The review board should convene on a regular basis to discuss how work is going on the many usability fronts, exchange ideas, and encourage one another's efforts (Martinsons, 1993).

8.5.3. Publicize the Usability Success Stories

Use the inherent competitiveness that exists between multiple departments and product lines to your advantage by publishing the usability success stories of other departments within your company or even those of your competitors. No division or team wants to have the impression that another component of the company or an external rival has an advantage over them. In particular, make sure others are aware if you are lagging further and further behind your rivals (Johnson & Westwater, 1996).

8.5.4. Link Usability to Economic Benefits

In order to ensure that the studies and tests being performed are cost-effective, it is recommended to report on the cost benefits whenever possible. It is important to adopt an attitude that ensures that UCD pays for itself. To create this link, a particular economic-based target can be used as the foundation for a UCD project. For instance, one objective could be to decrease the number of hotline calls that are related to usability issues (Wendel et al., 2012). To achieve this objective, research should be conducted to determine the nature and frequency of calls that are caused by usability-related problems. The cost of hotline calls to the company should also be determined, as well as the potential savings that could result from reducing the number of calls. These savings could include lost sales, additional customer support, and needing to send out fixes. The following is an example of such a calculation (Benitez et al., 2018).

"Let's say you know that each hotline contact costs the business roughly $45 in salary, phone bills, field repairs, and other expenses. You also know, thanks to some excellent sleuthing, that out of the 65,000 calls handled each month, roughly 30% (or 19,500) may be directly linked to usability problems. Hence, usability issues are directly responsible for $877,500 of the hotline's costs. You might save the organization $438,750 monthly or more than $5 million annually if you can cut usability-related calls by half.

This kind of study will go a long way to assisting everyone in understanding the value of UCD and will help develop a very clear aim. One may create a plan for correcting the issues by analyzing the type of issues that are creating the calls and why they are happening. Consider making it a goal to increase customer happiness or decrease the amount of documentation or informational website pages without sacrificing efficacy (Weiss et al., 2013).

By approaching problems in this manner, one would be surprised at the number of issues that exist within the organization and are waiting to be analyzed. It is recommended to combine the efforts of marketing and research and development in order to solve a specific problem. Often, this will be the first time that these departments collaborate on addressing a particular usability objective or issue (Menzi et al., 2017).

It is advisable to review product problem reports from all relevant groups, such as marketing and training. Data and information about problems can be obtained from different sources, such as hotline reports, letters and emails from customers, warranty cards, and marketing surveys within the organization or from external sources like product magazine reviews and beta site reports. By collecting and categorizing problem information, it is possible to move from a scattergun approach to a more targeted and focused approach to usability

(Schwab et al., 2001). To be more precise, research any usability issues with the present product before starting any projects that involve a "follow-on" product to it. Then, resolve these issues by factoring their resolution into the new product's usability goals. Sweeping up the error messages, for instance, should be an inherent usability goal for the new project if you are aware that the present product's online error messages are cryptic and the user guides lack clarity of the errors. Despite the fact that this seems like the most straightforward common sense, it's amazing how frequently politics interferes with and stops such an analysis from occurring (Donner & Tellez, 2008).

8.6. EXPAND UCD THROUGHOUT THE ORGANIZATION

The usability specialist may push himself farther after usability has established itself, and there are numerous advocates within the company, safe in the knowledge that all the efforts won't be undermined by a single setback (Sward & Macarthur, 2007).

This stage of development is when things really start to pick up in interest and fun. It is also the time at which this novel comes to a conclusion. The business will only be constrained in its subsequent efforts by the specialist's imagination and what the future holds in terms of new technologies once it has reached this level of recognition of the benefits of UCD in creating goods. For instance, UCD can be extended to cover the full product management life cycle and the entire user/customer experience rather than being restricted to the product development life cycle (Roth et al., 2015). A user-centered approach to these prepurchase and postpurchase stages, as well as how various corporate components interact with one another (or don't) from the client's perspective, can yield significant value. Say, for instance, that a customer wants to pick up furniture they had ordered online from a local retailer's store. Are both locations equally welcoming, accommodating, effective, and customer-focused? Are the two locations' inventory management systems interoperable to allow for seamless order transfer between them? and so forth (Zorzetti et al., 2022).

8.6.1. Pursue More Formal Educational Opportunities

It is advised that people who want to work in UCD but lack formal education in the discipline think about entering in a degree program in one of the behavioral sciences subjects, industrial design, human factors, or human-computer interaction. As an alternative, some corporate organizations and academic institutions provide certification programs in human factors (Richter et al., 2014).

Collaboration with a skilled usability professional who can advise and support the project's technical aspects is also advised. Suppose you are the sole practitioner in your company. In that case, it could be advantageous to schedule regular meetings with a coworker from another organization to share ideas, discuss strategies, and discuss progress (Dillahunt et al., 2014).

8.6.2. Standardize Participant Recruitment Policies and Procedures

To streamline the recruitment process, initiate relationships with diverse sources of participants, such as research companies and hiring agencies. Establish and enhance a database of users, detailing their participation in terms of who, what, where, and when. Keep in mind that if you need experienced participants, you may need to use the same people again and again. When the demand for participation grows, it may be advantageous to appoint someone to handle database acquisition and management (Le Lann et al., 2020).

8.6.3. Align Closely with Market Research and Industrial Design

It is advised that tight collaboration with market research and/or industrial design be maintained for the entirety of the product's lifecycle in the event that your company has departments dedicated to either of these fields. The three disciplines of human factors and usability study, market research, and industrial design work together in a way that is both natural and beneficial (Khan et al., 2012). For instance, forming a partnership with the marketing team in order to define the user, or employing marketing in order to either acquire participants for field study or carry it out with those participants already recruited. The specialist or specialists in industrial design can be of assistance in addressing issues with user interfaces, visual design, and developing an overall user-centered approach (Wormald & Rodber, 2008).

8.6.4. Evaluate Product Usability in the Field after Product Release

This examination goes beyond the traditional product life cycle, which concludes with product release. Do studies on how the company's product is used in the industry as well as outside the lab.

This could take a variety of shapes. One may collect information on how the item is being used by telephone or written questionnaires or by doing remote usability assessments. Integrate this information back into the creation of the next item by rendering it publicly accessible to the development team of the subsequent product (Paz et al., 2015).

After a development team completes and launches the current product, they frequently move on to another project. This causes a significant gap in the feedback cycle because new ideas are never observed in the light of day-to-day usage after being evaluated in the lab. As a result, any issues encountered by users are simply passed over to the following version (Rosenbaum, 2008).

8.6.5. Evaluate the Value of Your Usability Engineering Efforts

Do "before" and "after" studies to evaluate the impact of UCD. Then, undertake research on a current product to see how it ranks in regards to simplicity of use, contentment, and so on. Afterwards, examine the results of a comparable study on the next-generation product that has been exposed to usability testing or other approaches. This is a great strategy to gain a genuine foothold for usability throughout the organization and determine which approaches are most successful. Of course, share the findings and modify the technique based on what works and what doesn't (Wixon & Wilson, 1997).

8.6.6. Develop Design Standards

There is no reason to postpone this activity in any way; nonetheless, before the establishment of an ongoing program of UCD, many businesses struggle mightily with standardization. Within your own organization, the standards refer to techniques for depicting activities of the user-interface design, as well as guidelines for documentation formats and the layout of a control panel (Greenfield et al., 2012). The goal here is to guarantee that similar model principles are executed in precisely the same manner across all product lines. Even though standards can't cover every possible scenario, they are more than capable of handling the most prevalent ones, which frees up developers to focus on more innovative parts of new product creation (Tillinghast et al., 2011).

8.6.7. Focus Your Efforts Early in the Product Life Cycle

Without a doubt, active participation in the life cycle of a product can yield the largest benefits. Always try to influence products as soon as possible, even if you usually have to demonstrate the worth of UCD in the latter stages. Concentrate on preliminary exploration experiments of several design concepts (Brannon et al., 1993). Spend some time questioning people to determine whether the usage estimates are accurate. The early research has a substantially higher return than a test done after a significant portion of the design has been fixed. Do not be deterred by developers who say that research cannot be conducted until a more tangible product exists. It is never too soon in the life cycle of a product to think about usability (Labro, 2006).

SUMMARY

This chapter discusses how the field of user experience (UX) design has evolved beyond just usability testing to a more holistic approach to designing products that meet users' needs. The chapter explores the various stages of the UX design process, including user research, prototyping, and testing, and highlights the importance of involving users throughout the design process.

MULTIPLE CHOICE QUESTIONS

1. **What is the goal of usability testing?**
   a. To evaluate the usability of a product
   b. To design the user experience
   c. To gather user feedback for marketing purposes
2. **What is the difference between usability testing and user experience design?**
   a. Usability testing is focused on evaluating an existing product while user experience design is focused on creating a new product
   b. Usability testing is focused on evaluating the usability of a product while user experience design is focused on the overall experience of using a product
   c. Usability testing and user experience design are the same thing
3. **What is the main benefit of using personas in user experience design?**
   a. To create a visual representation of the target audience
   b. To provide a framework for usability testing
   c. To ensure that the product meets the needs of the target audience
4. **What is the purpose of a wireframe in user experience design?**
   a. To provide a visual representation of the final product
   b. To test the usability of the product
   c. To outline the basic structure and functionality of the product
5. **What is the difference between qualitative and quantitative data in user experience design?**
   a. Qualitative data is numerical data while quantitative data is non-numerical data
   b. Qualitative data is based on observation and feedback while quantitative data is based on statistical analysis
   c. Qualitative data and quantitative data are the same thing

Answers to Multiple Choice Questions

1. (a); 2. (b); 3. (c); 4. (c); 5. (b)

REFERENCES

1. Agarwal, N., Calvo, B., & Kumar, V., (2014). Paving the road to success: A students with disabilities organization in a university setting. *College Student Journal, 48*(1), 34–44.
2. Ashraf, G., (2012). A review on the models of organizational effectiveness: A look at Cameron's model in higher education. *International Education Studies, 5*(2), 80–87.
3. Atkinson, N. L., Saperstein, S. L., Desmond, S. M., Gold, R. S., Billing, A. S., & Tian, J., (2009). Rural eHealth nutrition education for limited-income families: An iterative and user-centered design approach. *Journal of Medical Internet Research, 11*(2), e1148.
4. Atkinson, P. E., (2012). Selling yourself magically-Persuasion strategies for personal and organizational change. *Management Services, 56*(4), 28.
5. Auger, J., (2013). Speculative design: Crafting the speculation. *Digital Creativity, 24*(1), 11–35.
6. Bendixen, R. M., Fairman, A. D., Karavolis, M., Sullivan, C., & Parmanto, B., (2017). A user-centered approach: Understanding client and caregiver needs and preferences in the development of mHealth apps for self-management. *JMIR mHealth and uHealth, 5*(9), e7136.
7. Benitez-Paez, F., Comber, A., Trilles, S., & Huerta, J., (2018). Creating a conceptual framework to improve the re-usability of open geographic data in cities. *Transactions in GIS, 22*(3), 806–822.
8. Benoît, C., Norris, G. A., Valdivia, S., Ciroth, A., Moberg, A., Bos, U., & Beck, T., (2010). The guidelines for social life cycle assessment of products: Just in time! *The International Journal of Life Cycle Assessment, 15*, 156–163.
9. Brannon, A. L., Schoenmakers, M. A., Klapwijk, H. P., & Haley, K. B., (1993). Product value matrices help firms to focus their efforts. *Omega, 21*(6), 699–708.
10. Brody, A. A., Arbaje, A. I., DeCherrie, L. V., Federman, A. D., Leff, B., & Siu, A. L., (2019). Starting up a hospital at home program: Facilitators and barriers to implementation. *Journal of the American Geriatrics Society, 67*(3), 588–595.
11. Bruce, K., (1998). Can you align IT with business strategy? *Strategy & Leadership, 26*(5), 16–20.
12. Carter, J. A., Liu, J., Schneider, K., & Fourney, D., (2005). Transforming usability engineering requirements into software engineering specifications: From PUF to UML. *Human-Centered Software Engineering—Integrating Usability in the Software Development Lifecycle*, 147–169.
13. Cooper, B. L., Watson, H. J., Wixom, B. H., & Goodhue, D. L., (2000). Data warehousing supports corporate strategy at first American corporation. *MIS Quarterly*, 547–567.

14. Dhamija, R., & Tygar, J. D., (2005). The battle against phishing: Dynamic security skins. In: *Proceedings of the 2005 Symposium on USABLE Privacy and Security* (pp. 77–88).
15. Dillahunt, T., Wang, Z., & Teasley, S. D., (2014). Democratizing higher education: Exploring MOOC use among those who cannot afford a formal education. *International Review of Research in Open and Distributed Learning, 15*(5), 177–196.
16. Donner, J., & Tellez, C. A., (2008). Mobile banking and economic development: Linking adoption, impact, and use. *Asian Journal of Communication, 18*(4), 318–332.
17. El Bassiti, L., & Ajhoun, R., (2013). Toward an innovation management framework: A life-cycle model with an idea management focus. *International Journal of Innovation, Management and Technology, 4*(6), 551.
18. Ellis, R. D., & Kurniawan, S. H., (2000). Increasing the usability of online information for older users: A case study in participatory design. *International Journal of Human-Computer Interaction, 12*(2), 263–276.
19. Friedman, H. S., (2000). Long-term relations of personality and health: Dynamisms, mechanisms, tropisms. *Journal of Personality, 68*(6), 1089–1107.
20. Göransson, B., Lif, M., & Gulliksen, J., (2003). Usability design-extending rational unified process with a new discipline. In: *DSV-IS* (pp. 316–330).
21. Gorry, J., Roen, K., & Reilly, J., (2010). Selling your self? The psychological impact of street sex work and factors affecting support seeking. *Health & Social Care in the Community, 18*(5), 492–499.
22. Greenfield, D., Pawsey, M., Hinchcliff, R., Moldovan, M., & Braithwaite, J., (2012). The standard of healthcare accreditation standards: A review of empirical research underpinning their development and impact. *BMC Health Services Research, 12*(1), 1–14.
23. Grossman, J. H., (1991). How to sell yourself: A guide for interviewing effectively. *SAM Advanced Management Journal, 56*(2), 33.
24. Grundlingh, A., (2008). "Are we Afrikaners getting too rich?" 1 cornucopia and change in Afrikanerdom in the 1960s. *Journal of Historical Sociology, 21*(2, 3), 143–165.
25. Gudipati, M., & Sethi, K. B., (2017). Adapting the user-centered design framework for K-12 education. *Taking Design Thinking to School: How the Technology of Design can Transform Teachers, Learners, and Classrooms*, 94–101.
26. Guiffrida, D. A., (2003). African American student organizations as agents of social integration. *Journal of College Student Development, 44*(3), 304–319.
27. Guthman, J., (2008). Bringing good food to others: Investigating the subjects of alternative food practice. *Cultural Geographies, 15*(4), 431–447.
28. Hansen, M. T., Nohria, N., & Tierney, T., (2013). What's your strategy for managing knowledge? In: *The Knowledge Management Yearbook 2000–2001* (pp. 55–69).
29. Harper, M., & Allen, S., (1997). Volunteer to enhance your career and the profession. *Journal of Accountancy, 183*(2), 41.

30. Howell, J. M., (2005). The right stuff: Identifying and developing effective champions of innovation. *Academy of Management Perspectives, 19*(2), 108–119.
31. Jansen, E. P., (2004). The influence of the curriculum organization on study progress in higher education. *Higher Education, 47*, 411–435.
32. Jiang, J. J., Klein, G. S., & Pick, R. A., (1996). Individual differences and system development. *ACM SIGCPR Computer Personnel, 17*(3), 3–12.
33. Johnson, G. I., & Westwater, M. G., (1996). Usability and self-service information technology: Cognitive engineering in product design and evaluation. *AT&T Technical Journal, 75*(1), 64–73.
34. Khan, O., Christopher, M., & Creazza, A., (2012). Aligning product design with the supply chain: A case study. *Supply Chain Management: An International Journal, 17*(3), 323–336.
35. Labro, E., (2006). Is a focus on collaborative product development warranted from a cost commitment perspective? *Supply Chain Management: An International Journal, 11*(6), 503–509.
36. Lampland, M., (2010). False numbers as formalizing practices. *Social Studies of Science, 40*(3), 377–404.
37. Lane, I. F., (2007). Change in higher education: Understanding and responding to individual and organizational resistance. *Journal of Veterinary Medical Education, 34*(2), 85–92.
38. Le Lann, L., Jouve, P. E., Alarcón-Riquelme, M., Jamin, C., & Pers, J. O., (2020). Standardization procedure for flow cytometry data harmonization in prospective multicenter studies. *Scientific Reports, 10*(1), 11567.
39. Lewis, III. R. R., (2005). Ecological engineering for successful management and restoration of mangrove forests. *Ecological Engineering, 24*(4), 403–418.
40. Lucchi, E., & Delera, A. C., (2020). Enhancing the historic public social housing through a user-centered design-driven approach. *Buildings, 10*(9), 159.
41. Lyall, C., & Fletcher, I., (2013). Experiments in interdisciplinary capacity-building: The successes and challenges of large-scale interdisciplinary investments. *Science and Public Policy, 40*(1), 1–7.
42. Martinsons, M. G., (1993). Cultivating the champions for strategic information systems. *Journal of Systems Management, 44*(8), 31.
43. Meloncon, L. K., (2017). Patient experience design: Expanding usability methodologies for healthcare. *Communication Design Quarterly Review, 5*(2), 19–28.
44. Menzi-Çetin, N., Alemdağ, E., Tüzün, H., & Yıldız, M., (2017). Evaluation of a university website's usability for visually impaired students. *Universal Access in the Information Society, 16*, 151–160.
45. Mizrahi, T., & Rosenthal, B. B., (2001). Complexities of coalition building: Leaders' successes, strategies, struggles, and solutions. *Social Work, 46*(1), 63–78.

46. Nesbit, R., & Brudney, J. L., (2010). At your service? Volunteering and national service in 2020. *Public Administration Review, 70*, S107–S113.
47. Paz, F., Paz, F. A., Villanueva, D., & Pow-Sang, J. A., (2015). Heuristic evaluation as a complement to usability testing: A case study in web domain. In: *2015 12th International Conference on Information Technology-New Generations* (pp. 546–551).
48. Philippidis, A., (2022). Into orbit: Satellite bio raises $110 M toward tissue therapeutics: Emerging from stealth mode, company focuses on manufacturing platform, pipeline growth starting with focus on liver conditions. *GEN Edge, 4*(1), 400–406.
49. Redish, J. G., (2007). Expanding usability testing to evaluate complex systems. *Journal of Usability Studies, 2*(3), 102–111.
50. Richter, D., Kunter, M., Klusmann, U., Lüdtke, O., & Baumert, J., (2014). Professional development across the teaching career: Teachers' uptake of formal and informal learning opportunities. In: *Teachers' Professional Development* (pp. 97–121).
51. Rosenbaum, S., (2008). The future of usability evaluation: Increasing impact on value. *Maturing Usability: Quality in Software, Interaction and Value*, 344–378.
52. Roth, R. E., Ross, K. S., & MacEachren, A. M., (2015). User-centered design for interactive maps: A case study in crime analysis. *ISPRS International Journal of Geo-Information, 4*(1), 262–301.
53. Schaltegger, S., Lüdeke-Freund, F., & Hansen, E. G., (2012). Business cases for sustainability: The role of business model innovation for corporate sustainability. *International Journal of Innovation and Sustainable Development, 6*(2), 95–119.
54. Schwab, A. L., Knott, R., & Schottdorf, W., (2001). Environmental and economic benefit of new fungus-tolerant grape varieties and their usability for different training systems. In: *Proceedings of the 12th GESCO Congress 2001 in Montpellier, France* (Vol. 1, pp. 201–204).
55. Sfikas, P. M., (1999). Volunteering your services. *The Journal of the American Dental Association, 130*(2), 278–280.
56. Sward, D., & Macarthur, G., (2007). Making user experience a business strategy. In: Law, E., et al., (eds.), *Proceedings of the Workshop on Towards a UX Manifesto* (Vol. 3, pp. 35–40).
57. Thursky, K. A., & Mahemoff, M., (2007). User-centered design techniques for a computerized antibiotic decision support system in an intensive care unit. *International Journal of Medical Informatics, 76*(10), 760–768.
58. Tillinghast, E. D., Hunt, W. F., & Jennings, G. D., (2011). Stormwater control measure (SCM) design standards to limit stream erosion for Piedmont North Carolina. *Journal of Hydrology, 411*(3, 4), 185–196.
59. Van, H. M. C., & Bingham, T., (2013). 'Surfing the silk road': A study of users' experiences. *International Journal of Drug Policy, 24*(6), 524–529.
60. Versteeg, G., & Bouwman, H., (2006). Business architecture: A new paradigm to relate business strategy to ICT. *Information Systems Frontiers, 8*, 91–102.

61. Walden, A., Garvin, L., Smerek, M., & Johnson, C., (2020). User-centered design principles in the development of clinical research tools. *Clinical Trials, 17*(6), 703–711.
62. Weiss, E., Mixtaj, L., Weiss, R., & Weiss, G., (2013). Economic evaluation of the usability of abandoned mining works. In: *SGEM 2013: 13th International Multidisciplinary Scientific Geoconference Science and Technologies in Geology, Exploration and Mining; Conference Proceedings* (Vol. 1, pp. 16–22).
63. Welch, T. D., Smith, T. B., & Niklinski, E., (2023). Creating a business case for success. *Nursing Administration Quarterly, 47*(2), 182–194.
64. Wendel, H. E. W., Zarger, R. K., & Mihelcic, J. R., (2012). Accessibility and usability: Green space preferences, perceptions, and barriers in a rapidly urbanizing city in Latin America. *Landscape and Urban Planning, 107*(3), 272–282.
65. Wixon, D., & Wilson, C., (1997). The usability engineering framework for product design and evaluation. In: *Handbook of Human-Computer Interaction* (pp. 653–688).
66. Wormald, P. W., & Rodber, M., (2008). Aligning industrial design education to emerging trends in professional practice and industry. *Journal of Design Research, 7*(3), 294–303.
67. Zorzetti, M., Signoretti, I., Salerno, L., Marczak, S., & Bastos, R., (2022). Improving agile software development using user-centered design and lean startup. *Information and Software Technology, 141*, 106718.

INDEX

C

I

J

K

L

M

N

O

P

Q

R

T

U

V

W

X

Printed in the United States
by Baker & Taylor Publisher Services